Guiding Your
Student Teacher

Guiding Your
Student Teacher

BY

DWIGHT K. CURTIS

*Head, Department of Teaching
Iowa State Teachers College*

AND

LEONARD O. ANDREWS

*Coordinator, Student Field Experience
College of Education
Ohio State University*

35302

Englewood Cliffs, N. J.
PRENTICE-HALL, INC.

PRENTICE-HALL EDUCATION SERIES

Harold Spears, *Editor*

Copyright, 1954, by
PRENTICE-HALL, INC.

L.C. CAT. CARD NO.: 54-12272

First printing......October, 1954
Second printing.......June, 1955
Third printing.......March, 1956
Fourth printing...February, 1960
Fifth printing...September, 1960
Sixth printing....September, 1962
Seventh printing......April, 1964
Eighth printing..September, 1965

Printed in the United States of America
37134—C

TO
teacher education students today
that they may be better
teachers in schools of
a democratic soci-
ety tomorrow.

Preface

This book is directed to you who guide student teachers. It is intended to help you in your important work, the guidance of college students as they become teachers. Your effective performance can play a major role in preserving and improving our country's democratic way of life. Improving the competence of young teachers can have a powerful influence, also, in raising the standards and prestige of our profession.

Your opportunity for service requires understanding and skill. The general principles to be followed are the same as those which apply at any level of learning, but the relationship between teacher and student teacher is a very intimate, personal one. As a result, the procedures may differ from those which you ordinarily follow in working with boys and girls. We have tried to collect and present practices which teachers have found effective with college students.

We offer a handbook for the busy teacher. Theoretical considerations have been minimized, but the treatment of practical problems is in no sense exhaustive. Rather, we have tried to illustrate the problems which you will face in working with student teachers and to suggest a few ways to go about solving them. We hope that with this manual as a basis, you will develop original ways to stimulate the development of these teachers-to-be.

In brief, the task of the teacher is to provide conditions in which the maximum growth of student teachers can take place. We hope that you will be successful in providing such a favorable climate.

The points of view expressed, procedures reviewed, and principles listed have been developed by the authors over a period of years from three main sources: (1) supervision of students in learning to assume the responsibilities of teachers, (2) supervision of teachers in learning to guide student growth in teaching, and (3) data collected from students and teachers concerning the effectiveness of supervisory procedures. Systematic research in the supervision of student teachers is extremely meager. However, we have quoted freely from other research in learning when this could be applied to the guidance of student growth in learning to teach. Other sources which have direct bearing upon aspects of supervision reviewed in this book are referred to in content or listed in the annotated bibliography at the end of each chapter.

Many students are quoted in this book. These quotes are taken, for the most part, from reactions given on the "Evaluation of Supervision" form (Appendix F), administered to hundreds of elementary and secondary student teachers during the last five years. Such reactions have sharpened our focus upon many aspects of supervision, intensified understanding of many others, and, in all, made us more keenly aware of the need for systematic research in the supervision of student teaching.

The authors appreciate the many insights gained in working with the staff of the Department of Teaching centers at Iowa State Teachers College and the supervising staff and cooperating teachers of Ohio State University. We are especially grateful to Miss Pearl Merriman, Supervising Teacher, Western College of Education, Bellingham, Washington, who critically reviewed the entire manuscript; and to Miss Gladys Hoffpauir, Supervising Teacher, F. M. Hamilton Training School, Southwestern Louisiana Institute, Lafayette, Louisiana, who reviewed the manuscript and contributed extensively to Chapter IV. Most of all, we wish to pay tribute to the many student teachers with whom we have worked in learning how to contribute effectively to their growth.

Cedar Falls, Iowa   Dwight K. Curtis

Columbus, Ohio   Leonard O. Andrews

Terminology

Terminology in the field of teacher education lacks much in precision and uniformity. Several terms are used interchangeably and rather loosely; others are common only in certain types of institutions or localities. For the sake of clarity a few of the more important ones are defined here, although variations in their use will be found in the literature.

Professional laboratory experiences include all those contacts with children, youths, and adults (through observation, participation, and teaching) which contribute directly to an understanding of individuals and their guidance in the teaching-learning process.

Student teaching is a period (or periods) during which a student receives guidance in learning to assume responsibility for the major activities of teachers in the public schools.

Student teacher is the term used for any college student engaged in the specific experience defined as student teaching.

Observation includes those situations in which individuals or groups watch an experienced teacher direct activities in any of the areas of teacher responsibility. *Demonstration teaching* is instruction planned especially for groups of observers.

Participation includes those activities in which students work with pupils, teachers, parents, community agencies, and so on, but are not responsible for directing the activities.

Cooperating teacher is the term now rather generally used to designate the public school classroom teacher who supervises student teachers. Ordinarily a cooperating teacher is considered to be a regular public school teacher, in contrast with a laboratory school teacher. *Supervising teacher* is still very commonly used, although it may be confused with the term *college super-*

visor. Sometimes campus laboratory school teachers are called *supervising* teachers, to distinguish them from the *cooperating* teachers in the public schools.

Campus laboratory school is the name generally applied to the school found on so many teachers-college and university campuses. The particular functions served vary greatly from institution to institution, but most such schools provide a laboratory for the teacher education activities of demonstration, observation, participation, and student teaching. The campus school is usually operated and controlled *entirely* by the college, although there are many off-campus laboratory schools over which the college exercises differing degrees of control in such matters as curriculum and selection of staff. These latter schools are often maintained under some joint contractual arrangement with public school systems.

Cooperating school is any school which assists a college with some phase of the teacher education program. This term is usually reserved for public schools that receive student teachers under some agreement with a college.

College Supervisor is any member of the college faculty who assumes responsibility for supervising or coordinating the direction of the student teacher's activities. This college staff member is responsible for assisting the cooperating teacher in planning the student teacher's activities, directing those activities from day to day, and evaluating student growth.

Usage of terms in this book

For clarity and simplicity several single words will be used throughout this book in place of more complex terms. The four words and their equivalents are as follows:

Pupils: Boys and girls in elementary or high school classes.

Teacher: The classroom teacher, whether in a public, private, campus, or other laboratory school.

Student: The student teacher.

Supervisor: The college faculty member immediately responsible for assisting the teacher in the supervision of the student.

Sources

There are four sources of information on student teaching that will consistently be of help to you. In addition, several professional magazines carry occasional articles, which can be located through the *Education Index* or similar reference sources. There are a few textbooks for students which are designed to be particularly helpful at the time of student teaching. Most of the best material in the field is well isolated in student teacher handbooks, manuals, and bulletins developed at different colleges, and in reports of conferences and workshops.

For you, the classroom teacher, the following four sources will usually be the most readily available and the most helpful:

1. *Association for Student Teaching* yearbooks and other publications. The yearbooks offer some of the best material available. Since 1937 a well-annotated bibliography has been kept up to date in the yearbooks and furnishes the best single guide to the literature of the field.

2. *American Association of Colleges for Teacher Education* yearbooks and other publications. This organization of institutions includes the colleges that prepare about half of the certificated teachers in the United States. Before the merger of 1948 it was known as the American Association of Teachers Colleges, which organized the study and published the report known as *School and Community Laboratory Experiences in Teacher Education.* This book reports extensively on practice in many institutions and provides a statement of principles. It also gives the first draft of the standards that were adopted by the Association in 1949.

3. *Educational Administration and Supervision.* This magazine, for many years, has reported almost monthly on developments in student teaching and related areas.

4. *Journal of Teacher Education.* This quarterly, which began in 1950, provides the only national journal devoted exclusively to the field of teacher education. Most issues contain articles on student teaching and other professional laboratory experiences, and include several departments to aid the busy teacher in keeping up with current developments throughout the country.

Contents

APPENDIXES

1

You Guide Student Teachers

STUDENT TEACHING IS GENERALLY REGARDED AS the most important single experience in any teacher education program. College students look forward to the period when they can take over the actual instruction of a group or groups of boys and girls. In the minds of these prospective teachers, there are two major reasons for the great importance of student teaching: it is something real and practical, and success in student teaching has a lot to do with getting a job and with success on the job. You may recall how much student teaching contributed to success on your first job.

The confidence that you and others have expressed in student teaching offers a real challenge to those working in and responsible for teacher education programs. Students have a right to expect colleges to provide teaching experiences that contribute to maximum growth in learning to assume the responsibilities of public school teachers. The profession faced the challenge realistically in the publication *School and Community Laboratory Experiences in Teacher Education*,[1] which included a set of standards, formally adopted by the association in 1949, setting goals for teacher education institutions to work

[1] John G. Flowers and others, *School and Community Laboratory Experiences in Teacher Education* (Oneonta, N.Y.: American Association of Teachers Colleges, 1948).

1

toward for years to come. But major strides are being made by colleges and universities to improve their student teaching programs. Several significant trends are:

1. Student teaching and other professional laboratory experiences are receiving a more important position in teacher education programs.

2. Student teaching experiences have been increased to include the major areas of teacher responsibility in school and community.[2]

3. More students are being placed in cooperating public schools for their student teaching experiences.[3]

4. Student teaching is rapidly becoming a cooperative enterprise between public schools and colleges.[3]

5. College programs in teacher education are becoming increasingly closer to the public schools for which teachers are being prepared.[4]

The last three trends bring the largest segment of the profession, the public schools, into the teacher education program. With more than a thousand colleges preparing teachers, this trend is, each year, including more and more public schools and public school teachers. If you are one of those teachers, we sincerely welcome you into the teacher education field.

The improvement of the profession of teaching lies in the hands of the public school teachers just as much as in those of the college faculties. Improvements, of course, can and should be made in the curricula and methods of instruction in colleges. Such developments will be of little effect, however, if the quality of student teaching is poor. Regular classroom teachers need to know what experiences should be provided, how to direct these experiences, and how to evaluate them. For many teachers

[2] *Developing Facilities for Professional Laboratory Experiences in Teacher Education,* Thirty-third Yearbook (Lock Haven, Pa.: Association for Student Teaching, 1954).

[3] *Off-Campus Student Teaching,* Thirtieth Yearbook (Lock Haven, Pa.: Association for Student Teaching, 1951).

[4] *Curriculum Trends and Teacher Education,* Thirty-second Yearbook (Lock Haven, Pa.: Association for Student Teaching, 1953).

this is a new demand, one to which their preparation has heretofore given scant attention.

This book is written in the hope that it will serve as a guide to you in the public schools and also to you in laboratory schools, who have previously carried the major student teaching load. In writing this volume for you we hold that:

1. Teachers who work with student teachers can make a real contribution to the teaching profession.

2. Working with student teachers is one of the most fascinating and challenging positions in the teaching profession.

3. Teachers should have help in meeting the complex problems of guiding student teachers who are learning to assume the responsibilities of teachers.

4. Students who have excellent experiences during student teaching can make a real contribution to the profession.

Let's ask five questions and see if we can clarify some aspects of student teaching before getting into specific helps for your day-by-day work with students.

What is student teaching?

What are your functions in guiding student teachers?

What competencies are desirable for one working with student teachers?

What effect does student teaching have upon pupils?

What is your relationship to the college supervisor?

WHAT IS STUDENT TEACHING?

This part of the student's program generally comes in the last year of the teacher education curricula. The student has fulfilled a part of the requirements for the degree or diploma, has background in general education and professional education (subject-matter fields and education courses), and has met any special requirements or prerequisites to student teaching. He is not yet sure that he has the personal and professional qualifications for success in teaching; this he will now have opportunity to discover.

The purpose or function of student teaching across the country, generally speaking, is to provide opportunities, under guidance, for the student to develop and evaluate his competencies in the major areas of teacher activity in the public schools. Specifically, he has opportunities to:

1. Appraise his basic personal qualifications for teaching
2. Apply and test his professional knowledge, understandings, and skills
3. Participate in and assume responsibility for teacher responsibilities in public school teaching
4. Have direct contact with examples of the major phases of a public school's operation
5. Develop both personal and professional competencies under optimum conditions
6. Evaluate his competence and readiness to enter the profession
7. Prepare, as nearly as possible, to meet types of demands he will face as a beginning teacher.

One view of the function and importance of student teaching may be obtained by considering some of the attributes of a profession. Three that would be considered very essential in teaching are *professional knowledge, professional skill,* and *professional judgment. Knowledge* would include content of courses, the conclusions drawn from research sources, the information gleaned from personal experience, and the opinions of leaders in the field. *Skills* would include a wide range of competencies: instructional, clerical, administrative, personnel, scholarship, leadership, and managerial, to name but a few. Student teaching allows a prospective teacher to try his hand at these skills and to identify his weaknesses.

The third attribute, *professional judgment,* plays a vital role in the success of any teacher. Some people seem to possess a sixth sense, a type of intuitive response in judgment situations which is right a surprisingly high percentage of the time. This very phenomenon has probably given rise to the idea that "Teachers are born and not made." Whether a person starts with a good set of normal reactions or has to learn new patterns consciously, professional judgment is still a competence that must be developed through experience.

Another view might be the problem approach of any professional worker. He must attack problems by making a *diagnosis*, determining a *prognosis*, giving *treatment*, and evaluating results. A student has opportunities to apply these procedures over and over again. Each learning problem of a class or an individual must be studied to identify the causes. A plan of action must be developed and carried through the treatment stage. Even though the public would never include school teachers among workers who must make split-second decisions, these four phases are often wrapped up in one almost instantaneous reaction to a class or an individual. Every experienced teacher knows of children whose attitudes toward school, life, and other people have been powerfully affected by sharp and sudden reactions. Sound professional judgment could save many a beginning teacher from serious mistakes.

Under controlled and supervised conditions a student can try out his ability to diagnose, make a prognosis, and check his ideas before proceeding with treatment. Mistakes can be corrected quickly, and experience can be studied and evaluated continuously. When student teaching is viewed in this light, its importance rises sharply—both to the student teacher himself and to the hundreds and thousands of children his work will influence.

To provide these opportunities effectively for even one student requires the cooperation of many different persons. To the immediate classroom teacher, however, more than to anyone else, comes this important professional challenge: to make certain that the student has these opportunities within a climate favorable for maximum growth.

WHAT ARE YOUR FUNCTIONS IN GUIDING STUDENT TEACHERS?

Perhaps we first should clarify your dual role in working with student and pupils. Your attention, your professional concern, and your loyalty are divided between the student and the school in which you are teaching the minute a student enters your room, your club, your parent conference, or the school lunch room. In reality, the dual nature of your work is between pupils and student. This sort of arrangement requires that you keep the best interests of both in mind.

YOU HAVE LEGAL RESPONSIBILITY

Your legal responsibility as a classroom teacher in the public school is the instructional program of boys and girls and such other responsibilities as the school authorities may delegate. If you teach in a campus laboratory school, you are equally responsible for the student and the pupils. However, our experience has been that laboratory school teachers feel their first responsibility to be to the pupils. They also feel, for the most part, that the best thing for the pupils is also the best thing for the student.

You may delegate certain activities to the student and temporarily delegate teaching responsibility, but you can never fully abdicate all your responsibilities. Legally, the student teacher is an assistant teacher to whom you give certain opportunities and duties only temporarily. Yours was the full responsibility before the student came; yours is the full responsibility after he leaves. The student may direct all of the teaching-learning activities during a part of the time he is with you, but at all times you must keep thoroughly informed concerning the work in progress and the development of the pupils. *The full, final, and legal responsibility for the guidance of pupils in the school remains with you during the entire time that the student is there.*

This legal status could be, and unfortunately at times has been, interpreted by teachers to mean that they never have a right to give any real teaching responsibility to the student. Nothing could be farther from the facts. When a school system enters into a contract with a college providing for student teaching, the teachers are immediately given the right to delegate teaching responsibilities. The restriction on the teacher is against abdication of all of his rights and duties. The parents must have assurance that the pupils' interests are being carefully watched and protected. You want to assure yourself that the student is really ready before he assumes responsibility for any major activity.

YOU CREATE A CLIMATE FOR STUDENT GROWTH

It is understood that you want to work with a student, otherwise one would not be assigned to you. Therefore, since you are the major element, approximately half of the climate essential for student growth is present. Your attitudes toward the student, your interest in him, your ability to guide growth effectively, and your ability to establish quickly wholesome interpersonal relations determines whether or not you can create a climate conducive to optimum growth. Any strong professional person who has the necessary personal qualities for developing and maintaining good personal relations can certainly learn to guide student teachers effectively.

Your attitude and manner of working will determine whether or not you can establish a close partnership, a team relationship. If you become the senior partner and take the student in with full status as a junior partner, both can join forces in working for the best interests of the pupils. When this relationship is skillfully promoted, the distance between teacher and student will narrow rapidly and emotional tensions will evaporate. One important word of caution must always be emphasized: A team relationship, no matter how fine, must never be allowed to prevent the student from having sufficient opportunity to work independently. Here are several comments, made at the close of student teaching, which illustrate students' reactions to a skillfully maintained, cooperative partnership:

"My teacher once said she learned from her student teachers, and was pleased when they taught something by a different method."

"The teachers never gave us any jobs they didn't actually want themselves."

"When I made suggestions as to how a student could be motivated, they were tried."

Dickson found that two-thirds of all difficulties in supervision of students reported by students, teachers, and supervisors were directly concerned with human relationships.[5]

The question remains, "Can you develop or stimulate the development of other requisites of a wholesome climate for student teacher growth?" For example, can you stimulate necessary faculty interest and enthusiasm for students? This is essential if the student is to have opportunities for experiences outside the school program under your direct supervision. The faculty in the school has much to do with whether the student can acquire a feeling of being wanted, of being useful, of being professionally accepted, and of having security. Your attitude toward the student can't alone provide sufficient climate to overcome undesirable attitudes on the part of other faculty members.

The pupils also play an important part in creating climate. They can often be very cruel with students, as you probably know. Since the pupils are a part of the program, why shouldn't the student teaching situation be discussed quite frankly with them? Certainly, in schools where pupil-teacher planning has reached a high level of operation there should be no difficulty.

Students fear pupils much more than they fear you and the other teachers. At the same time, the major criterion of success in teaching is the ability of the student to work effectively with boys and girls. Therefore, if there is to be a climate conducive to maximum growth, it is exceedingly important that the pupils, insofar as possible, display attitudes of interest, courtesy, cooperation, and appreciation.

One teacher in a public school, not satisfied with the climate that was created for the student by pupils, asked not to have a student teacher next term. She talked the problem over with

[5] George Edmond Dickson, "Human Relations Problems in the Stanford Elementary Student Teaching Program" (Doctoral dissertation, Leland Stanford University, 1949).

the pupils in her sixth grade and, together, they listed the situations that certainly would not make the student feel at home. Teacher and pupils then decided that, during the next term, they would list the ways in which they were handicapped by not having a student with them. Some of the handicaps listed were as follows:

1. We couldn't go to the flour mill because there weren't enough teachers to go with us.

2. We didn't receive nearly as much help during our study periods.

3. We didn't always have an official for our games at recess.

4. When our committees needed help, we had to wait longer for our turn.

5. It's better having ideas from two teachers instead of just one.

6. When we had two teachers, you (the teacher) could work with us more.

7. We had more interesting things to do when we had two teachers.

8. We can just get more done all of the time when we have two teachers.

Observation during the next term demonstrated this to have been a successful procedure in spite of the fact that the student was generally weak.

There is another value here that cannot be overlooked. The individuals who profited most from this experience were the pupils, and it may have been the best lesson they had in the public schools in the development and maintenance of good cooperative relationships. Thus, when you enlist pupil cooperation in creating a good climate for a student, you are giving pupils valuable experiences in interpersonal relationships.

YOU HELP THE STUDENT DEVELOP FOCUS AND PURPOSE

When your student teacher comes, will he know what responsibilities he must assume as a public school teacher? The only evidence we have supports the conclusion that few students know what responsibilities they will have, other than to "teach classes."[6] You have heard students say, "I'm going to teach science next year!" This may have been the same student who, as a high school pupil, said, "Mr. —— didn't teach me anything." Ask yourself, "Why has the emphasis changed from teaching *me* to teaching *science?*"

To say that students do not have purpose would be incorrect. The purpose they have, however, may be misguided, non-guided, or sketchy. Several years ago a young lady asked to be assigned to kindergarten for her student teaching. About two weeks later she came to the office and wanted to be assigned to first grade. She was asked why the request to be reassigned was being made. Her response illustrates our point: "Kindergarten isn't academic enough!" When questioned further, she explained that she wanted to "teach science, social studies, health, arithmetic, and subjects like that." When asked why she had not prepared to teach high school pupils, she responded, "You have to know too much!"

You, of course, know the areas in which students must be prepared to accept responsibility as teachers, and plans for your student will provide for experiences in each of the areas. But your knowledge, your plans, and your focus give no assurance that the student will have proper focus. The student's growth while he is with you will partially depend upon his knowing what he must be prepared to do as a teacher, his continued focus upon preparation for those responsibilities, and his desire to achieve growth in meeting those responsibilities. The climate or setting is planned and ready for the student. Now you must consider ways by which you can get the student focused upon areas in which preparation must be made and in which competencies must be developed, then give attention to his development of purpose.

The student who has a full-time assignment may see you meeting responsibilities in all of the areas during the first week. Those who have less than full-time assignments will probably

[6] Informal studies conducted by the authors.

see the range of your activities by reviewing your daily schedule (not class schedule). Your schedule should show responsibilities for school hours and out-of-school hours, for week ends as well as school days—that is, a complete picture of your professional activities. We hope your daily responsibilities are not so extensive that they will overwhelm the student. Those of some teachers are. You may find that working with student teachers greatly reduces the breadth of activities in which you can participate or assume responsiblity, both in and out of school.

It would be helpful for the student to have such a list of teacher responsibilities as a part of his professional gear during student teaching. These may be in a handbook or a mimeographed list. They serve to acquaint him with the areas and to suggest types of responsibilities available to him in each area. We suggest organizing such a list under the following areas:

1. Pupil growth in the educational program
    A. Classroom program
    B. Extraclass program
2. Pupil guidance and counseling
3. Intrafaculty activities
4. Administrative relationships
5. Parent relationships
6. Community relationships
7. Professional self-growth

The real focus of the student during student teaching must be upon the development of competencies necessary to work effectively in each area. A list of such competencies should be supplied the student at the beginning of the term and reviewed carefully with him in conferences. No doubt you will use the same list of competencies in evaluating student growth. This is another reason why he should have the list at the beginning of the term and why each competency should be carefully explained. (See Appendix F for a suggested list of competencies.)[7]

[7] Also see *The Evaluation of Student Teaching*, Twenty-eighth Yearbook (Lock Haven, Pa.: Association for Student Teaching, 1949). Chapter I reviews the "California Statement of Teaching Competencies."

Student focus has been determined, but how can you stimulate student purpose? You can help the student to see what teacher responsibilities are and what competencies are essential to growth in those responsibilities through discussion and through demonstration of the conditions listed below:

Enthusiasm in meeting your daily tasks. Your cheerful disposition, concern to do a thorough job, sincere feeling for the pupils, professional interests, attitudes toward your work and others, desire to do more than required, and drive to meet responsibilities, all have a "catching" effect upon students. The student's general approach, interest, and attitudes generally reflect those that you demonstrate while he is with you.

Success which teachers demonstrate in teacher competencies. If you are highly successful in consistently demonstrating skill in pupil concern for his growth, the results will certainly be attractive to the student, unless you make the procedures you use seem quite difficult and mysterious. Your highly developed competencies must be evident, but the student also must see other teachers working successfully in their jobs. One of the values in having the student work with several teachers is that he may see that they are equally effective in working with pupils, parents, community, administration, and other staff members, but with different personalities and quite different approaches. Thus, for example, he can see that teachers may meet individual differences of pupils effectively but in different ways. This removes the stereotype and may stimulate student imagination.

Ample conference time for informal discussion. This is a time for pep talks, if they are needed. Real skill may be required in getting the student built up to the point where he wants to get into things for all he's worth. We want to emphasize one point here: student purpose, once developed at a high level, may not stay constant. It may be high at the beginning of the term, then start sagging and continue to sag throughout the term. You must be reading his mind constantly through his actions and reactions. You may waste much effort, unless you work toward maintenance of purpose. Informal discussion in conferences is one of the best ways to keep close to the student's attitudes and to keep his spirits up.

Success in first activities. A taste of success may be the magic that gets purpose up to a high level. This is one reason why we shall emphasize that a student should start with activities in which a failure will not wreck his spirit.

YOU ARE RESPONSIBLE FOR THE STUDENT'S GROWTH

The teacher is normally expected to guide the student by:

1. Orienting him to the school and the community and to the particular areas in which he will assume responsibility

2. Providing a graduated series of induction experiences for him

3. Permitting him to assume responsibility as he demonstrates readiness

4. Communicating your own over-all plans for your pupils to him, and, especially, assisting him in gaining a true perspective of your long-range instructional goals

5. Providing encouragement and guidance to aid him in achieving maximum growth

6. Assisting actively in the evaluation process, both in promoting student self-evaluation and in aiding the student by your own analyses and suggestions

YOU ASSIST THE COLLEGE IN SELECTIVE RETENTION

The colleges need your help in continuing the process of selection during student teaching. The fact that any good program of selection must be a continuous one, from admission to graduation and certification, places a very important responsibility on all those teachers who guide students in their professional experiences with children. You can help students identify their weaknesses and plan ways to strengthen themselves. You can take an active part in weeding out the unfit and the potential failures, for yours is a joint responsibility with the college faculty for the improvement of the profession. We owe it to the children of America to send out capable young teachers and to eliminate those who are not likely to be successful as leaders of youth. Our responsibility is to the state, to the parents, and to the profession. As the competency of teachers rises, so will the prestige of teachers and teaching, as well as our opportunity for service.

YOU PREPARE THE STUDENT FOR HIS FIRST JOB

The success of the student in his first year of teaching will depend, more than anything else, upon how well you have prepared him to teach successfully in a public school. You must know public schools—how they operate, their functions, their organizations, the attitudes of communities toward education—and must be able to suggest ways for improvement of self in readiness for a job in public education.

WHAT COMPETENCIES ARE DESIRABLE IN WORKING WITH STUDENT TEACHERS?

Please don't be frightened by the competency list that follows. Few teachers are highly effective in all of the competencies. However, if you are going to work with students you should develop as many as possible. The list is arranged in the form of a checklist, and each statement is in question form. Rate yourself on each item, using a three point scale as follows: H—highly effective; A—average, just so-so in effectiveness; or N—not effective. Practically, no teacher would be able to rate himself highly effective on all items; certainly not at the time of beginning to work with students, and probably not even after having had two or three.

The checklist is designed for several purposes. If you have never had a student teacher it will give you a chance to study the attitudes that are important and helpful, the responsibilities that you might carry, and the scope of the whole experience. Again, you might review it as a check on your progress while a student is in the middle of his experience with you. After the completion of a student's assignment, the list might be used as a quick evaluation of your efforts. Much of the concern for the day-to-day teaching of boys and girls has been omitted because it is always an obvious responsibility of both teacher and student. Special emphasis has been given to desirable points of view, relationships, and ways of aiding the growth of your student.

IN YOUR PERSONAL RELATIONS WITH YOUR STUDENT, CAN YOU:

1. Respect the personal integrity of the student?

2. Accept him both as a student and fellow teacher?

3. Establish and maintain informal, friendly working relations with him?

4. Encourage him to express his own opinions and to feel free to come to you to discuss his problems?

5. Encourage him to make his own decisions, based on careful study and defensible standards, rather than asking you to make decisions for him?

6. Originate and suggest new ideas without dominating his thought and action?

7. Observe your student at work and record observations without disturbing his emotional balance and poise?

8. Make a practice of suggesting a positive approach toward solving his problems, instead of just repetitiously reminding him of them?

9. Maintain your confidence in him and be optimistic about his eventual success, even during those periods when he becomes discouraged?

10. Take a sympathetic interest in his personal problems, without undue inquisitiveness, and be tactful and helpful in assisting him in his adjustment to personal problems, responsibilities, and limitations?

CAN YOU PROVIDE GENEROUS OPPORTUNITIES FOR GROWTH THROUGH:

1. Observations of well-planned lessons which you have designed to illustrate important principles and procedures?

2. Proper utilization of the student's background experiences for the enrichment of the teaching-learning activities?

3. A series of carefully selected induction experiences which lead into responsible teaching by easy stages?

4. Many demonstrations of sound teacher-pupil relations

based on a thorough understanding of the psychology of child growth and development?

5. Aiding your student in setting up levels of achievement appropriate to his development?

6. A generous period of independent teaching, so that your student will have a chance to develop the self-confidence and skill he will need on his first job?

7. Independent responsibility by your student for planning, organizing, and directing a major unit of instruction with a minimum of review and modification?

8. Maintaining an open mind toward your student's suggestions and acting on those which appear promising?

9. Practice in self-evaluation induced by withholding your judgment and encouraging your student to analyze his own procedures and results?

10. Continuous adjustment to his changing needs and progressive development?

IN PROMOTING YOUR STUDENT'S GROWTH IN PROFESSIONAL COMPETENCE
CAN YOU:

1. Adjust the length and activities of the induction period to meet his needs?

2. Evaluate your student's early teaching skillfully enough to encourage him and still suggest ways for improvement?

3. Refrain from imposing your standard of "correct and incorrect procedures" on your student?

4. Encourage him to use a wide variety of teaching procedures?

5. Encourage him to develop new ideas and put them into practice?

6. Assist him in observing the facts of child growth and development and in identifying psychological principles as they apply to teaching and learning?

7. Assist your student in setting reasonable standards of performance for his classes and encourage frequent evaluation of their appropriateness?

8. Use the presence of deviates—mental, physical, or social—

to stimulate your student's professional initiative, without engendering idle curiosity or defeatism?

9. Assist actively and continuously in the evaluation process and refrain from being a real "critic teacher?"

10. Develop a system of continuous evaluation, including anecdotal records of your observations, and share your judgments with your student at appropriate times and conferences?

IN YOUR PROFESSIONAL RELATIONS WITH YOUR STUDENT, CAN YOU:

1. Clarify his responsibilities and privileges and give him security in knowing what is expected of him the first day, the first week, and periodically throughout the assignment?

2. Clarify his relationship to the administration, other teachers, pupils, and parents, and give him an understanding of the proper channels of communication and ways of working?

3. Make a place for him in the professional and social life of the school staff?

4. Make definite arrangements for the time, place, and frequency of conferences?

5. Develop a "team relationship" so that he feels he is the "junior partner" in a going concern?

6. Assist him in arranging for profitable observations and opportunities for further experience throughout the school and community?

7. Assist him in securing opportunities to discuss professional matters with the administrative personnel and other staff members?

8. Refer him to sources of information and illustrative material and to agencies that offer personal and professional services which he may need?

9. Counsel him concerning his professional plans and ambitions without dominating his decisions?

IN SETTING AN EXAMPLE OF HIGH PERSONAL STANDARDS, CAN YOU:

1. Remain content to influence your student primarily by modest example, rather than by incessant precept and lengthy harangues?

2. Practice self-evaluation on a wholesome, objective basis

and encourage your student to share with you his judgment of your work?

3. Follow acceptable standards of language, dress, social amenities, and interpersonal relations?

4. Maintain your own sense of humor without laughing at his mistakes and personal limitations?

5. Live a well-rounded life and thus retain a mature perspective toward personal and professional matters?

6. Exemplify maturity and emotional stability in the way you react in emergencies and carry on in the face of emotional tensions and outside personal cares and responsibilities?

IN SETTING AN EXAMPLE OF GOOD PROFESSIONAL ETHICS, CAN YOU:

1. Keep your perspective and maintain good working relations with your student, colleagues, college faculty, parents, and public?

2. Refrain from dumping your own "busy work" on the student with the weak excuse that he needs lots of experience with routine?

3. Secure and analyze personal data on your student and use it in a thoroughly professional and confidential manner?

4. Maintain complete objectivity if it becomes necessary to discuss with him some unprofessional behavior on his part?

5. Accept gracefully the standards of social and moral behavior which are expected of teachers by the community?

6. Evaluate objectively the advantages and disadvantages of teaching, but exhibit enthusiastic loyalty toward your work and the profession of teaching?

WHAT EFFECT DOES STUDENT TEACHING HAVE UPON PUPILS?

The needs of the pupils come first in student teaching. In this book we are primarily concerned with the growth of students, but we must never lose sight of the pupils. Whenever a pupil program shows signs of serious deterioration because of the presence of such teacher education functions as student teaching, the student or students must be removed or the program altered until adequate safeguards can be provided. Such drastic action is seldom necessary if the students have developed readiness for the experiences included in student teaching. Actually, when wisely guided, almost all students can make a positive and significant contribution to the learning of the group. One of your major responsibilities is to evaluate your student's readiness and to select activities that he can carry with profit, for the pupils as well as for himself.

Parents, administrators, and teachers sometimes worry about the effect of student teaching on pupils. A good professional program of student teaching can provide a superior learning situation. When the student and teacher are both vitally concerned with improving the teaching-learning situation, when both are working as a team to use all their abilities in solving learning problems, the public need have no fear for the pupils' welfare.

Two rather different personalities in a classroom can stimulate more pupils to maximum effort. The youth of a student often becomes an advantage in working with certain children. The concern of the teacher should be that all possible efforts are being put forth to provide a good environment for learning. The way in which a team relationship can work in the lower grades is illustrated by this observation made by a young woman student: "My teacher doesn't have a chance to take notes on my teaching—she is so busy all the time with the children. I just don't know how she will be able to get along after I leave!" *Competence of the teacher as well as of the student must be measured finally in terms of the pupils' growth.*

WHAT IS YOUR RELATIONSHIP TO THE COLLEGE SUPERVISOR?

If you are a public school teacher supervising students, you were selected for this service by the college or by the college and your school officials cooperatively. By your agreement to cooperate with the college, you accept responsibility for the growth of the student assigned to you and for cooperation with the college in your work with the student. Ordinarily, this co-operation chiefly involves a working relationship with the super-visor designated by the college.

Since the responsibility for the student must be carried jointly by you and the college supervisor, it becomes very difficult to set forth precisely the functions of each person. Particular cir-cumstances in the college and public school influence the respon-sibilities that each assumes; also, easy informality and flexibility can provide a basis for frank discussion and the building of a team spirit between the teacher and supervisor.

The college supervisor often has some knowledge of your student even before he is assigned to you. The supervisor may have had the student in class. He may have had a part in the student assignment to you, although many factors are influen-tial in making assignments and the process varies according to local conditions. Most college officials have the student teach-ing assignments approved by the proper school authorities. We hope that you were asked if you would like a student teacher and that you received information about him several days in advance of his coming. Sometimes the supervisor has a chance to confer with you before the student's arrival; however, pres-sure of numbers often prevents this.

From this point on the supervisor's major responsibilities are two-fold, to the teacher and to the student. He directs or coun-sels the teacher concerning the general planning of the student's experiences, and he may assist in the day-to-day guidance of the experiences. His work with the student may be through weekly group conferences, observations of the student at work in the school, individual conferences with the student, and confer-ences with the teacher and student. When local conditions per-mit, two other kinds of group situations can aid greatly in facili-tating working relationships. Many supervisors arrange seminars for teachers which permit sharing of experiences and sugges-tions. The three-way conference, including supervisor, teacher, and student, is an excellent device for checking program and facilities and for making long range plans and evaluating progress.

The final evaluation of the student and the reports which must go to the proper college offices are a responsibility of the supervisor. The teacher is usually asked to cooperate in making the evaluations or requested to supply information and personal judgments which can be used by the supervisor. Laboratory school teachers generally are given full responsibility for student evaluation.

The above description of the working relationship between the college supervisor and teacher may not fit your particular situation. The important point is for you to make sure that you know what your responsibilities are and what the responsibilities of the supervisor are before you start working with student teachers.

Student teaching in teacher education programs of the colleges and universities of the United States varies in all respects. Widely divergent practices are found, for example, in the following:

1. The nature of experiences provided
2. Provision for individual differences
3. Significance accorded student teaching in the teacher education programs
4. Quality of supervision by the college supervisor and teacher
5. Responsibilities assumed by teachers and college supervisors
6. Working relationships between college and cooperating public schools
7. Focus or emphasis in the teacher education program and particularly in student teaching
8. Types of services provided teachers by college personnel.[8]

You owe it to yourself, your pupils, your school, your community, and your future students to determine as quickly as possible, preferably before receiving your first student (1) what the college expects in the student teaching program and (2)

[8] Flowers and others, *op. cit.*, pp. 144-187.

what your functions and responsibilities are in that program in relation to the other public school and college personnel with whom you will be working.

SUGGESTED REFERENCES

Curriculum Changes and Teacher Education, Thirty-second Yearbook. Lock Haven, Pa.: Association for Student Teaching, 1953. This yearbook reviews the impact of public school curriculum change upon institutions preparing public school teachers and reports teacher education programs designed to prepare teachers to meet such changes effectively.

Developing Facilities for Professional Laboratory Experiences in Teacher Education, Thirty-third Yearbook. Lock Haven, Pa.: Association for Student Teaching, 1954. Especially, Chapter II, "Facilities Pertaining to Good Working Relationships"; Chapter IV, "Facilities Pertaining to Good Contractual Relationships"; Chapter V, "Facilities Pertaining to Good Supervision of Student Teachers"; Chapter VI, "Provisions Made by Cities to Regulate and Facilitate Student Teaching Programs"; and Chapter VII, "Facilities Pertaining to the Improvement of Professional Laboratory Experiences."

Flowers, John G. and others, *School and Community Laboratory Experiences in Teacher Education.* Oneonta, New York: American Association of Teachers Colleges, 1948. Chapter II reviews curriculum patterns that students follow preceding and following student teaching. Chapter III reviews types of experiences that your student may have before coming to you as a student teacher. Chapter IV describes the place of student teaching in teacher education programs and proposes desirable experiences for students during the student teaching period. Chapter V defines present and desirable practices in providing for professional laboratory experiences following student teaching. Chapter VI gives many valuable suggestions concerning the nature of your work in guiding student teachers. This reference, better than any other, should clarify your place and function in the teacher education program.

Off-Campus Student Teaching, Thirtieth Yearbook. Lock Haven, Pa.: Association for Student Teaching, 1951. Chapter II reviews the place of off-campus laboratory experiences in teacher education programs. Chapter VI gives reactions to off-campus student teaching by the student teachers, off-campus school staff, the community, and the pupils. Chapter I reviews essential features of competencies by which student growth may be appraised.

2

Your Student Teacher

WHAT KIND OF INFORMATION ABOUT THE STUDENT can be helpful to you before he arrives? Teachers have a variety of ideas. Some want detailed reports, some none at all. The following are illustrative:

1. Teacher "A" asks to have each of her students fill out a lengthy information sheet covering the items listed below before she holds a pre-student teaching conference. She feels that this information gives her the type of background she needs so that she can have clues to approaches in the first conference and can help the student get acquainted. For example, to know that the student was raised on a farm and has been self-supporting through college prompts her to see that he does not have unnecessary expense in coming to the school for the pre-student teaching conference. This helps immediately in establishing a wholesome attitude toward the teacher.

Educational background:
    Elementary School
    High School: date graduated
    Colleges attended: dates, expected date of graduation
Professional preparation:
    Majors and minors
    Course patterns pursued

Special professional laboratory experiences
Special scholastic honors and recognition
Scholastic performance
General experiences:
Employment: kinds and amounts
Military
Community service: recreational or religious, youth organizations, camps, social service
Leadership responsibilities
Social and group activities
Travel
Personal characteristics:
Age
Health, physical development, and limitations
Intellectual interests and pursuits
Recreational interests
Hobbies and special personal skills: music, entertainment
Marital status, children
Place of residence during student teaching
Family background:
Parents: birthplace, citizenship, national origin, occupation
Community background and experiences
Siblings: number, sex, age, education experience, occupation
Autobiographical statement:
Often the student is asked to write a general sketch of his life, with emphasis on those facts and relationships which influenced his development and adjustment at various stages, his vocational plans, interest in teaching, and ambitions for the future.

2. Teacher "B" feels that any information preceding student teaching may create unwarranted judgments. The best way to collect information from the student is by conference, observation, and working with the student as he progresses through the term. In student teaching his actual background is less important than the way he can use his background in teacher activities.

3. Teacher "C" only asks for an autobiographical sketch and

uses this information to detect attitudes more than anything else. She feels that basic attitudes are likely to creep into such a sketch which might not appear in conversation or observation for weeks later. She insists, however, that she doesn't isolate attitudes that aren't there and that no prejudices are formulated before the student arrives. Of course, the general background is valuable and especially the high points brought out by the student, which may indicate interest, personality characteristics, and perhaps future goals.

4. Teacher "D" gets the general information that she wants following the first conference. A blank[1] is handed to the student and he is expected to mail it back. She likes to meet the student and establish a good relationship first, feeling that this approach contributes to more sincere and complete responses than could be obtained otherwise.

Your problem in getting information helpful to you in guiding students in their growth in assuming the responsibilities of a teacher has two aspects: (1) Obtaining background before the student arrives that will help you plan or prepare for the student, guide him wisely beginning with his first day at your school, and provide a basis upon which to build understanding of him as he works with you during the term or semester; and (2) Obtaining insights while working with the student during the term or semester which are necessary to provide for maximum growth of the student.

Getting acquainted with your student is not easy. The short time that he is with you complicates matters severely. For some of you the student teaching period may be only six weeks full-time or part-time; for others it may be only one hour per day for one term. Situations of this nature make it almost essential that you obtain some information before the student arrives.

We are suggesting the following three types of information that should be especially helpful to you, ways by which you may be able to obtain the information desired, and how this information may be helpful to you:

[1] See sample in Appendix A.

The educational program of the college which your student attends.

The placement of students by the college which your student attends.

The specific background of your student.

THE EDUCATIONAL PROGRAM OF THE COLLEGE WHICH YOUR STUDENT ATTENDS

You know what college he attends, but which college actually makes much less difference than the program provided for him in that college. He may be enrolled in a college in which the emphasis of the total college is upon preparation for teaching, or he may be in a college in which teacher education is only one of many emphases. You might anticipate that, in general, the student from the school which devotes all resources to the preparation of teachers would have the most highly developed attitudes toward the profession, understanding of the nature of a teacher's work, and philosophy of education. However, this is not always so.

The most helpful information you can obtain will have to do with the more specific aspects of the college environment. These should apply to all students from the college with which you work and should give you a better understanding of any student who might come to you.

THE ACADEMIC PROGRAM

A picture of the total college program can be misleading unless it is based upon an understanding of the emphasis in each part. For example, you might know the course requirements and electives, both general and professional, for students who plan to teach in primary grades. But until you become familiar with emphases in the program, such as art for child expression vs. teaching of art skills, or helping the child grow in creative expression vs. growth as the child wishes, you cannot anticipate the student's basic philosophy in teaching. Therefore, we are asking several questions concerning the college program and suggesting reasons why you should seek information to answer the questions.

What is the nature of the general education program? This program may be a variety of specific courses in fields such as science, social studies, art, music, English, industrial arts, home economics, and languages, or it might be composed of broad courses such as *Art in Contemporary Culture, Literary Expression, American Civilization, Social Problems of Modern Man,* and *Trends in American Social Life.*

You would expect the student who had the latter type of general education background to be better qualified for teaching units which encompassed fields of knowledge. For instance, a student teaching in intermediate grades should be better qualified to teach highly integrated social studies or science units. That is, in a unit on *The Westward Movement of the American People,* he should see possibilities for increasing understanding and appreciation by bringing in relevant experiences from the fields of art, music, science, literature, and so on.

Knowing children as you do, you realize the importance of your student having familiarity with and feeling for many fields. Students do not need to know all the answers, but they should be sufficiently familiar with different fields so that they can see (1) possibilities for contribution to anything the pupils may be studying at the moment, (2) possibilities for pursuing any particular question raised by a pupil, and (3) opportunities for pupils to develop broad interests in the world around them.

Are majors and minors broad or narrow? This question is closely related to the former. In fact, in some schools, some of the general education courses may be used in fulfilling requirements for the major and minor.

If your student has a major in social studies, he is certainly better equipped to teach social studies in high school and elementary grades than if his major were in economics. Likewise, a student whose major is science is better equipped than if his major were physics, chemistry, biology, geology, or agriculture.

This is especially true if the student is teaching in elementary grades and junior high school, or in senior high school general science classes.

The student with the broad major background should be able to see and utilize the total learning experience rather than just a part of it. For example, if the seventh grade science class is studying a unit on *How Is the Earth Changed?* it would be desirable for the pupils to consider earth changes in general, such as flora, fauna, soil, minerals, climate, weathering, diastrophism, glaciers, and the like. This requires a broad science background on the part of the student. If his preparation in the major field is broad, he is much more likely to direct the pupils in studying the total picture rather than a few aspects; for instance, the biological or chemical.

In elementary student curricula the major may be in education and not in major subject fields. Such majors may be narrow or broad. For example, some colleges offer majors both in primary and intermediate grades while some have one curriculum which includes all elementary grades. Unless courses in the former type program treat all elementary grades, with emphasis on either intermediate or primary, the student in each area may be severely handicapped. The student preparing to teach primary grades may have difficulty in student teaching in third grade unless his courses have also included at least some consideration of intermediate grades.

Another problem which may be faced by a student preparing to teach in elementary grades is lack of understanding in science, social studies, art, music, industrial arts, and so on. This may result from too much of the student's program being required in general education and methods courses. In fact, no more than one-fifth to one-tenth of the student's program may be outside general education and methods courses. If you have had students with this type of background you know how handicapped they are in providing rich, meaningful learning experiences for boys and girls.

What is the program in psychology and education? Perhaps

your student started his teacher education program with a practical course in orientation to the teaching profession. In this course, he may have observed pupil and teacher activities in elementary and secondary schools. For example, before starting to prepare for teaching in primary grades, secondary school science, or physical education, he may have had a chance to *see* the pupil program in action in each area. At the same time he may have reviewed his own interests, talents, and emotional characteristics, and may have decided which area seemed best suited to him.

In the same orientation course, he also may have explored the major areas in which teachers are responsible in the public schools.[2] Thus, before the student started his teacher education program he could find out *what he is preparing himself to do.* You may have gone all the way through a teacher education program without finding out what teachers must be prepared to do in the public schools, but you found out quickly when you started out on your first job!

Perhaps the only orientation your student received was as a pupil in elementary and secondary schools. But the value of this orientation is often over-rated. Most students can recall only vaguely the curriculum, organization and practices of the elementary schools and high schools which they attended.

What about the psychology and education courses beyond orientation? Does the student study child growth from a book alone, or does he study children and use books and other sources of information as resource materials? As a part of his education courses, does the student observe pupil learning, work with teachers in their school activities, work with the community groups, and so on, or does he only study *about* those things? You would expect that a student who had studied and worked *with* children, rather than only studying *about* children, would have developed a sensitivity toward and a feeling for pupils that other students might not have.

[2] See Chapter I, p. 11 and Appendix A.

What opportunities are provided for student experiences with children? The student's background with children and youth may make a real difference in his understanding, attitudes, and facility in getting started. The following types of experiences are illustrative. What program is provided by the college with which you work?

1. Observation in a campus laboratory school as part of professional courses. This observation may be an inherent part of professional courses. Emphasis may be placed upon the nature of learning, characteristics of the learner, the teaching-learning process, measurement of learning, and so forth. Also, the student may have opportunity to observe many types of teacher and pupil activities. Such observations, however, may provide meager understanding of public school situations. For example, there may be a select pupil population in the laboratory school limited in number to facilitate research and experimentation. We do not mean that there is no value to be gained through observations in laboratory schools. Students need to see newer practices, the most advantageous teaching conditions, the best instructional materials, and well-qualified, experienced teachers planning and working with children. It does mean, however that other observations are necessary. How are rural schools and those in less-favored communities fulfilling their obligations in public education?

2. Observation in public schools. Students in some colleges have opportunity to visit public schools; visit with the administration, teachers, and other personnel; observe class and extraclass activities; study the class and extraclass program, policies, philosophy, pupil personnel, and nature of the school district or parish; and learn something of the way in which the school is financed. These students may spend a day in each of several schools selected to provide variety in philosophy, size, organization, and type of district or parish. Students in some schools do not have access to campus schools, and all observations are made in public schools. Others have access to both campus schools

and public schools. However, the type of school observed probably makes less difference than the direction provided in observation.

3. Participation in school and community. Some colleges require students to participate in a public school before student teaching. The student may be assigned to a public school before the college opens or for a two- to six-weeks period during the quarter or semester before student teaching. In these situations the student works directly with a teacher and may progress to the point of assuming responsibility in class and extraclass activities. In fact, some students may progress farther during a period of this type than others progress during student teaching. Participation may be a part of many professional courses. In such courses, the students are required to work directly with pupils and teachers in different kinds of situations. Some schools also require courses which are chiefly observation and/or participation preceding student teaching. Experiences in the community are sometimes required, either in connection with professional courses or as special prerequisites to student teaching. These community experiences acquaint the student with and give him experiences in the out-of-school professional activities of teachers; also, they give him some understanding of the relationship between school and community.

Three factors will determine the effectiveness of pre-student teaching experiences: the degree of student readiness for such participation, the quality of teacher guidance, and the type of school and community. These three factors are even more significant when the student engages in apprentice activities as a high school pupil or does substitute teaching prior to student teaching. The latter may have serious consequences. One student, a potential teacher, was ready to change her college course after her first teaching experience. On the last day of school before the Christmas holidays, she had attempted to substitute for her mother, a fifth-grade teacher. In short order, she recognized her inability to cope with the Christmas spirit of the thirty-eight bright-eyed youngsters. She did not know how to utilize their interest and enthusiasm and, fortunately, was unable to squelch it. The same cannot be said of her own. It was totally destroyed by the eager children. Summed up in her own words: "I left the classroom that afternoon weary but wiser. I was truly sorry for the parents who were duty-bound to welcome home each bundle of burning energy. Never again would I want to teach!" Many carefully planned, pleasant, and successful contacts with children were needed to offset this single undesirable experience.

You have no way of knowing what ideas a student will bring to student teaching, what biases or prejudices have been inculcated or long-harbored, or what misinformation he will bring from past experiences. Therefore, you must be very sensitive to his attitudes and to his understandings revealed in ideas expressed, methods of procedure, and ways of thinking. No matter what attitudes or ideas exist preceding student teaching, the student must enter the student teaching situation with an open mind toward school organization, policies, practices, method, materials, and so forth. The approach is to find out, to understand, to adapt; not to revolutionize. You are the one who can best direct your students to this approach.

Are subject-matter courses professionalized? Your student may have had courses such as *Science for the Elementary Teacher* I, II, III; *Literature for Primary Grades; Mathematics for Elementary Teachers; Industrial Arts and the Child.* Such courses are referred to as professionalized if the student is building background and understanding in the areas and also discovering how those areas might contribute to pupil growth. On the other hand, your student may have had courses in any of the above fields but with no concern for the use of the understandings developed in relation to his future responsibility for directing pupil learning.

If you are a secondary school teacher, the same situation might exist. You may have noticed that your student teacher, in social studies, let us say, has little concept of how to teach pupils using social studies materials. Basically, your problem in guiding the student may be in getting his focus upon *teaching the pupil*, if his focus when he came to you was upon *teaching the subject*; if he failed to recognize that, in the process, something happens to the pupil.

What is the student teaching program? Is there more than one assignment? If so, what experiences are to be provided the student in each? Suppose, for example, that the first part of the student teaching assignment is provided in the campus laboratory school and the second in a public school, as is the case in some colleges. You should have some picture of the student's experiences in the first assignment if you teach in the public school. In the first assignment the student may, in general, work only with the teacher, as an assistant in the classroom. If so, you would expect your student to have a better background in classroom teaching than in other areas of teacher activities.

Perhaps there is no campus school in the college with which you work and all student teaching is in one assignment. In such case you have responsibility for all of the student's pre-service teaching experiences. Or, the student may have a student teaching assignment following his guided experiences with you. Regardless of the pattern, you should understand it, so that the best possible use can be made of the student's time while he is with you.

The following types of assignments are predominant in teacher education today:

The limited assignment: Many colleges still have student teaching organized to last only a few weeks, or have only a one- or two-period or an hour-a-day assignment. You could provide neither the breadth of experiences nor the flexibility you would like under such a plan. You would find that the program must be limited pretty largely to student direction of classroom experiences, induction must be briefer for all but the weakest of students, and planning with the student must be greatly reduced.

The initial student teaching assignment: This type has a try-out or exploratory function as one major purpose. The student should be allowed to grow at his own rate and to explore teacher activities widely. This would allow you to concentrate upon developing readiness to assume teacher responsibilities. An important final objective is the identification, by the student, of areas needing study and of objectives for the next assignment. Since the pressure for reaching a standard for certification is not present, there is more opportunity for the student to develop an objective approach to his work, free from the strain of excessive concern over grades.

The final assignment: Here the pressures are just the reverse of the one above. A final evaluation, a decision on certification, and a prediction of fitness to teach must all be reached at the end of this experience. The student would have to be moved along as rapidly as possible, and he should have an early understanding of the standards to be used in evaluating his growth. This kind of pressure is not wholesome for many students, and would have to be minimized in every way possible. If there were any doubt in your mind that the student could succeed, there would be little time to lose just hoping for the best. You would have to apply remedial measures quickly. If more experience were needed to recommend a student for certification, an early decision could probably be sold to the student much more easily than at the end of the term. This would be especially true if graduation were also involved.

The full day assignment: Flexibility and breadth are the special gains of the longer period spent in the school. To take advantage of them, early planning is important. You need to keep your perspective as broad as the whole field of education itself, and to set your sights on experiences you want your student to have. Many suggestions will be made throughout the book to help you capitalize on the opportunities of long assignments.

THE COLLEGE EXTRACLASS PROGRAM

If you have worked with a student teacher you recognize the value of a strong background of interests outside curricular work. Those who have had experience with the responsibilities in clubs, student government, and some type of counseling are in a better position to work in similar activities when they come to you. They not only have interests developed but also have had experience in group direction of activities and personal relationship problems involved in such activities.

Special interest groups or clubs are common in fields which offer majors and minors for secondary teachers and for teachers in special fields, such as art, music, and physical education. However, the same situation applies less often to elementary majors, unless they also have majors in academic fields. Thus, elementary teachers from a particular college may have little or no opportunity for the development of special interests.

Another aspect of the extraclass program of the college that should be of real concern to you is the social life. Is there variety in social life activities? Does the college sponsor large group activities and encourage groups and organizations to sponsor large and small group activities? Also, does the college and do groups sponsor activities involving both students and faculty? You are well aware that the social development of the student makes a real difference in his success in student teaching.

THE SELECTION AND RETENTION OF TEACHER EDUCATION STUDENTS

First, does the college select students who enter the profession? We hope you are associated with a college that can select those who are entering teacher education curricula. But the method of selection also makes a difference. Are they selected on the basis of scholarship alone, upon the basis of scholarship and personality, or upon the basis of personality, scholarship, and known success in interpersonal relationships with pupils, teachers, and adults in general? The college with which you work may have other methods for selection which have been found to be predictive of future success in teaching.

Second, does the college have a strong selective retention program preceding student teaching? In other words, are students screened out of the teacher education program? If so, how? The criteria may be grades below "C" average and serious moral conduct. Your college may include emotional instability, physical disability, poor interpersonal relationships, and lack of success in working with boys and girls. The last mentioned criteria is not commonly applied because, preceding student teaching, students ordinarily do not have sufficient experience with boys and girls to make judgment possible.

Third, does the college select those who enter student teaching? Most colleges use criteria for selection at this point, but the most frequent is scholastic record and completion of required courses. This situation exists even though we know that there is little relationship between courses taken and student teaching success. A study on requirements for admission to student teaching in 125 colleges of the American Association of Colleges for Teacher Education showed the following:

Per cent of institutions reporting use	*Factors determining admission*
84	Completion of a sequence of education courses
65	Scholastic rank in education courses
65	Scholastic rank in major teaching field
57	Completion of a certain number of hours in the major field
51	Judgment of the director of student teaching
44	Physical examination
43	Judgment of member(s) of the faculty
37	Character
34	Social maturity
32	Test of speaking ability
24	Judgment of selection committee
24	Personal appearance
18	Success in previous experiences with children
10	Score on teaching aptitude test
10	Score on personality test (Minnesota M.M.P.T.)[3]

These results indicate clearly that the heaviest emphasis is on academic readiness. Faculty judgment and recommendation come next in importance. Various personal and physical exami-

[3] Charlotte Junge, "Readiness for Student Teaching," *Off-Campus Student Teaching*, Thirtieth Yearbook (Lock Haven, Pa.: Association for Student Teaching, 1951), pp. 31-32.

nations and judgments are now being made in many schools. The difficulty of getting data in usable form from the student's previous experiences explains why this factor ranks third from the bottom, being used by only 18 per cent of the colleges.

THE COLLEGE GUIDANCE PROGRAM

In some colleges, student guidance is an integral part of the total program. In others, a guidance program is practically non-existent.

Perhaps the college with which you work considers the guidance program a necessary part of teacher preparation, and perhaps you are a part of it. It considers that religious life, social life, interest development, curriculum, student teaching, and family life are all parts of a total program focused upon the preparation of the student to be a successful teacher. The thread that runs through all of the parts and holds them together is guidance.

This places a real responsibility upon the student's advisor, for it is he who may be responsible for coordinating all aspects of the student's growth in preparation for teaching. The total guidance program in your college may be so successful that, in general, you know ahead of time that your student will be a fairly well-adjusted individual.

Another aspect of guidance has to do with the development of responsibility in self-direction. Suppose the college were to plan for the student and direct his activities rigorously, according to faculty or arbitrary rules. When the student comes to you with this sort of background, he may have difficulty in developing independence in assuming responsibility for teacher activities. He may wait for you to tell him what to do, fear responsibility, or just not see what needs to be done. We wonder just how much of the lack of imagination and creativeness in student teaching may be due to the overdirection and regulation of college students! Surely the average citizen is not so lacking in imagination.

Getting information concerning the above areas may be difficult. The following suggestions might help:

If you teach in a public school—

Get as much information as possible from and through the college supervisor who works with you.

Get acquainted with college personnel and obtain information through visits with them.

Visit with the guidance director or dean of student personnel.

Gradually accumulate background concerning the college program from your student teachers.

Collect informative materials concerning the program, such as the college catalog, college bulletins, mimeographed materials, and so on.

If you teach in a campus or off-campus laboratory school—

Get information from campus friends or the persons responsible for the particular parts of the program about which you need insights.

Get information from student teachers.

Use descriptive printed materials concerning the college program.

THE PLACEMENT OF STUDENTS BY THE COLLEGE

Perhaps in your state the student who receives a two-year diploma may expect to teach his first year in a small community or consolidated school. The elementary student receiving the B.A. degree, in general, may expect to teach the first year in a city system. The student receiving the B.A. degree to teach in a secondary field or special field, in general, may expect to start in a smaller community or consolidated school. Perhaps the student who works with you may expect to be placed first in a particular type of school. If so, information concerning such probable placement would be especially helpful to you in planning for the student from the first day on.

Briefly, both you and the student must have similar ideas of the types of positions in which he may be teaching on his first job. With this understanding, you can both keep in mind, as you work together, that his first job may be similar or dissimilar to the one in which he is doing his student teaching. His experiences in student teaching must always be paralleled by the reminder that his first teaching situation may be different in certain respects.

The matter of supervision is one illustration. Suppose you and the student are in a large city system but you are fairly confident that the student will be teaching in a small school. You have supervisors in different fields in your school system and they work rather closely with you. The school to which he may go would probably have little or no supervision. *He would have to seek supervision.* This you can prepare him to do while he is with you. Guiding student preparation for teaching in a particular type of situation or in particular types of situations presumes, of course, that you are familiar with conditions that exist in public schools.

THE SPECIFIC BACKGROUND OF YOUR STUDENT

Obviously, most of this information must be obtained after the student starts working with you. And, if relationships develop as they should, getting acquainted with him will pick up momentum as the student teaching period proceeds. There are two aspects that we would like to emphasize to help you get acquainted with students.

Obtaining written reports of student's background

There are many forms used across the country, and the sample in Appendix A may be used as an illustration. We should like to call several features of this form to your attention:

Only information that would *generally* be helpful in working with student teachers is requested. No attempt is made to ferret out many peculiar conditions.

The form does not require extensive writing and can be filled out in a brief period of time (necessary on registration day or advance assignment for student teaching).

The information requested includes the areas of curriculum, college extraclass activities, experiences with children, special interests and talents, social activities, leadership activities, professional activities, and future plans.

The information serves only as clues, which can best be expanded in informal conferences and visits before and during student teaching.

The information is sufficient so that you need not use excessive time in gathering information during the first conferences.

The form provides a broad coverage of information that can be used as points of departure in helping you and the student get acquainted.

You may work with a college that uses no such form to provide information for you. If you teach in a public school and would like such information, you and the college supervisor might work one out together. If in a laboratory school, you could work through your principal or the student advisors. When you cannot get information of this type before the student arrives, you could ask him to supply such information after he starts working with you. Be sure to explain why you want the data.

There is danger of hasty judgments concerning students if information is obtained before the student arrives. As a result, some teachers prefer to get their first impression of the student when he comes to the school and to collect data later. Actually, there is just as much danger in formulating hasty judgment in your first meeting with the student as there is in getting information ahead of time. Making hasty judgments during any of the time that he is working with you is equally as dangerous. At no time in working with a student can you be absolutely sure of your judgment regarding him as a person or his work. There are always intangibles and illusive contributing factors in a student's behavior. It does not behoove us to judge any student quickly, no matter how much we think we know about him. The best judgments can be made after weeks of patient, understanding work with the student under the best personal and professional relationship climate you can provide.

We should mention at this point that judgments of others concerning a student who is coming to work with you should not be used in formulating impressions before the student arrives. The person who could come nearest to giving you a valuable judgment would be the teacher who has guided him in student teaching experiences immediately preceding his assignment to your school. Even then, the judgment of the other teacher was based upon student performance in a particular situation. The conditions might have been quite unlike those under which he will work with you. Thus, the only way you can be safe in making judgments is in continuous, sincere attention to the guidance of his growth in learning to become a teacher.

Obtaining information through pre-student teaching conferences

We urge you to visit with your student before he reports for the first day of his student teaching assignment. You might visit with him at the college, but we recommend that he come to your school. His orientation to the environment in which he is going to work begins while the two of you are getting acquainted. More than one visit to your school is desirable, but if there is only one, it should come immediately preceding the beginning of his assignment. For example, he might come on Saturday before he reports on Monday, or, he might come anytime during the week preceding the day he reports.

You would want to have the conference in your classroom or office, but the pupils should not be present. Conversation would be informal and concerned with nonpersonal matters, such as the material on bulletin boards, the view from the room, the recent flood in town, the historical features of the community,

the size of the school, the recent concert at the college, or, perhaps, the baseball fortunes of your favorite major league team.
The objective is to make the student feel at ease by finding a
topic or topics of conversation which he can discuss freely. You
want to find out all you can about the student, but the best
way to succeed is to focus attention first on things other than
himself. The next step might bring the focus upon the school,
the room program, and you. Information that you obtain from
him during the first conference will be obtained in relationship
to other topics of conversation. The first conference reported
below illustrates the point.

The student (Betty) came to the school on Wednesday evening
by bus. A severe electrical and wind storm had developed while she
was en route and a taxi brought her to the school. She went immediately to the office and was quite apologetic concerning her
appearance. The secretary assured her that Miss Sloan would understand and took her to Miss Sloan's room. Betty found Miss Sloan and
the custodian busily gathering up papers that had blown about the
room as the result of an open window. Betty was properly introduced to Miss Sloan and the custodian and started to apologize for
her appearance, then forgot about herself and quickly assisted with
the paper collecting.

As Miss Sloan was sorting the arithmetic papers she was saying,
"This sometimes happens when you place too much responsibility
on pupils. They were in a hurry to get home ahead of the storm and
so didn't get one window shut. I went down stairs with the first ones
to see that they did not try to get on the buses and the storm struck
before I got back to the room. Did you get in much of the storm on
the way over?"

Betty responded, "We came in ahead of the storm but the lightning was severe. I'm scared to death of lightning and wind."

"Didn't you have a tornado close to your home this summer?"
Miss Sloan asked, hoping to get Betty talking and at ease.

Betty reviewed the nature of the storm and dwelt at length on the
damage caused. Miss Sloan noted that she overdramatized the conditions, showed an emotional approach, and, as a result, exhibited
lack of poise and stability. Miss Sloan was thinking, "Now this is a

characteristic that I'll need to watch. I wonder if she will be inclined to get upset easily if a child gets sick at school, spills ink on the floor, loses a book, strikes another child, or refuses to cooperate?" Note that Miss Sloan made some observations, attempted to analyze the observations in terms of teacher behavior, but was *withholding* judgment until further observation. She *was* getting acquainted with Betty without personal prying.

Miss Sloan shifted the conversation to the recent concert at the college, but Betty couldn't talk about this because she had not attended. She stated that she had gone home to a high school football game that evening. In this school students are admitted to concerts on activity tickets, so a clue was obtained regarding Betty's interests.

The conversation was shifted to Betty's home town and she expressed enthusiasm for the activities of the community, especially her church. Her comments also showed very strong home ties, and most of the community activities in which she participated also involved her parents. No mention was made of community activities with other young people or leadership on her part in community activities. Miss Sloan was afraid that here was a girl who might not have attained an independent personality apart from her parents.

Miss Sloan cautiously moved the conversation back to the college and to Betty's activities there. Betty explained that she didn't belong to any organizations, that she wanted to be free to get home when she wanted. Anyway, she thought clubs and sororities were boring. One college teacher she liked very much. She had spent a lot of time in this teacher's home.

Later, in discussing the room program, Betty suddenly asked, "Do you mean that you still use a geography textbook in the school here?" Then, "We were told in class that a teacher can't teach by units and use textbooks!"

Miss Sloan explained calmly that "in public school teaching one can't always have everything he would like and can't always do everything just as he would like." She further explained, "We do have other books, pamphlets, clippings, bulletins and lots of audio-visual aids. You will find out how we use a textbook later."

Notice that Betty was revealing her characteristics, attitudes, habits, interests and problems without Miss Sloan having to ask direct questions. Miss Sloan certainly was gathering impressions that would be helpful, not only in getting Betty started, but all through the student teaching period. In your pre-student teaching conferences you can be just as observing and find out just as much if you are skillful in conversation.

Further suggestions concerning the pre-student teaching conferences might be helpful to you:

Exchange ideas but do not become involved in argument or sharp differences of opinion.

Arrange a group meeting with other students and teachers in the school and serve refreshments.

Arrange for the principal to come in for a minute to meet and welcome the student.

Give the student any printed material concerning the school, such as teacher handbook, pupil handbook, statement of philosophy, general statement of curriculum, or rules and regulations.

Give the student a copy of the community bulletin, if available from the chamber of commerce.

Locate the classroom in relation to auditorium, toilets, building entrances and exits, playground, gymnasium, office, and so on.

Establish a friendly relationship between student and teacher.

Stimulate his interest in becoming a part of the group.

Prepare him for the first day of his assignment.[4]

OBTAINING INFORMATION AFTER YOUR STUDENT ARRIVES

There are three major ways by which this can be accomplished. No one can give you the picture you want by itself. We urge your use of all procedures suggested below and any more that you have discovered.

Developing informal conferences. The conference can be informal without giving the student the idea that working with you is a "soft touch." Students are not likely to express them-

[4] See suggestions for first-day activities in Chapter 3.

selves freely in formal conferences, and it is through informal discussions that you get many clues as to causal factors in student performance. Your student may be harboring some fear that you never would be able to isolate in a formal conference atmosphere. But in unguarded, relaxed moments, while both are discussing things informally, many comments are made which reveal the inner self. Much will be said about the mental health of the student later, but informal chit-chat with you is one of the best releases of inner tensions and one of the best mental health governors that has been discovered.

With mutual respect established, the informal conferences provide the opportunities you want to get acquainted with your student in a manner that will enable you to really know him. It is somewhat comparable to the painter who starts with a rough sketch and gradually adds, bit by bit, a meaningful interpretation of what he sees. So with you, bit by bit is added to the brief information you have concerning the student when he arrives, and by the end of the teaching period you can know him.

Providing social situations. Informal social gatherings enable you to meet the student on even terms. A skating party, picnic, tennis match, theatre party, hike, or bird-watching trip with a few other staff members and students can help tremendously in getting acquainted. But a word of caution: It is best that there be a group and not just the two. The group should not consist of an even number of men and women, otherwise an awkward situation might result, especially for the student. No situation should ever be created that would give any student the idea of a "date" with the teacher.

Observing and working with students. You can get most of the additional information you need while observing and working with your student. In fact, you will always get more clues by observing him in action than by talking with him, although comments do assist you in interpreting student performance. You may have gathered all sorts of background concerning the student's ability to work with pupils, but you may find him "all thumbs" in his actual working relationships with pupils. Unless you have established good working relationships with him, you may never discover why, other than that he "just can't."

Our chief concern here is that you work with the student, study his activities, talk with him informally about the activities he is directing, attempt to analyze his problems, and then decide how to proceed. You are getting to know him; there will be time later to formulate judgments concerning his growth and probable future success. You can defeat all of your purposes, and his, too, by judging when you should be doing everything possible to get to know him.

In summary, we have emphasized several points that you should keep in mind in getting acquainted with your students:

1. An understanding of the college program and environment is essential to help you understand *all* of your students.

2. An understanding of the placement possibilities helps you to understand better the student's probable needs in his first teaching position.

3. General background information may be obtained from the student before he arrives for student teaching, but this is not to be used for pre-judging him in any respect.

4. Mutual respect must be established before you can really become acquainted with your student.

5. Informal procedures are most effective in obtaining insights that enable you to know your student well enough to help him specifically.

6. Getting to know your student continues through the student teaching period.

SUGGESTED REFERENCES

Flowers, John G. and others, *School and Community Laboratory Experiences in Teacher Education*. Oneonta, N.Y.: American Association of Teachers Colleges, 1948. Especially Chapters II and III, which give a picture of student background in professional education and professional laboratory experiences preceding student teaching.

Off-Campus Student Teaching, Thirtieth Yearbook. Lock Haven, Pa.: Association for Student Teaching, 1951. Chapter III reviews factors and requirements for admission to student teaching.

3

Getting Ready for Your Student

YOUR RESPONSIBILITIES HAVE BEEN REVIEWED, and you know something about the student for whom you are to assume responsibility. You may have visited with him once or twice, but to say that you know him well enough to be sure that your plans for him will work would be drawing conclusions without sufficient evidence. However, preparations for his arrival must be made. Those of major importance are:

Planning to acquaint the student with the school.

Planning a tentative program for the student.

Planning for the initial activities of the student.

Planning for a series of conferences with the student.

Planning to acquaint the student with the community.

There may be other planning that you do at this point. You can hardly be over-prepared for the student's presence the first few days in your school.

PLANNING TO ACQUAINT THE STUDENT
WITH THE SCHOOL

Students may have come to your room before and perhaps you have worked out effective approaches to their orientation; certainly you have changed the procedures that did not work.

49

To get your student off to a good start we recommend that you follow the procedures suggested below.

ENLIST ASSISTANCE OF PUPILS

In a laboratory school the children become accustomed to working with student teachers. The purpose of the school and how it functions in its relationships to the college is explained to the pupils, and it becomes increasingly more meaningful as they progress through the grades. This also may be true of a cooperating public school in which a student teaching program has been underway for some time. If student teaching is being introduced into the school's program for the first time, the need for preparing the pupils is most acute. They should know why these young teachers are planning to teach in their school. You can point out the many advantages which this program offers them. At the same time, you can make clear the responsibilities which go with the privileges of having the student's assistance. The pupils must have the same respect for the students that they have for the other teachers. In fact, they must recognize them as teachers, not students. If they are properly prepared, the pupils should take pride in cooperating with the teacher education program.

Some teachers find that the "acquainting" procedures are made much more enjoyable and profitable for all concerned by planning with the pupils for the responsibilities. Explanations concerning the student will vary according to age of pupil, little explanation being necessary in kindergarten and primary grades. At these ages, the new teacher situation might be explained thus:

Another teacher is coming to work with us. She will be here Monday. Her name is Miss Olson (write on board). When I talked with Miss Olson, I discovered that her home is at Trenton. You remember that Billy lived at Trenton before he came to our school. I also found out that she plays a violin and likes to sing. It will be fun having her in our music class.

We need to decide how to get acquainted with her. She will want to learn all of our names as soon as possible. How do you think we might help her learn our names? (Discussion, decision, and responsibility determined.) I've told her about some of the things we do in our room. What are some of the things you think she would like to know about? (List, decide which items are to be used, decide how Miss Olson is to be informed, determine pupil responsibility.) She might like to know about our art room. Can you think of other things that we could tell her about our school? (List, decide upon items to be used, decide how Miss Olson is to be informed, determine pupil responsibility.)

"Telling Miss Olson" when she arrives could become a monotonous drudgery for all. This situation, however, presents excellent opportunities for individual planning, group planning, class planning, oral expression, written expression, committee discussion, excursions, proper introductions, pupil acquaintance with school, and use of the opaque projector. Just think, there would be a week or more when you wouldn't have to worry about opportunities for functional learning! You would have wonderful opportunities for making experience charts, organizing information, promoting pupil responsibility, meeting individual differences in abilities, and guiding pupil-teacher planning. But caution: don't wear out Miss Olson before she arrives!

You may have the most difficult situation of all; one in which the pupils extend themselves to the limit to make the student miserable. If this is your first experience with these pupils, you should follow a procedure somewhat like the one discussed above, but adapted to the age level of the pupils. The important point is to arrange for the pupils to assume responsibility for the beginning stage of student acquaintance with pupils, program, and school.

In intermediate grades, junior high school, and senior high school, you can explain the nature of student teaching in more detail. Pupils should know the extent to which the student can assume responsibility in the school, the authority he will have in discipline cases, and so on. Generally, boys and girls are remarkably understanding, helpful, and considerate, especially when they are in possession of the unvarnished facts and have definite responsibilities. Sometimes, in campus laboratory schools or even some public schools, student teachers are so numerous that they are just taken for granted. In such a school, pupils in any grades from three to twelve may gang up on the student. A frank discussion concerning the function and problems of the student teacher, when the student is not present, will often be enough to put them back on the track.

In intermediate grades and junior and senior high school, preparation for the student teacher might include discussion of ways to present information concerning the following items:

The pupils in our school

Our teachers, principal, custodian, secretary, and nurse

Our school district

Our school organization

Our class schedule

Our work in this class

The materials and equipment we use

Our clubs

Our student council

Our athletics

Our social activities

Our standards of conduct

Our homeroom program

Our rules concerning absence, tardiness, and violation of standards of conduct

Our reports to parents.

Committees plan the information they are to give, perhaps only enlarging upon the points given in the student handbook. They also plan the way in which the information will be given. The reports are made to the student in an informal manner, perhaps with the student and pupils sitting around a table. They have the necessary materials, such as a map of the district, the school schedule, the standards of conduct, and so on. Committees may also show the student about the building, the school grounds, and the community. You and your pupils may have other procedures you like better. The important part is that the pupils not only share in the procedures but have definite responsibilities.

The familiarity of personnel with student teaching in your school will influence your plans. Even in schools where there are many student teachers, it is desirable that all personnel know the names of student teachers who are coming and to whom they are assigned. This information can be given in faculty meeting. Also, such a meeting would provide opportunity to discuss tentative plans for the student's program. If you had arranged for him to work with other people, for his office space, and for any out-of-school activities, these can also be reviewed. You might want the custodians and other school personnel in the staff meeting or you might want to talk with them separately.

The first student in your building or in your community would require additional planning. Several staff meetings might be needed to review the student teaching program and the responsibilities of the student, the staff, the community, and the college. The college supervisor or other college representative should be present at these meetings, and the agenda for the meetings should be planned by you and the college representative. You might want to have such a clarification meeting each fall before the first student arrives, if you have new teachers or administrators in the school.

Plans should be made for students and faculty to meet, if possible, during the first week of each term that students are in your school. Some schools have informal meetings at which refreshments are served. Other schools have semi-informal gatherings in which refreshments are preceded by short talks from the school administrator, a member of the teaching staff, and a member of the custodial staff.

Your general plans should be focused upon making the student a definite part of the school. He should have a mailbox in the office, a standing invitation to smoke in the room used by other school personnel, a desk or table where he may keep his materials, and a place for hat and coat in the cloakroom. Such arrangements must be made before the student arrives, so that he can be assured of a place in the school community. Students are sensitive about these matters, as would be expected. The following comments are indicative:

They treated you as a fellow teacher. I felt I was a part of the whole school.

I felt very free to go to other members of the faculty.

The teachers created an excellent environment by respecting everybody's opinion.

I was never introduced to another faculty member.

Two of the teachers seemed quite obstinate in their own opinions; completely dogmatic.

Have essential information concerning the school assembled

This type of information can be made up in mimeographed form and placed in a folder. Some teachers prepare such a folder for each student. A statement of the philosophy of the school and requirements for graduation; a copy of absence and tardy blanks, the report to parents, and the pupil handbook; a list of classes and extraclass activities available in each year of high school; the student council constitution; and a list of fire drill regulations, regulations concerning bicycle and automotive traffic on the school grounds, and any other rules and regulations should be in the student folder. Questions concerning the above items and many other general areas will require answers. If you have the information ready at the outset, the student can get his information independently, leaving you to discuss more intangible items, such as availability of films, pupil and parent attitudes, and the nature of discipline in the school.

PLANNING FOR STUDENT USE OF MATERIALS
AND EQUIPMENT

If you are a social studies teacher, you may have the courses of study which you follow in your file. Also, you may have sample units, lesson plans, bibliographies, and tests. These should be well organized in the file where you keep them. One teacher always took them out and placed them on her desk to show the student, then put them away after the student left. Instructional materials used in the teaching-learning process should always be left in their proper places and the student taken to them. Make sure that other materials, such as projectors, record players, and playground equipment, are in their places before starting out with the student. The impression gained by seeing instructional materials well organized and in place is extremely important. If your files and other storage areas are labeled and the organization in each explained to the student, he will be able to study the materials when time is available. This procedure is better than trying to tell him *about* everything in the files in one or two conferences.

If you are an elementary teacher, personnel folders and other confidential information may be in your room or in the elementary school office. If you are a high school teacher, they may be in the counselors' files or in the principal's office. In any event, the folders should be well organized and available for use. Some elementary teachers file all materials—that is, anecdotal records, test results, samples of work such as handwriting and composition, and records of parent-teacher conferences— in one folder in each pupil's cumulative file. Other elementary teachers keep composition samples for the entire grade in one folder, reading test results in another, parent-teacher conference records in another, and handwriting samples in another.

In high school, if the cumulative records are in the principal's office or the office of the guidance director, they should be kept in usable order and should be completely accessible to the student. If records from the elementary school are incorporated in the individual folders of the high school pupils, they are most helpful to the student teaching in high school. They can be helpful to the student, for instance, in tracing a reading problem.

Staff and administration in some schools are reluctant to permit students to use cumulative record files, especially to discover the mental maturity of pupils. Schools that have permitted students free use of cumulative record files, however, have been of real service in providing experience in the use of confidential information. We are aware of only a few rare instances in which problems have arisen from student use of confidential information. Again, these files are not studied intensively the first day or two but are used as the student feels need to use them.

Do you have a list of equipment, such as movie projector, film strip projector, opaque projector, maps, science equipment, and playground equipment? Do you have the location listed for each item? Having this type of list for supplies and equipment is a real help to students.

If some of the equipment and supplies are located in rooms or offices of other teachers, or if you share instructional materials with another teacher or other teachers, arrangements should be made for the student to have the same privileges in sharing the materials. The student, of course, should be informed of the procedures that should be followed in checking out materials or in sharing materials with others. This is one situation in which he can cultivate the development of good working relationships with faculty members and other school personnel.

Forms used in requesting films, projectors, and any other items should be available, so that explanations can be given before he has need to make such requests. The sooner the student becomes oriented concerning the location of materials and discovers how to proceed in getting needed materials, the sooner he will develop a feeling of belongingness and security in your school.

PLANNING A TENTATIVE PROGRAM FOR THE STUDENT

When you know the background of the student, what sort of program he is supposed to have, and the experiences available to him, you are ready to start planning with the faculty and other school personnel: if in a public school, which teachers would be willing to work with him, to what degree could he assume responsibilities if working with them, and, finally, what quality of supervision might he have? This places a terrific burden of decision on you, a burden that must be shared by the college supervisor.

Your planning at this stage would, therefore, involve ascertaining:

1. The experiences available
2. The staff responsible for the experiences
3. The quality of supervision
4. The degree of responsibility that the student might assume
5. The willingness of the staff members to cooperate
6. The communication that could be expected between you and other teachers working with your student
7. The approval of your plans by the school administrator.

After you have determined what experiences and supervision are available to the student, you are ready to project a possible program for him. One teacher, Mr. Gill, on the basis of all information obtained, prepared this tentative program for his student, listing the experiences in which he hoped to assign the student specific responsibility:

Classes:
General science (8) ....Mr. Gill
Biology (10) ....Miss Pence
Algebra ....Miss Hanks
Extraclass:
Camera Club ....Miss Pence
Homeroom ....Mr. Gill
Study Hall ....Mr. Gill
Faculty relationships:
Report card committee ....Mr. Fair

Administrative relationships:.
  Hot lunch program ....Mr. Dix, Principal
Parent relationships:
  Conferences ....Mr. Gill
  Reports to parents ....Mr. Gill, Miss Pence and
                                     Miss Hanks
  PTA ....Mr. Gill
Community relationships:
  Youth Center ....Mr. Younkin
Professional self-growth:
  Professional file ....Mr. Gill

Mr. Gill prepared a similar tentative list of participation activities, as follows:

Classes:
  Physics ....Mr. Nusser
Extraclass activities:
  Assembly Committee ....Mr. Kent
Faculty relationships:
  Faculty meetings ....Mr. Gill
  Social committee ....Miss Horn
Administrative relationships:
  Monthly attendance report ....Mr. Dix, Principal
Parent relationships:
  PTA ....Mr. Gill
  Parent homeroom meetings ....Mr. Gill, Miss Pence and
                                     Miss Hanks
Community relationships:
  Education-Business
  Committee of Chamber
    of Commerce ....Mr. Gill

Mr. Gill planned the above program for a student who was assigned full-time in a public school for one semester. If your student is to be in your school a shorter period of time or only a part of each day, you would not plan such an extensive program of responsibility and participation. Also, you may find the student weaker or stronger than anticipated and may have to change the schedule accordingly. To illustrate: Mr. Gill found his student to be weaker than expected, so he shifted biology, study hall, reports to parents, and camera club to the participation list. He omitted from the participation list physics, assembly committee, social committee, monthly attendance report, parent homeroom meetings, and education-business committee of the Chamber of Commerce.

PLANNING FOR THE INITIAL ACTIVITIES OF THE STUDENT

Have you ever walked into a meeting where you were a stranger, where everyone looked you over and tried to size you up, and where you were ill-at-ease and unsure of yourself? We hope that your student can be spared this unhappy predicament by becoming acquainted with you and by being assigned first-day activities that definitely identify him with the group. The following schedule illustrates what we mean by being identified with the group on the first day.

A student in fourth grade in an elementary school:

8:00-9:00 Assist the teacher in readying the room for the pupils, adjust shades, and help get materials ready for classes. Meet and talk with pupils as they come in, be with pupils preparing materials for classes (unless this bothers him), be with pupils tidying displays on tables, get pupils spotted on seating chart. (Pupils should not congregate around student.)

9:00-10:00 (Social studies) Using seating chart, get pupils located while they are reading from references or having discussion. Be around room noting the references pupils are using and how they're using them, but be sure not to bother. Help teacher respond to pupils who indicate they need help. (Be careful of this because the pupils may only want to be noticed and to receive attention from the new teacher.) Go on tour of building with a committee of pupils during last thirty minutes of period.

10:00-10:30 (Music) Sit and sing with the group and participate in other music activities of the group.

10:30-10:45 (Recess) Go to playground with the pupils and play with them or officiate if they play a competitive game.

10:45-11:50 (Science) Sit in group during discussion and respond when called upon by teacher. Be around room noting problems pupils have in preparing a letter to industrial firms for additional reference materials.

11:50-1:00 (Lunch period) Go with group to lunch room, eat with pupils, and go to playground with pupils after lunch. Go through building with committee of pupils to meet other teachers, principal, custodian, nurse, librarian, and school secretary.

1:00-1:40 (Arithmetic) Observe class participation as pupils attempt to discover process of division by one digit number. Note the quality of thinking exhibited by the pupils; also note difficulties exhibited because some pupils had learned the mechanical process earlier. Make notations on seating chart.

1:40-2:05 (Spelling) Sit with group planning bulletin board while others receive spelling dictation.

2:05-2:50 (Art) Help pupils and teacher distribute art materials. Note artistic development of pupils and apparent special talents of some. Make notations on seating chart.

2:50-3:15 (Literature) Accompany teacher and pupils to library. Notice books selected by pupils, the type of assistance given by teacher and librarian, and the development of pupils in library routine.

3:15-3:30 (Dismissal) Be in room and hall with pupils. Find things to talk with them about.

A secondary student teacher with a major in social studies:

7:45-8:00 (Pupil arrival) Student in room with teacher going through file for possible bulletin board pictures, charts, and so on. Visit with pupils as they come in during last five minutes.

8:00-8:55 (American government) Student is identified by the teacher, who announces that he will work with the group making the large chart showing county government organization.

8:55-9:00 Start tour of building with boy and girl from the American government class.

9:00-9:55 Continue tour, leisurely discussing the school program, pupil activities, uses of the different rooms, the equipment in music and other areas, trophies, lunchroom, library, and so on. The last part of the period is spent in the library examining materials available, organization of materials, etc. and visiting teachers (if free), the custodians and the school secretary.

9:55-10:00 Student returns to teacher's classroom.

10:00-10:55 (American history) Student is identified and teacher announces that he will sit at tables with group and participate in the discussion. He is asked specific questions (prompted at pre-student teaching conference) and asks pertinent questions (also prompted).

10:55-11:00 Student circulates through corridors with pupils.

11:00-11:55 (Activity period) Visits Community Club with teacher and participates in planning trip to the city council meeting on the following morning.

11:55-1:00 (Lunch period) Eats in school lunchroom at table with teacher and pupils. Following lunch, visits with teachers in the faculty room.

1:00-1:30 Visit with principal and two selected pupils. Principal reviews some history and developments of the school, existing school-community relationships, the philosophy of the new school, and the like.

1:30-2:00 Student and pupils go to auditorium to listen to orchestra practice.

2:00-2:55 (Journalism) Teacher and student visit journalism class and work with individual pupils in refinement of articles prepared for school newspaper.

3:00-4:00 Conference with teacher. Review activities of day and plan activities for following day.

Thus the student immediately becomes involved in many activities, is a participating member of the groups with which associated, and is helped to forget self.

Before beginning your work with a student you need to have worked out a time schedule, a plan for the first two or three weeks. Although subject to change, it will serve as a guide to you, the student, and the pupils and will provide time for all points to be reviewed. A copy of this schedule should be available to the student when he first visits the school. The entire plan should be discussed briefly with the student, so that he can see how he is going to find out about everything. At the end of the schedule, or perhaps during the first two or three weeks, the procedures should be evaluated with the student so that subsequent schedules may be improved. See sample schedules in Appendix B.

PLANNING FOR A SERIES OF CONFERENCES
WITH THE STUDENT

Tentative planning should be done after you have somewhat sized up the student following the pre-student teaching conference. As you observe the student during the first day, you are in a better position to plan the conferences ahead, although the plans for the next day will need to be somewhat changed at the end of each day. All of your plans for student conferences should remain flexible.

During the first two weeks, the conference plans should emphasize acquainting the student with the items listed below, although not necessarily in the order given:

1. The interests, abilities, and backgrounds of the pupils

2. The personnel, organization, and responsibilities in the school

3. The policies and practices of the school

4. The building arrangement and the location of supplies and equipment

5. Community-school relations and standards expected of teachers

6. Class and extraclass offerings and schedules

7. The philosophy of the school concerning pupil standards of conduct, homework, methods of teaching (as textbook versus unit), teacher grooming, and contests

8. The over-all course of study in the classes in which he will teach and the program in these rooms during the preceding part of the year

9. School routine, such as attendance and tardy reports, reports to the nurse, fire drill, and so on.

Plans would also deal with activities of the student for each succeeding day and would provide ample time for the student to ask about anything he wants.

PLANNING TO ACQUAINT THE STUDENT
WITH THE COMMUNITY

Your student should become acquainted with the members of the school board, the pastor of his church, and other personnel who work closely with the school. Depending upon the field in which he teaches, he should become acquainted with potential resource persons. Many laymen in the community have much to contribute to the education of the community's children. Interviews with the older citizens can provide interesting background information essential to an understanding of the historical setting. The student also has another need for knowing the people in the community. What are the mores and customs? In what social activities do they engage? What are the places of interest to be visited? Your student will appreciate the help that you can give him in making such acquaintances possible. As soon as you know that a student is coming to work with you, you can start planning to get him acquainted with these people. Sometimes a handbook of the community is prepared by the Chamber of Commerce, Service Club, or other organization. If none is available, this may be an interesting project for your school. The student teacher who assists in gathering data would be even better acquainted with the community than those to whom the handbooks are given.

You cannot anticipate all preparations that need to be made for each student. In fairness to the student, the pupils, and the staff, however, tentative plans are necessary. Perhaps the most important outcome will be the favorable climate that has been started in the school by planning with pupils and other school personnel. You have contributed to receptive, understanding attitudes toward the student who is coming to the school. Preparation for his arrival should make him welcome, and the cooperative working relationships created as a result of your planning should have a stimulating effect upon the total school.

SUGGESTED REFERENCES

Feyereisen, Kathryn, and Verna Dieckman, *Guiding Student Teacher Experiences*, Bulletin No. 1. Lock Haven, Pa.: Association for Student Teaching, 1952. Helpful suggestions are given concerning planning that should precede student arrival.

4

Your Student Gets Started

YOU MAY RECALL THE QUESTIONS THAT WERE running through your mind, the fears that haunted you, and the information that you needed about the school at the beginning of your own student teaching. Recalling your unpreparedness, you are aware of the student's problems and are prepared to supply all of the ballast necessary. Getting a good start is a major factor in student success.[1] We recommend that you follow the induction procedures listed below to help your student get oriented most effectively. Each is discussed in some detail in the remainder of the chapter.

The student's orientation should be meaningful.

The student should immediately become a working member of the school.

You and the student should develop good working relationships.

The student should understand teaching-learning processes.

THE STUDENT'S ORIENTATION SHOULD BE MEANINGFUL

In your desire to get your student oriented there is an inherent danger of providing overdoses at the beginning of his experi-

[1] Kathryn Feyereisen and Verna L. Dieckman, *Guiding Student Teaching Experiences*, Bulletin No. 1 (Lock Haven, Pa.: Association for Student Teaching, 1952), pp. 1-10.

ences. The suggestions reviewed briefly below should help the student.

A PASSING INTRODUCTION TO A PERSON IS NOT ENOUGH

To be told that this is Miss Brown, the school nurse, is practically meaningless. A friendly smile and greeting gives the student very little with which to work, other than a friendly feeling. Where is her office? What are her hours? How are her services made available? The meeting should be informal, purposeful, and meaningful.

It is desirable that you or your pupils be with the student in meeting school personnel, so that the student can be properly identified. Pupils know all of the teachers, the principal, and other personnel, especially the custodians and schoolbus drivers. This gives pupils responsibilities for getting their new teacher started, and most often they are eager for the opportunity. Pupils usually like responsibility and conduct themselves with quality performance. Briefly, using pupils in this manner provides wholesome conditions that are conducive to student development of an among-friends feeling.

ACQUAINTANCE WITH PERSONNEL SHOULD BE MADE IN TERMS OF IMMEDIACY OF NEED

From the very start your student must work closely with certain members of the school staff. In your preparation for getting him acquainted, plan for early meetings with such staff members. Since the student has need for the meeting, he is more likely to make the most of such opportunities to know his fellow-workers. He should meet the other staff members with whom you have planned for him to work before he goes to their classes or other activities.

The physical education student generally works closely with the principal and custodian, so these two should be on his list early. The music student should become acquainted early with the teachers with whom she will be teaching. There are four persons with whom any student should become acquainted immediately: the principal, the school secretary, the school nurse and the custodian.

ACQUAINTANCE WITH SCHOOL POLICIES, PRACTICES, ORGANIZATION, AND CURRICULUM SHOULD BE MADE IN TERMS OF IMMEDIACY OF NEED

The student can avoid mistakes and embarrassing blunders if he fully understands how he can best conform to the school's accepted practices. Since each school has its own policies and practices, the student may not be expected to know specific rules and regulations of your school. The same applies to curriculum, personnel records, tests, text and reference books, and evaluation of pupil growth. Also, each school emphasizes certain rules and regulations, such as pupil conduct in corridors, pupil conduct in study hall, penalty for absences and tardiness, type of response in class, teacher supervision of corridors, teacher promptness in filling reports, and teacher hours in the school.

You need to decide upon the order in which the student should become acquainted with the various aspects of the total school and with your responsibilities in the school. It might help you to list the items you want to review each day or during each conference. If the student is teaching with you only one hour each day and you have no scheduled time for conferences, then you should arrange for conferences after school, evenings, or Saturday mornings. Systematic planning to review school policies and your own policies is necessary before the student is faced with a situation in which a policy is involved. A situation of this kind may set back a weak student to the point where weeks are required to re-establish his confidence.

THE TEACHER SHOULD DISCUSS ALL POLICIES AND PRACTICES WITH THE STUDENT

The student may not agree with the policies and practices of your school. Suppose you have rigid discipline in study halls and he came to believe, through discussion in education classes, that pupils should, for the most part, control their own conduct. If he reads the study hall rules without first reviewing them with you, it is possible that he will develop a serious prejudice against your policies. However, if you can review the policies and the reasons why your school uses such policies, the student is more likely to accept them without unwholesome reactions. This is especially helpful if the policies of your school and/or your policies and the beliefs of the student are at wide variance.

In this connection, a note of caution should be sounded. Be careful not to argue with the student concerning the differences that exist between his beliefs and the practices and policies of your school. Also, never let yourself get caught on the defensive. Points of difference in educational philosophy or practice *must be treated objectively.* He may even get emotional about his beliefs, but you can't afford to. This he must learn from you, so that he can see, before he goes into the field to teach, that differences in philosophy and the implementation of philosophy cannot be reconciled within a school by emotional argument and defensive tactics.

INDIVIDUAL DIFFERENCES AND BACKGROUND MUST BE CONSIDERED IN THE
RATE OF ORIENTATION

Only as you know your student are you able to plan and work successfully with him. If the student is lacking in background of experiences, the orientation should be slow and worked out in detail, with the student helping to make plans. A feeling of security is essential to his progress. The same is true of the student who is timid or reserved. Focus this student's attention upon the job at hand, thus removing him from prominence in the picture. Until this is accomplished, the rate of orientation is necessarily slow.

THE STUDENT SHOULD IMMEDIATELY BECOME
A WORKING MEMBER OF THE SCHOOL

Your plans for the student's first day are made and tentative plans are made for the first two weeks. Suggested plans for a student during the first two weeks, shown in Appendix C, are designed to illustrate types of activities or experiences that may be used to acquaint the student with the school and community as rapidly as possible. For applying the suggested schedule to your situation and for using the schedule you evolve, we make the following suggestions:

THE STUDENT PARTICIPATES IN THE SCHOOL PROGRAM IMMEDIATELY

Refer to the schedule of student activities in Appendix C and note the amount of time that the student is actively participating from the first day as compared to the amount of time that he just sits. Perhaps you cannot work out his schedule so that he is participating all of the time, but you can cut to a minimum the amount of time that he is sitting outside the group. Regardless of the field or the elementary grade in which you teach, the student can immediately become identified with the educational program.

The student can profit from using the same materials that are being used by the pupils—books, references, art media, science apparatus, physical education equipment, and so on. He becomes increasingly aware of the problems which confront the children when they are working. He becomes acquainted with and understands their developing skills and abilities. This places him in a better position to assist individuals or groups in the selection and use of materials of instruction. He is even more able to assist the teacher in selecting and locating materials to be used.

One student, after helping the teacher assemble all of the materials necessary for working out a Halloween street scene for a display, became so interested in the idea that she got other college students to work with her in the dormitory in setting up a larger but similar display for one of the sorority houses. During this experience many suggestions and new ideas were tried. On the following day, the teacher was delighted when the student brought in a host of ideas and literally baskets of material. Had she thought of using the separated parts of pine cones for thatching roofs? Why not use Spanish Moss for cobwebs in decorating the haunted house? These and many other suggestions proved most feasible. The student had tried them out and knew that they would work.

Identification with the total school may be difficult. It is possible that there are so many students in your school that immediate attendance of staff meetings, student council meetings, or lunch hour supervision by all of the students is completely impossible. In such case students might be assigned to these group activities on a rotation basis during the term. This would mean that orientation or getting acquainted could not be realized immediately but would continue through the term. A similar situation would exist for students teaching only one or two hours per day. In fact, immediate acquaintance could not be realized to the fullest extent unless the student were teaching full-time.

Another aspect of becoming identified with the school immediately has to do with faculty cooperation. It is quite possible that faculty members may not want the student to observe and participate in the activities for which they are responsible. If this be the case, student identification with the total school may not be possible. Before the term is over, however, the student may convince everyone that he is a safe bet and may work his own way into groups that were previously closed.

An art student, the only student in a public school, had quite a knack for lettering. He watched for opportunities to letter bulletin board signs, signs concerning school activities, and place cards for school functions. This gave him an opportunity that he used to good advantage and before the term was over he literally had access to the whole school. He was warned, however, not to start such wooing tactics on his first job. He could easily become a lettering slave.

The student assists in the experiences planned for him

Getting acquainted and assisting should start the first day of student teaching. However, the student will want to get acquainted with the faculty, pupils, school organization, school policies and practices, and location of materials and equipment as quickly as possible. Therefore, the major part of his activities in the first week or two are focused upon getting acquainted.

At the same time, he should be helping or assisting you. The student and you, for example, help the kindergarten children remove and hang up their wraps, or the student helps you distribute the specimens to be studied in biology class. Note that the student is working with you, not for you. It is a "we" arrangement, a partnership developing. For emphasis, the student learns how to work *with* you by working *with* you, not by working for you.

Assisting you is such a critical part of the student's development that some explanation of the term "assisting" is necessary. A teacher was asked by a mother how many words her boy missed on his Friday paper. The teacher responded that she didn't know because the student was checking the papers! In this particular case the teacher pronounced the words, used them in sentences, and directed the spelling study periods but the student checked the spelling papers. Further, the student working *for* this teacher corrected the papers and workbooks in arithmetic, reading, and language. In no case did he work with pupils in the correction of errors made on papers or in workbooks. This was a clear-cut case of misunderstanding the meaning of assisting. The student, in this instance, was a "flunky." He was checking, checking, checking for the teacher, long after he had learned how to check.

The student teaching period is so short in relation to the understandings, skills, attitudes, poise, and self-evaluation necessary for the first job that time cannot be wasted on "flunky business." We are especially concerned that assisting activities really count in the development of the student. Also, we do not want the student to enter the profession and become a flunky to his pupils. He has far more important things to do. Every day, teachers are performing a host of menial tasks and routine chores that should be a part of the educational experiences of the pupils in assuming responsibilities for their learning environment.

Many times you have asked yourself, and you will continue to ask yourself, "Is this an assisting activity or a flunky job?"

We are suggesting a series of questions which might help you decide. If you can answer *yes* to all of the questions, then you may feel sure that the activity you have in mind for a student is an assisting activity for *him*. Always, the questions must be answered in terms of the individual student. A particular activity might be an excellent assisting activity for one student and a deadening flunky job for another. Also, an assisting activity may become a flunky task after the student has developed proficiency in the task.

Does the activity immediately identify the student as a co-worker with you? Pupils need to see the student in a partnership with you and the student must feel that relationship. He is not working for you and he is not working for the pupils; he is working with you. This initial concept is most important for pupils and student to see. It is also a point of view for you.

The student who is asked to pick up the paper from the floor each evening, dust the reading table and the display tables, feed the goldfish, water the plants, or count the used towels after gym class may have difficulty in seeing how these activities contribute to the educational program of the boys and girls. Each activity mentioned above is a part of the cooperative responsibility of pupils, teacher, and student. The pupils are certainly being deprived of opportunities to learn how a group cooperatively assumes responsibility for developing and maintaining a pleasant, organized working environment.

The student who is asked to work with a committee in keeping the reading table in order, plan with a pupil who is preparing a special report, work with a committee in checking supplies to pupils in physical education, assist a pupil with his solo part in a choral number, or help you prepare a demonstration for science class should recognize immediately that he is sharing the responsibility for the educational program with you.

Examples of activities that should identify the student with you as a co-worker:

1. Working together in selecting references for a unit in seventh grade science

2. Planning with student for sharing responsibilities during lunch hour

3. Jointly preparing test to be used by you at the end of unit taught

4. Jointly checking spelling papers

5. Cooperatively assisting pupils in distribution of materials for art class

6. Accompanying you to school office for supplies

7. Helping collect bulletin board materials to be used in social studies class

8. Accompanying you on home visit.[2]

Does the activity immediately identify the student as an essential part of the school? The student needs to feel that he has an important part to play. He is asked to read a reference for accuracy of facts, evaluate the deception (or attempted deception) of the backfield in practice, confer with a high school science teacher concerning use of magnets in a fourth grade science unit, help pupils prepare for a skit in assembly, assemble different sizes of blocks to be used by first grade pupils in their development of concepts of size, or assist kindergarten children in putting away materials. Not one of the above is menial or slave-like, but each plays an important part in the school program.

The pupils may recognize the importance of the activities of the student, but, to be sure, you should point out casually what the student is doing. This may be done while planning by saying, for instance: "I will work with the pupils who are preparing the map and Miss Hall will work with the committee painting the frieze." "While we are looking for information today, Miss Hall, Barbara, and Jo will look for the maps we need." "Miss Hall will go with Mary and Phillip to get the jumping ropes and the rest of us will go to the playground." Care should be taken that the student is doing things with the pupils, not for them or not for you. In other words, avoid saying, "Today Miss Hall will get

2 For list of "assisting activities" see Appendix D.

some maps for us (or get the play equipment or fix the bulletin board)."

Pupils get the idea too easily that things are done *for* them (and justifiably we suspect). The presence of a student makes one more person to do things for them. The dangers of this situation are obvious, and you will probably have to warn the student many times not to do for the pupils what they can do for themselves. They may have difficulty in recognizing that doing something for the pupils, although making a real contribution in one way, is really depriving pupils of opportunities for independence in growth. Too many of us, for example, may spell the word for the child when he should learn how to find the correct spelling, evaluate the pupils' performance when he can and should do the evaluating, point out the mistake the pupil is making in stitching the sleeve in the blouse when she should be able to find her error, or carry the sweater in from the playground for the child who forgot it.

Examples of activities which identify the student as an essential part of the school program:

1. Helping pupils prepare to show a set of slides to class
2. Helping teacher plan reading materials for exceptional pupils in United States history class
3. Accompanying committee of pupils to ask principal's permission to take excursion
4. Demonstrating use of light meter to junior photography club
5. Scouting opposing team, reporting observations, and making suggestions for defense
6. Playing instrument in band when pupil is absent
7. Keeping time for drill in typing class
8. Planning with pupil committee for pep assembly.

Is the activity a real learning experience for this student? This is the point at which you have to decide whether the student needs the experience or whether it is for him monotonous routine with no growth involved. Taking the class roll and making an accurate report to the office may be learned in one or two days, or the student may require repetition for a month or more before becoming able to make an accurate, neat report. Our experience has been that students learn *how* to perform a task much sooner than they are able to perform the task well. Therefore, student growth involves the meeting of standards in performance, not just knowing how a certain thing is to be done. A student may have responsibility for room lighting for weeks before he demonstrates sensitivity to changing lighting conditions during the day.

Most students should be able to learn, by one or two experiences, the techniques required in feeding the fish or canary, watering the plants, closing the windows after school, rearranging the library books, and arranging the desks in order. These activities, then, could no longer be considered learning experiences. The only justification for student performance of these tasks would be on the basis of sharing routine with you. When and if the student assumes complete responsibility for the room, he should assume responsibility for all routine matters, but that does not mean that he alone will take care of all routine matters at one time.

Will the activity be likely to aid this student in developing poise and confidence in teaching? You are the individual closest to the student in these professional experiences and, therefore, you should be a better judge of the effect of an experience upon the student than is the student himself. He may think he is ready to step before the class to conduct a ten-minute discussion of current events, but your judgment may indicate otherwise. You may have seen him at a loss and flustered in meeting questions raised by individuals and groups. He is certainly not ready to face the entire group until he can face small groups and individuals with poise and confidence.

You may have many students who show uneasiness with children. They may not have had the experience of working with pupils before their student teaching and therefore cannot anticipate pupil responses. Or they may be retiring by nature. In any event, you need to be most careful not to push them into contact with pupils on their own until they show confidence in working with you and the pupils. They should start working with pupils, of course, but only in your presence. For example, you and the student would be in the hall when pupils come in the morning, work with the bulletin board committee, accompany the pupils to the playground, sit with the committee assembling the school newspaper, work with the group in planning a school party, or move about the science laboratory together while the pupils are working. After this, you should be able to judge the development of confidence by the student in working directly with pupils and others in the school.

The student next assumes minor responsibility with an individual or group. For example: during band practice he may help the trombone section with a difficult measure; in a science class he may work with a committee preparing for a demonstration; in an agriculture class he may help a pupil locate specific information; in a mathematics class he may help a pupil see through a particular problem; or in journalism class he may work with a committee in proofreading. This type of activity might be termed "bit" teaching. He is now, under your watchful eye, assuming responsibility for instruction, even though only a small part of the total program at any given time.

You should move the student from one assisting activity to another and also increase the number of assisting activities as student confidence increases. The biggest test of confidence, however, is the jump from bit teaching with individuals and small groups to bit teaching with the whole group. The student may appear quite ready, but the first trial may be all but disastrous. Don't blame yourself or the student too quickly, because this is the most suddenly dangerous ground over which you and the student will travel together. Perhaps it was wrong type of bit teaching before the whole group. For example: the activity may have been largely discussion, whereas it might have been better had the activity involved more pupil writing and less discussion. When you see the mistake, the next assignment may be made accordingly. With another student, the type of bit teaching may have been well selected but the student might not have been prepared to carry on for the allotted ten minutes and may have tried to ad lib during the remainder of the time. In this situation, perhaps the ad lib didn't work.

The assisting phase of the student's development requires tremendous judgment and each student presents different problems. Your ability to judge needs, abilities, and growth of students in general increases as you work with them. You will discover real satisfaction in noting your increasing success in guiding the student effectively from one experience to another.

YOU AND THE STUDENT SHOULD DEVELOP
GOOD WORKING RELATIONSHIPS

We have already emphasized the importance of good working relationships. We should look now to the ways by which this may be accomplished. The procedures given below do not exhaust the possibilities; they may suggest others, or you may already be using many others.

OBSERVATION OF STUDENT

Students know that you will observe their work with pupils, their relationships with other staff members, and their relationships with parents. That is your responsibility. They look to you for suggestions to improve their work and their relationships. At the same time, however, constant observation by the teacher bothers students more than they may admit. Your problem is to discover observation procedures that give you the information you want and also contribute to the student's development, poise, and confidence. We suggest the five reviewed below.

Insofar as possible, observe the student indirectly. Some teachers watch the student indirectly from the time he first comes to the room until he is successfully assuming complete responsibility. While the student is getting acquainted and assisting with groups and individuals, for example, he and you are both active in the room. There is little occasion for you to more than glance at the work he is doing. Even though you are not participating with pupils, you can find it convenient to be reading, working with materials in a file, or anything so that you will not appear to be watching the student constantly.

The above procedure can work just as well when the student is working with the total class in bit teaching. Place yourself where it will be unnecessary to look at him. Suppose the group is in a circle. You can sit in the circle close to him but not next to him. Here you can be as interested as any of the group but can look at all members of the group, not just the student. If the group is in a semicircle, you might sit facing the group. The same could be done if the class were in straight rows. There is also the practice of being busy when the student tries his first bit teaching with the total group. In this case, it would be necessary for you to excuse yourself from the group. You could explain that, "Mr. Smith is going to show you how an artist might start a picture while I get the materials ready for us to use today." You are the best judge of the amount of observation that is desirable.

Create an atmosphere in which he wants you to observe him. The student recognizes that he and you are working together as a team in the room. You are planning together, asking for the advice of the other, making suggestions to the other, enjoying the experiences that the other reports in his work with the pupils, and generally sharing the pleasures and problems encountered. In this atmosphere, brief observation spans (only a few seconds) may bother him very little. Rather, he may be looking your way to note whether or not you are seeing something—a problem, an achievement, or an incident—so that he can share it with you. This type of atmosphere contributes to the student's development of confidence.

Show interest in the student's work with the class, a group, or an individual. One of the major problems in observation is created by the student's inability to determine your reaction to the proceedings. It is so easy to be too serious. A smile when the student thinks he's facing trouble may give him the necessary confidence or assurance to proceed. A serious or worried expression may be the final blow. Live the experiences with him and let him know that you are.

Share in observation by observing each other. Observation in student teaching is a two-way process; you observe the student and the student observes you. He learns how to observe you and, in so doing, better understands how you observe him. Ask him to observe you while working with a group or the total class. Indicate specifically what it is that he is to look for, such as: interest of pupils in the topic or problem discussed; kinds of pupil questions asked, whether superficial or thoughtful; reaction of pupils to pictures used; or teacher responses to questions not pertinent. Discuss the results of his observation and let him see that you are not hurt by criticisms. He must recognize that observation is necessary for one person to help another improve his teaching effectiveness. Very soon the student will be in a public school in which there may be supervisors. You are helping him both now and later.

Also the student can take lessons from you concerning how to work with pupils while being observed. You can demonstrate that you are always concentrating on the pupils with whom you are working, not constantly looking over the pupils to catch the eyes of the student observer or other observers who might be in the room. Pupils are very conscious of too-frequent attention between teacher and observer and, as a result, often lose interest in the work of the group. This should be re-emphasized before he starts bit teaching with the total group.

When observing, one sees both the desirable and the undesirable. The student needs to know that you saw the good points in his work. Seeing and reviewing the good may help him more than reviewing the parts needing improvement. Perhaps you have found that the student is often well aware of weak points in his teaching, but, as he says, "I can't seem to do everything right at once even though I know better." The results of observation must always include the good or the good and bad, never just the bad.

THE STUDENT-TEACHER CONFERENCE

We consider the characteristics reviewed below to be most important in making the conference a valuable aid to you and the student.

The conference is a mutual arrangement. For the most part, the conference will include only you and the student. It provides an opportunity for you to develop and maintain mutual understanding. The student needs to understand you, your philosophy of teaching, the school philosophy, and why you handled a particular problem in a certain manner. The conference gives you an opportunity to clarify anything that the student sees in school but does not understand.

The conference deals with real problems. For the first time in the teacher education program, the student may be seeing and dealing with reality. How to proceed in a given situation must be a procedure that really works. Hypothetical solutions now are tried, not left dangling. He is finding that some work and some do not work. Why didn't the pupils respond as he had thought they would? Why did the pupils ask such superficial questions in the discussion? The student must attempt to discover, with your help in conference, why the projected plans did or did not work. You are then ready to help him project plans which remove the difficulties discovered in previous experiences. In the conference you attempt to agree upon causes for success and to see that these causal factors are considered in future plans. Also, you attempt to agree upon causes for unsuccessful teaching and to see that these causal factors are removed from future plans.

The conference clarifies the procedure by which the student grows. The procedure varies according to specific assisting or teaching situations, but, generally, it follows the steps given below. By discussing successive experiences, the procedure becomes a way of thinking. This process is basic to successful teaching both now and later. The steps are:

1. Understanding the specific purpose of the teaching-learning process

2. Planning for the specific teaching-learning process

3. Assisting or assuming full responsibility for the teaching-learning process

4. Evaluating the effectiveness of the teaching-learning process

5. Understanding the conditions that developed in the teaching-learning process

6. Making next plans in light of experience

7. Repeating above steps.

Discussion in the conference is objective. The conference is a frank discussion of any problem or point of interest that arises. Perhaps the best way to get this idea across to the student is through your example. You will be discussing pupil abilities, achievement, interests, and problems; pupils' home backgrounds; teacher relationships; parent relationships; administrative relationships; and community relationships. These discussions present ample opportunity to demonstrate your ability to be objective and to insist upon objectivity by the student.

A student reported in conference, in a sarcastic tone, that he could see why other teachers didn't like to work with a certain member of the staff. The teacher responded, "You're safe in saying that to me because it will not get back to the individual. But suppose you were to say that to another teacher here and it were to get back to the individual. In our conferences, we will discuss many such problems, but always in an attempt to understand them and in terms of how we can help the individual or work effectively with him." During your conferences, you will want the student to evaluate your work and you'll have to evaluate the work of the student. Therefore, it is necessary for you to get the objective approach established as soon as possible.

Another help in developing objectivity is in the approach to the teaching-learning activity conducted by you or the student. You may be assuming major responsibility during the first several weeks that the student is in your room. This gives you opportunity to discuss *your* teaching objectively. For example, if you have a problem causing you much concern, why not ask the student to help you? The focus is upon the teaching-learning process, not upon you as an individual. *The concern is not upon your personality as a personality but upon your personality as it affects your activities as a teacher.* If the student can develop this attitude before you and he start evaluating his effectiveness in the activities of a teacher, half the battle will be won. Both will be able to talk more freely and also more specifically about the teaching of either. You must demonstrate your ability to be objective and to have your teaching evaluated frankly if you expect the student to accept objective evaluation of his work.

There are regularly scheduled conference periods. The student needs to know when he can talk with you and how much time will be given to the conference. Many questions will arise as he gets acquainted, assists with the teaching, eventually assumes responsibility, and participates in the other activities of a teacher. He should jot down the questions in a notebook and have them organized for the conference.

It is best for both if the conference periods are at frequent intervals, at least once per day. Each can review a situation more specifically soon after it occurs. This is most important for the student, because so much is happening so fast that details are likely to be lost. He observes a social studies class and attempts to write down all of the things that he wants to ask about. The discussion moves too rapidly, however, so he finally jots down brief notes and attempts to remember other details. After school, or as soon as possible, he should recall and organize the points he wants to ask about. Otherwise, he will probably not remember enough of the details to understand the situations that he wanted to ask about.

The number of regularly scheduled conferences depends upon their length and upon the needs of the student. We recommend that neither you nor the student be in conference longer than an hour after school. Some teachers prefer scheduling the regular conferences in the mornings before the opening of school.

You may prefer scheduling them on Saturday morning or, if you are teaching in the secondary school, a vacant period may be more convenient. If you have no open period you may have to schedule them before or after school.

Conferences may occur spontaneously as opportunity arises or conditions demand. Plans may need to be changed on short notice. Perhaps the student needs to talk with you before carrying out an assisting responsibility assigned for the next day. He may really need help in planning or may just be scared. Nevertheless, he should have a chance to talk with you. You may recognize, while observing a student in an assisting activity or in teaching, that you must talk with him before he proceeds the next day. If you recognize that the student was not ready for the assignment, you may need to change plans for the next day.

Conferences requested by either of you need not be long. Perhaps a few minutes will settle the problem. The time given should be time needed. On occasion, the discussion might start on the day when the situation arises and continue on the next day. If the problem were concerned with the student's teaching or assisting, perhaps discussion should be continued before the student assists or teaches again.

The time for such conferences presents a serious problem in some schools. If you are an elementary teacher responsible for all classes, the lunch hour, playground, and recess, you may have difficulty in finding time to talk with the student. This is especially true if he is assigned for only one or two hours per day or a half day. You will want to avoid disrupting the pupil program, but in some cases this may not be possible. You could announce a free reading period or some other activity not requiring your constant attention so that you could talk to the student on the particular day before he leaves your room.

The problem of scheduling special conferences at your request or the request of the student may be no less difficult in the secondary school. Again, avoid interfering with the pupil program if possible. You may be faced with the problem of giving the student conference time before his next assisting or teaching assignment. In such case you must give him time or not let him proceed.

STUDENT AND TEACHER PARTICIPATION AS MEMBERS OF THE GROUP

When the student seems well enough acquainted with the pupils and at ease with them, you might ask him to sit as a member of the group. He should be encouraged to ask questions and to contribute information during the discussion. If he does not volunteer, you might ask for information, interpretation, or suggestion; but be sure that he is prepared. You may have to plan his class participation with him beforehand. This type of participation often helps the student develop a feeling of security and belongingness in the group.

You have now helped the student further to accept your presence and participation in the room when he is assisting or teaching. He has learned to participate with you in teaching and should now be able to accept your participation in the group when he is teaching. This position enables you to assist the student when he finds himself in a bad spot. A question may be asked which causes the student to hesitate. You might say something to a pupil which will give the student time to collect his thoughts, for instance, "Bill, are you asking a question that we should be able to answer by reading the reference on that point?" or "Bill, is your question asked in such a way that it can be answered?" or "Bill, I think you're forgetting that we don't ask questions that are not pertinent to the problem being discussed."

You also are in a position to get the discussion back on the track when it seems to be moving off the main topic or problem; to suggest further points when the student appears lost; to correct an inaccurate statement or point made by pupil or student; or even to take over the discussion if the class seems to be getting completely out of control. If you are sitting outside the group as an observer, it is most difficult for you to meet the above situations. The last two are serious and need to be met immediately.

Have you had a student give inaccurate information, interpretations with no supporting facts, or opinions with extreme bias when you were in no position to do anything about it? Coaching from the side gives the pupils the idea that you are correcting the student or that he can't succeed without your help; it generally harms the student instead of helping him and, most often, makes the whole situation worse. If you are going to be in a position where you can help, you should be a participating member of the group. You can move into this position any time you think the situation would be helped, but it is best if you have started out being a participating member. For a period of weeks before student teaching is over, however, the student should have been completely responsible for the teaching-learning process without you as a regularly participating member of the group. Some students, however, do not reach this degree of competency.

THE STUDENT SHOULD UNDERSTAND
TEACHING-LEARNING PROCESSES

How does a child learn? A college student who has not observed or worked with children may consider this a simple process, easy to see and to stimulate. Students who have seriously studied learning by observing or working with pupils in the process may approach learning situations with fear and trembling. You can be pretty sure that most students will be able to use the terminology and recite principles of learning, but will be unable to detect learning when they are in the midst of it. Neither will they be quick at determining procedures to facilitate learning in specific situations.

To emphasize the attention that you must give to student understanding of learning, we impress two conditions: (1) college students in their professional courses may have, for the most part, studied pupil learning apart from pupils, and (2) students must study the practical aspects of learning intensively while with you. This is a real challenge for you. Also, it makes your position in the teacher education program extremely important. Your major job in this connection is to help the student understand the nature of learning, how it can be brought about, and how its presence or absence can be determined.

THE STUDENT WORKS WITH YOU IN DIRECTING LEARNING

There is actually more learning going on in the classroom environment than the student will understand or be able to identify for years to come. But if he has just come close to classroom learning, you first must be sure not to confuse him by expecting him to see everything at once. For example, as he observes your vocal music class he will not realize that you complimented this child because he was really trying today, that you asked the pupils to evaluate their singing of a particular measure to determine whether or not they could detect a mistake made by a few, that three times during the twenty minutes you asked for volunteers for a quartet to give the pupils confidence in singing before a group. You must recognize that the student may enjoy watching you teach but may have little understanding of the processes he sees.

There are many procedures you can use to help the student. We recommend the following as especially helpful.

"Think aloud" as the student assists you in planning and working with pupils. You and the student are planning for recreational activities for a fifth grade. You are concerned not only with developing pupil skill in ball handling, but also with developing attitudes. During the planning process you might "think aloud":

We'll name captains to select squads rather than counting off. Otherwise the best ball handlers might space themselves in the line so that they'd all be on the same team. That's too discouraging to the other boys.

To start with, we'll say something about the need to help each other learn. This may make the good ball handlers more patient with the poor ball handlers.

During the last few minutes of the period we'll leave the relays and use these skill development exercises. We'll reorganize the squads so that boys of comparable skills will be in the same squads. That will take care of individual differences in skill development.

You could have listed each of the above items but have said nothing about *why;* that is, what your purposes were in each procedure or how you expect these procedures to effect growth. The student may get more insights concerning the how, the why, and the what-happened from your thinking aloud as you work with him than in any other way, unless it be by his thinking aloud. You may repeat the same explanation many times in different situations. For example, you may use the expression, "By asking 'why' we're always forcing the pupils to think through the information. This also helps them remember."

Insist upon the student "thinking aloud" to you when he is planning with you. Did you ever have a student list a series of procedures he had planned to follow in a lesson without being able to explain why he would use any one of them? Most of us have. The trouble may be that his previous abstract treatment of learning does not equip him to see the relationships between the process and possible results as they actually exist in working with pupils. Or, he may still think of teaching as a process in which one uses tricks and techniques, each of which will produce a given result! Finally, and most difficult for you to cope with, he may not have the ability to see relationships of the high order necessary to understand teaching and learning.

Some teachers feel that insisting upon a reason for each procedure the student plans to use will be discouraging to him, will thwart initiative. We have not found this to be the case unless the student is moved too rapidly into complex teaching situations, such as the large teaching unit. However, there are dangers in the practice and therefore we recommend that you observe the following:

1. Ask for the most apparent or obvious in the beginning. For

example, in planning for high jump practice a student started his lesson with a demonstration by himself and two of the boys. He gave no explanation for this (stopped thinking out loud) so the teacher asked for a reason. He said that it was to show the boys the exact form to be used. Then he laughed and remarked, "Really it wouldn't be worth-while practice unless they could see what they were supposed to do at first—'practice wouldn't make perfect'." The teacher let it go at this but could have asked exactly how the demonstration was to be used and why. The latter, more analytical approach, comes later.

2. If necessary, put the words in his mouth at first. A student had planned for a spelling lesson in fifth grade and on the plans had indicated that the words would be used in sentences. When asked why, the student said that the pupils enjoyed hearing them used in sentences. Her teacher pointed to the words "too" and "reign" and asked how they would know how to spell them. The student then explained that several words might be spelled differently but have the same pronunciation; if pupils don't know the meaning of the word they don't know which spelling to use.

3. Add further explanation if the student is not sure or gives a partial explanation. After all, you and the student are working together. Why shouldn't you both be giving explanations. Your explanations along with his give him just that much more insight as you go along. In other words, he may grow faster if you contribute to his thinking than if he does all of the out-loud thinking. The student who had planned to work with a group in preparing a graph for science class had both science and arithmetic books listed. He had arithmetic books listed so that "the pupils could see exactly how the graphs were made." His teacher added, "The pupils might also need to decide which kind of graph would best show the information. That is one thing they have to learn in showing the information by graphs."

Ask the student to give special attention to your use of specific procedures. You want to be sure he recognizes a procedure or method or evidence of learning. Before class you might say,

"Today in the American problems class, you will see me spend-
ing quite a bit of time making the assignment for the next week.
See if you can determine why" (differentiated assignment to
provide for differences in reading level of pupils). Or, "Try to
find out how I am helping the pupils to remember the important facts in social studies class" (increasing retention in the
learning process).

In this manner, you can help the student recognize the
method, understand many ways by which it can be used, and
analyze the results of the method as you use it. Also, you can
help him understand how learning takes place, what elements
contribute to learning or prevent learning, how to determine
degree of learning, and how to determine the nature of concepts
acquired by the pupils as the lesson proceeds.

This way of helping the student to understand learning requires much skill on your part. You must have developed proficiency in the use of the methods, in analyzing the learning that
results from your methods, and in determining what methods
might be used to increase learning. You must also be proficient
in the use of a variety of methods. Chances are that few students will develop to the point where they can have experiences
in all of the methods demonstrated by you. We say this with
confidence, because we believe that students should understand
and show proficiency in the methods they use, rather than having a little experience with many methods and developing little
proficiency in any.

The following are illustrative of ways by which you can have
the student study your direction of the learning process:

1. Ask the student to list ways by which you give attention
to the learning of each pupil during discussion period in health
class. (It is understood that each of these assignments will be
discussed in conference.)

2. Ask the student to list evidences of incorrect concepts or
hazy concepts and to suggest ways by which they might have
been prevented.

3. Show the student samples of good questions that you in-

tend to use during class. Ask him to write down others that you did use in class and suggest how they might have been improved.

4. Ask the student to observe illustrations of how you got the discussion back on the track after a pupil or pupils had made comments or raised questions which temporarily sidetracked the discussion.

Use references including psychology and methods books, periodicals, and bulletins. The student has not had and will not have a better time to study theory and practice together. He now has the explanations of theory and is seeing theory in action. Further, he has you to help him see sense in motivation (both intrinsic and extrinsic), pupil purpose, pupil retention, social behavior, and pupil-teacher planning. The student who said, "Oh, I see now what they mean when they say junior high school pupils are unpredictable," illustrates the thing that happens daily as one concept after another is seen in action.

Your problem in connection with references may be serious because so many students do not keep their textbooks. If you are far from the college campus and the student lives in your community, the only books available will be your own, those in the professional library of the school, or those that you might borrow from friends. Nevertheless, this is the time for students to learn that one studies as one teaches and that the study of current professional materials is never-ending for the alert teacher. In this connection, we are making two recommendations that should be helpful to you.

1. The student looks for specific information that has bearing on a specific aspect of learning. As you discuss observations of pupil interest, the student could well spend some time gathering information regarding specific interests of the particular age child, both boys and girls. Or, a discipline problem may arise and the student would have occasion to look for suggestions concerning the treatment of that particular type problem. There should be no going to the references unless there is definite need or reason.

2. You and the student are studying together. It is not a one-person study of the problem in *your* teaching-learning situations, and neither is it in *his* teaching-learning situations. You both pursue the problem, then share information and decide upon next procedures. No student should ever say of you, "Boy, I sure rounded up a lot of information for him."

Observe other teachers to get a broader perspective of teaching-learning procedures. The student should see how other teachers plan with pupils, secure pupil interest in the work at hand, guide pupil thinking, formulate questions, secure wide pupil participation in discussion, make assignments, and evaluate pupil learning. If possible, they should discuss their observations with the teachers observed.

There is a real value in wide observation, besides helping the student to understand teaching-learning processes. The student sees many types of classroom personalities, perhaps all equally effective. He sees many illustrations of how teachers motivate pupils. All of this helps him to recognize that each teacher directs teaching-learning processes in his own way and that there is no standard procedure which can be applied for this or that type of situation.

The student who comes to your school must be identified immediately as a member of your school. You can provide for this belongingness by making him feel welcome, by making him a working part of the group, by providing experiences that assure growth, and by developing an informal, objective, uninhibited working relationship between student and teacher. In the student's participation, assisting, and bit teaching we recommend that the following things be kept in mind:

1. You should retain the over-all responsibility for the teaching-learning situation, even though the student is assigned specific responsibilities with individuals, groups, or the total class.

2. The assisting activities should be planned by you and the student or by you, the student, and the pupils.

3. The student should assume responsibility for a routine task no longer than is necessary for him to learn how to perform the

task effectively, unless you and the student are sharing routine responsibilities as planned, or while the student is assuming over-all responsibility for the class.

4. The student should assume responsibility for assisting activities *for purposes of learning*, not to relieve you of responsibility or work.

5. The activity should be one which contributes toward good working relationships between you and the student or between the pupils and the student.

6. The student must see that the activity contributes directly to the educational program.

7. A specific assisting activity assigned to a student should identify him as an inherent part of the school.

8. The assisting activity should be one which contributes to the student's development of poise and confidence in assuming the responsibilities of the teacher.

SUGGESTED REFERENCES

Burr, James B., Lowry W. Harding, and Leland B. Jacobs, *Student Teaching in the Elementary School*. New York: Appleton-Century-Crofts, Inc., 1950. Part One gives specific suggestions designed to help the student to get ready for student teaching and to make a good beginning with teacher, pupils, and others.

Feyereisen, Kathryn and Verna Dieckman, *Guiding Student Teacher Experiences*. Lock Haven, Pa.: Association for Student Teaching, 1952. Pages 1-10 give practical suggestions that will help you get the student off to a good start.

Flowers, John G. and others, *School and Community Laboratory Experiences in Teacher Education*. Oneonta, N.Y.: American Association of Teachers Colleges, 1948. Pages 233-236 offer specific suggestions concerning the student activities during the first two weeks.

Grim, Paul and John Michaelis, *The Student Teacher in the Secondary School*. New York: Prentice-Hall, Inc., 1953. Chapters I and II review in detail what the student should do at the beginning of the student teaching period to get oriented to the job before him.

Michaelis, John nd Paul Grim, *The Student Teacher in the Ele-*

mentary School. New York: Prentice-Hall, Inc., 1953. Chapters I, II, and III review the responsibilities of the student in getting acquainted, making preparations for teaching, and studying the children.

Schorling, Raleigh and Max Wingo, *Elementary School Student Teaching.* New York: McGraw-Hill Book Company, Inc., 1950. Chapter I gives specific suggestions to the student concerning his activities at the beginning of the student teaching period.

5

Your Student's Readiness To Teach

STUDENTS COME TO YOU WITH VARYING DEGREES of readiness for growth in assuming teacher responsibilities. Regardless of the college program, personal and professional readiness of students varies widely. This range in readiness presents a real challenge. You have to determine specifically wherein a student is or is not ready and then decide what you will do to contribute to his growth. This begins the first day a student is with you and continues through the entire student teaching period. You must determine the student's readiness before you assign more complex types of assisting activities or increased responsibility. The problem is complicated because a particular student will seldom be equally ready for all activities; he may have little difficulty with one type and great difficulty with another. Further, provision must be made for the development of readiness for each type of responsibility he is expected to assume during student teaching. Skill in determining readiness and in providing for growth in it can greatly enhance the effectiveness of your work with students.

No part of the total student teaching process is more crucial than this: your sensitivity toward and treatment of student response to the school and community environment from the first day of student teaching to the last. You may have had a student who was afraid of his shadow, or one who was all ego. A bad start with any group of pupils, kindergarten to twelfth grade, may result in damages that are almost impossible to repair.

Your observation of student readiness to begin student teaching should be organized in some fashion. Perhaps it would be helpful to focus your observation upon and gather evidence from student response or reaction to the following, considered to be major factors in student readiness for success in teaching:

Interest in teaching.

Breadth of interests and experiences.

Maturity and emotional stability.

Ability to attract, interest, and get along with pupils.

Skill in human relations.

Intellectual and professional energy.

To say that evidence of a high degree of readiness in each of the above factors would assure student success would be misleading. However, they are widely accepted as factors which definitely influence the degree of success that a student may achieve in student teaching and in the teaching field.[1] They would be significant points around which to organize your observations and activities to promote readiness, because they can be used during the entire student teaching period and in student evaluation. Evidences of readiness in each are reviewed below, followed by suggestions that may help you contribute to student growth.

INTEREST IN TEACHING

During the first day, you may observe such responses as the following:

1. The student seems to be unaware that the pupils are in the room; he has a faraway stare while you teach.

2. The student glances at his watch.

---

[1] Charlotte Junge, "Readiness for Student Teaching," *Off-Campus Student Teaching*, Thirtieth Yearbook (Lock Haven, Pa.: Association for Student Teaching, 1951), pp. 28-39.

3. The student does not recall what happened in the discussion.

4. The student's facial expressions indicate appropriate reactions to pupil activities and responses.

5. The student overflows with penetrating questions at the close of school conference.

6. The student suggests a reference that is apropos to the lesson he observed.

7. The student shows no animation when working with pupils.

8. The student is eager to talk with pupils.

9. The student helps when a pupil needs an extra hand in science experiment.

10. The student frowns when a pupil objects to a decision of the group.

11. The student offers to help a first grade pupil find his mitten.

12. The student merely glances through the references used by the pupils.

To say that the above responses *only* reveal presence or lack of interest would be oversimplifying the matter. Readiness factors are interrelated and highly complex. You recognize, however, that some of the responses in the above list would certainly indicate lack of interest and others would indicate presence of interest. Through close observation of student response to teaching-learning processes, to school personnel, and to general school environment you may ascertain a general picture of his interest readiness. Also, you may be able to isolate something of the nature of interest present.

Even though a student exhibits interest, the nature of the interest may be misleading. For example, you may discover that it is really interest in obtaining pupil approval, your approval, or maintaining a straight "A" grade in college. Give the student the benefit of the doubt but don't get caught off guard. The student has just come to you from an environment that is quite unlike teaching boys and girls. Through no fault of his own, he may not have had the opportunity to become interested or to develop interest in assuming the many responsibilities of a teacher. They may be unknown to him through direct experience. Real interest is developed on the job, not by reading and talking about the activities of teachers.

Another example would be the student who intends to teach only a year or two, to use teaching as a "stepping stone" after a year or two, to get money enough ahead to get married, to satisfy the parents, etc. Your job now becomes very complex. You are confronted with the problem of stimulating a sincere interest in teaching.

You can contribute to the development of student interest in several ways:

Be interested in all of your responsibilities. If you dislike certain aspects of your work, be careful not to show it. Be certain that you say nothing to reveal any pet peeves, gripes, or dissatisfactions that you or the other teachers have. This practice should be strictly observed by all teachers in schools where there are student teachers. Your own enthusiasm for teaching is your best approach. The following statements made by student teachers when asked to evaluate this aspect of their supervision indicate the significance of your interest.

Ran down the school—pointed out all weak points—forgot good points.

They held it to be worthy, but in some particular instances made you stop and wonder if all teachers become unfriendly and unprofessional.

They increased my opinion of teaching even more favorably than I had placed it, which was high.

All seemed proud to be teachers.

These teachers think that teaching is terrific.

They all spoke very highly of their work. I never heard any gripes about not getting enough money or wishing they were in a different type of work.

Anybody who watched Miss _____ would be interested in teaching or want to be a teacher. Those children respond to her as if by magic.

You can tell by the way he teaches that his whole heart is in it.

He surely holds his profession in high regard and makes you feel the same way.

If what I'm seeing is teaching, I don't want it.

Capitalize upon student abilities and interests. These should be discovered early so that they may be used to stimulate development of student selfconfidence and pupil confidence in student. The student may have a flair for sign painting. If so, he might work with the committee preparing a display table or preparing the bulletin board for a new unit of work. The second grade student teacher who was raised on a farm might start working immediately with the committee looking for pictures of horsedrawn machinery. The fourth grade student teacher who plays the violin might accompany the children when they sing. The science student teacher who worked at a weather station might start working immediately with the committee to prepare the weather prediction for the high school daily bulletin. The student needs to discover that his background of information, abilities, and interests can apply directly to his success in meeting the responsibilities in teaching.

Capitalize upon pupil interest and enthusiasm. Place the student in activities for which pupils show enthusiasm. His interest can be just as catching from pupils as from you. The star tackle did not want to be bothered with elementary physical education; he wanted to be a big-name coach. His teacher, however, wanted him to become interested in and concerned with the total public school physical education program before he left college. How did he go about it? On successive days (planned program was changed) his teacher asked him to assist with fifth grade in swimming, third grade on the trampoline, and first grade in tumbling. You guessed the result. On the third day, he was observed after class helping some first graders with bothersome knots while putting on their street shoes. Taking the youngsters back to their classroom, he was holding the hands of three boys in his right hand and the hands of three boys in his left hand!

Very often, if you've done a good job in setting the stage with the pupils, their immediate interest in the student may quickly overcome student indifference. The other members of the faculty, the custodian, and even a parent or two might be enlisted in the first few days to stimulate student interest.

Give the student increasing doses of satisfaction. Let him work first with pupils who really need help and who also really show appreciation. For example, helping a pupil with a knotty problem in sentence construction, in figuring out why the sleeve doesn't fit properly on the dress, in trying to find out why the white rat nutrition experiment didn't produce the results anticipated, or in trying to find specific information concerning the effect of slope upon rate of run-off, will certainly do something for a student, especially when he senses pupil satisfaction and appreciation. You will want to be as sure as possible that satisfaction will be derived in each situation. On the first home visits, for example, take him to families that can be depended upon for a welcome, friendly reception.

We do not intend that the student be unduly protected, but give the fire a chance to get started. You are building student interest and that interest will be tested soon enough, especially if the student has serious problems to overcome on the way to becoming a successful teacher.

Commend whenever possible, no matter how insignificant the assisting task. This may be done by recognizing the contribution of the student in talking with the pupils, in talking with the principal, or in talking with the parents being visited. Be careful not to over-commend. Also, be objective about it. Students often become selfconscious or become unable to go ahead without praise if praise is lavish. You can destroy the good by overdoing. Suggestions for improvement are given more easily if preceded by mention of the points well done.

A kindergarten teacher had observed the student working with a child in finger painting. The two were working at a table alone. The child was making many small figures on the 12 × 18 sheet of paper, but the student was attempting to get him to use large strokes and develop a large pattern. Finally the student demonstrated on another sheet. The child somewhat got the idea and created a larger pattern. However, the student was not satisfied, so he changed parts of the pattern and then asked, "Now, doesn't that look better?" The child did not respond, but went immediately to wash his hands. A few minutes later he was overheard saying to some of the children, "*You* don't know how to build a house. Here, *I'll* show you!" In talking with the student, the teacher expressed confidence in her use of finger paint and in her demonstration of how to get interesting pictures by filling the page (fortunately the student had done something right). It was then possible for the teacher to call attention to the fact that the picture was no longer the child's after the student had changed it.

Give the student assurance of your confidence in him. Giving assurance of confidence is a delicate matter because there is a difference between confidence in the student and confidence in what the student does. By your attitude toward the student, your tone of voice in talking with him, your exhibition of patience, and your straightforward and friendly approach you can point out weaknesses in his work without crushing his ego.

Difficult problems may arise in a student's development of confidence if he does not disassociate confidence in himself and in his work. At the risk of having student interest develop more slowly, therefore, talk frankly with the student concerning his work. If you "soft pedal" his mistakes in order that interest and confidence may be developed more rapidly, you are creating an even more serious problem. When you get around to serious criticism of his work, he may wonder why he is making more mistakes now than when he began! Such a question may be expected from any intelligent student.

In most cases interest is not dynamic; it lacks direction and purpose. Thus, *in most cases your concern will be to use procedures necessary to build student interest to the point of enthusiasm, zeal, and dynamic drive. The result and chief ingredient of this pepped up interest is intensity of purpose, which is of foremost importance in student teaching, just as it seems to be in life generally.*

BREADTH OF INTERESTS AND EXPERIENCES

In many colleges, the students have opportunity to observe and work in the laboratory school before student teaching. However, experiences your student has had with children in school and out of school, attending faculty meetings, making home visits, working with school committees, and assisting in the school office may be no index to his readiness. Lack of interest, lack of capacity for growth, or other conditions may have prevented the growth that might be indicated by *breadth* and *intensity* of experiences preceding student teaching.

The following list, made by a music teacher at the end of a student's first week, shows evidences of lack of breadth in interests and experiences:

Was not familiar with songs in music series for elementary grades.

Was surprised that boys in junior high school did not want to sing solo parts.

Did not want to play the piano for choral accompaniment; had never been interested in piano.

Didn't feel well enough prepared to help any of the pupils with instruments.

Couldn't help pupils in pep band because she didn't have time to learn numbers.

Didn't want to work with fourth grade committee on song for assembly; wanted more time to observe.

The above student was sincere in her reactions, and the teacher knew pretty well what should be done. The really serious problem is the student who attempts to hide his lack of background and his narrow interest. Pupils very quickly detect superficiality and pretense in a student.

The suggestions given below illustrate types of procedures you might follow with students who lack breadth of interest and experience in teacher activities.

Note the student's characteristics and assign activities which he may be able to handle successfully. The student who is unsure of himself, timid, or hesitant should be given activities apart from the pupils. Observe his reaction to pupils in the classroom just before class. They will certainly engage him in conversation. Does he seem ill at ease, look to you as if crying for help, try to move away from pupils, try to talk them down using a louder voice as the conversation proceeds, pretend to be quite busy, or ask them to take their seats? If any of the foregoing, he is certainly not yet ready to assist by working directly with pupils. Better keep him working at tasks which contribute to the educational program but not in a working relationship with pupils. Specific assignments in the room give him continued opportunity to become accustomed to being around pupils. Continue to observe pupil reaction to him and his reaction to the pupils when they do associate informally in the classroom, corridor, or playground.

Beginning and continuing classroom activities for him might include revising a bibliography of references, sorting pictures to file with units, checking names of pupils who made contributions to discussion period, keeping score during games, working mathematics problems along with pupils, and studying unit being taught by you.

Move the student into direct work with pupils on a trial basis. The first assignment might be to help pupils select a map for use in a report, prepare a demonstration in science, set up volleyball nets for physical education, arrange tables for committee work, organize slides to show in class, or arrange articles of clothing in ensembles. These are brief, perhaps only a few minutes in duration, and none extend beyond a single class period.

An advantage of brief assignments is the opportunity you have to evaluate the student's performance with him, and to give him time to relax before he tries again. Also, you may have made an assignment that placed him in the position of making a decision, enforcing conduct standards, demonstrating to pupils, giving an interpretation, or providing initiative for which he was not ready. Perhaps he hadn't realized how far he could or should go in providing leadership, and felt that he was on the spot. The brief assignment brings out his questions, uncertainties, and fears so that they can be discussed before a situation has developed too far. Further, you have a chance to reassess your judgment in the type of assignment that was made.

Increase number and type of brief assignmnts as student shows growth, confidence, and desire to advance. A brief assignment with pupils may give the student little responsibility or it may give him a large degree of responsibility; it increases as the student demonstrates that he can assume responsibility.

Little	*Much*
Assist pupil in looking for lost article.	Inspect individual lockers as they are cleaned by pupils.
Assist pupil in repairing kite.	Assist pupils in planning a skit for assembly.
Return papers to pupils for corrections.	Supervise pupils in the preparation of a demonstration for physics.
Accompany pupil to report lost article to office.	Work with pupils in preparing an editorial on school policy.

The activities in the right-hand column require judgment, poise, self-assurance, understanding, and definiteness not required in the other list. If you discover that you are moving the student too rapidly into assignments that carry too much responsibility, you can hold back and give additional assignments in activities requiring less responsibility. The student's success, as determined by your standards and by pupil approval, gives you the best indication of his readiness for the next step —full responsibility for the total group.

Move the student into work with total group by brief assignments or bit teaching. Some teachers prefer to move the student into co-teaching situations before placing him on his own in front of a class. For example, you and the student could prepare a demonstration in science, give the demonstration before the class, and answer questions. Situations of this type may give the student confidence because of your presence. (Occasionally you might like his support, too!) Also, you are in an excellent position to pick up quickly when the student hesitates, to provide vocabulary or complete explanations, to make a response in place of the student in case a pupil asks a question or makes a remark that is not pertinent, or take over completely if the student's knees and voice indicate. You also have opportunity to give the student rein as he demonstrates ability to carry the discussion, or to take over as he indicates inability. If you do have to take over, you can do it with less sting than when the student is in front of the class by himself. Perhaps the most sudden shock, the greatest damage, and the biggest repair bill occurs when the student does not succeed the first time he attempts bit teaching before the entire class.

When you feel confident in the student's ability to handle bit teaching on his own, try a type of assignment that will not test him too far. Always follow the practice of moving the student into more complex situations as gradually as possible. It is better to move forward slowly than to move too rapidly and then have to retreat. The student might review very briefly a new reference obtained for social studies. In this case, he would be before the class but would not have to engage in discussion with pupils, one of the greatest fears of students.

The next step might include some discussion; for example, the student could demonstrate uses of the kerosene lamp to the third-grade pupils studying pioneer history, permitting them to ask questions; or he could review plays used by the next basketball opponent, give demonstrations, and answer questions. If the discussion does not work well and the student seems unable to cope with the situation, you should probably remove him from discussion work with the total group. He could concentrate further on individual and group work, co-teaching work with you, and work with the class involving little or no discussion. When you think he is again ready to try bit teaching with group discussion, give him another trial. In case this performance indicates lack of readiness, repeat procedure of reversion to other activities and another trial as suggested above. *A student must not be moved to responsibility for the teaching-learning processes of the total group over a period of time, as in unit teaching, unless he is successful in bit teaching activities with the total group.*

The types of experiences the student has in the teacher activities preceding student teaching may also influence or create problems. For example, the student may have observed in a laboratory school where pupil control is successfully used, but when he comes to student teaching he may find a more rigid type of control which he has not seen used. Neither he nor the pupils have had experience with pupil control. Trouble is certain to arise if he tries informal pupil control. Equally difficult problems arise when the student has observed teacher-imposed control and in student teaching finds himself in a school where pupil control is practiced. There is no certain answer to this problem. Our advice, however, is for the student to establish himself successfully in the type of control practiced in the school before he attempts variations from that control.

MATURITY AND EMOTIONAL STABILITY

Maturity and mental health are qualities which seem closely related but are difficult to define. A mature individual might be described as one who is aware of his own strengths and weaknesses, who is sensitive to and observing of the mores, standards, and demands of his own social group, and who desires to do his best and take full responsibility for his actions. Other characteristics of maturation and emotional stability would certainly be poise, self-confidence, self-control, sense of humor, ability to evaluate one's work, and ability to accept and profit by criticism.

Fear and nervous anxiety of students is especially characteristic of elementary teacher candidates on two-year curricula. Most move out of this acute stage, some within a few days. But, we cannot expect them to have the poise and stability of veterans.

What symptoms of lack of maturity and emotional stability might you observe in the first few days, or on the first day if possible? Here are a few:

The student tries to keep up with the high school pupils in use of slang and current jive.

The student falters and appears not sure of himself in speaking with children.

The student is loud and raucous in the presence of pupils (inside, he probably feels quite insecure).

The student wears "loud" flashy ensembles in school.

The student almost continually watches you for approval.

The student nervously plays with anything in reach.

The student does too much talking and too little listening in conversation with pupils.

The student is apologetic about everything he does and feels that he does nothing right.

Having observed symptoms or evidences, what can you do? We suggest the following:

Provide for frequent conferences. If your attitudes are such that confidence can be built up by frequent conferences, don't spare yourself at this point. The student needs all of the reassurance and support you can give him, but be careful that he doesn't become too dependent upon you. We suspect that too many students are delayed in maturation and development of emotional stability because the jacks have been taken from under them too soon.

Some people believe that, even though the student is literally paralyzed with fear, he should be plunged into the water at the deep end of the pool; that he should take over the class after a few days and sink or swim. We do not believe in this procedure, but advocate the process whereby the student is gradually moved along by a stairstep effect. The induction period can be planned so that even the most immature student picks up the load gradually by doing increasingly difficult tasks.

Provide for increasing success. Avoid moving the student into many situations in which he has exhibited most fear or uncertainty. Perhaps he has more fear for adults than pupils. You can postpone some meetings with other staff members, so that he will not be meeting so many so soon. Let him develop a feeling of security with you, the custodian, the principal, the school nurse, and any other persons with whom you work daily. You might arrange that he have only brief contact with these for the first two or three weeks.

Determine seriousness of problem. You may have to decide whether or not a student has a chance to develop the needed maturity, or the emotional balance necessary. In the vast majority of cases you can isolate single characteristics, help the student identify them, and work with him for improvement. After you have worked with a dozen or more students in the classroom, you will probably be able to sense at once whether or not they have what it takes and can make the grade. Snap decisions are dangerous if you act on them too quickly, but shrewd judgments, when kept to yourself, may even enable you to plan your student's experiences in such a way that his readiness will grow without his ever realizing that you spotted his weakness so early.

We are concerned here, also, with the presence or absence of psychoneurotic tendencies, the ability to meet new or problematic situations and to continue working at a high level of effectiveness under strain. Unfortunately, most colleges have an occasional student who has a borderline mental illness and must be excluded from teaching on medical grounds. Allowing students with recognizable psychoses to go on into teaching is dangerous on two counts: first, teaching is strenuous; second, such persons should not risk working under such severe emotional strain. We have no right to allow such people to have daily contact with highly impressionable children. If you feel that you have a student whose problem is of such a nature, you should contact college authorities immediately. The decision is for them to make.

ABILITY TO ATTRACT, INTEREST,
AND GET ALONG WITH CHILDREN

An individual's ability to work effectively with children depends largely on his genuine interest in them and on his understanding of them and their problems. Some experience in working with children in groups is important. Valuable traits are personal magnetism, enthusiasm, patience, fairness, cheerfulness, kindness, and resourcefulness. There is strong evidence that children's impressions of students are quickly formulated and not changed materially through the student teaching period. This is especially true of a strong initial approval or a strong initial dislike.[2] The importance of experiences with children and youth preceding student teaching is evident here. Many teachers are convinced, even though the evidence is largely subjective, that the recent emphasis on pre-student teaching experiences with children and youth is paying big dividends. Follow-up of many cases makes us very cautious about predicting an individual's probable success with children until after he has had a real chance to try his hand.

Rowena Lund was an excellent student in the field of business education and had had experience in accounting. Never was a student more sincere—never did a student try harder to succeed. Her skill in ordinary human relations was excellent, and her ability to explain difficult processes in bookkeeping was far above average. Everybody expected her to become an outstanding teacher. But, no matter how hard she tried, her relations with pupils in classes deteriorated steadily. The difficulty was finally identified but no one knew how to help her remedy it, short of having her live her 21 years over again. She never

[2] Walter D. Smith, *Social Attraction between Elementary School Children and Student Teachers* (unpublished doctoral dissertation, University of Michigan, 1950).

made a single intuitive response to a pupil that didn't seem to irritate the learner sooner or later. The more she taught the farther the class drew away from her; the more she tried to improve the more she rubbed the fur the wrong way. Certainly student teaching was too short a time in which to work herself out of her natural pattern of response to senior high school pupils.

The above is an extreme case and you may never encounter one if the college with which you work has a good guidance program. But you probably will have many who have some difficulties. You know from experience that a teacher who tries too hard to be liked by the pupils loses their respect. This is a common weakness of student teachers. Naturally the student is anxious to get along well with pupils, but he may have had so little contact with them, either in school or out, that he just doesn't know how to proceed.

What are the responses of your student? Does he put hands on the pupils, spend excessive amounts of time just kidding with them, blush when a high school girl giggles at something he says, try to report the wildest experience in a talk-fest, or do just what the pupils want him to do? If so, he hasn't learned how to live effectively with pupils in school situations. We recommend the procedures reviewed below.

Direct the student's observation of results of teacher action. Ask him to observe in other rooms to see if he can determine the characteristics to which the pupils seem to respond most effectively. Your demonstration can be most impressive because you can demonstrate exactly what you want him to see.

Direct the student's observation to the results of his action. The student should continue to work with individuals and small groups, and you should continue to observe and attempt to get him to see which tactics he uses are effective. As rapidly as possible, he should learn to evaluate his growth in pupil-student relationships and to suggest approaches that might get more desirable results.

Prospective teachers need extensive contact with boys and

girls of the general age group they expect to teach long before they assume responsibility for teaching a group. More than that —*students must face the fact that they must really like children and want to work with them.*

SKILL IN HUMAN RELATIONS

A person is strong in human relations when he meets people graciously, enters easily into conversation with them, shows a genuine interest in other people, respects their opinions even when they differ from his own, willingly compromises differences, and exhibits faith in his fellow men. Important traits are sincerity, geniality, friendliness, courtesy, tact, tolerance, appreciation, and optimism.

You have ample opportunity to observe your student's skills in human relations during the first few days that he is with you. Does he show sincere friendliness or do you seem to detect some or much superficiality? Does he show immediate intolerance toward some pupils in the room or toward other teachers? Is he really interested in other people, their ideas, and the things they are doing, or does he seem to give the appearance of being concerned only with the promotion of self? Is he immediately critical of the conditions in the school? When he meets the custodian, does he exhibit a sincere warmth of interest and friendliness or give the impression that he is on one level and the custodian on another?

The quicker you detect student weaknesses in human-relations skills, the quicker you can set the student right. This can best be done in the conference, which is another good reason to have daily conferences the first week or two if possible. In reviewing problems with him, be fairly sure that you are observing the real thing and not a mirage. Artificialities and superficialities may be caused only by tensions or not knowing just what to do. Or they may be caused by a student suddenly trying to bridge the gap between immature and mature responses to situations.

Regardless of the causes, you need to talk with him about

traits he has exhibited that may cause him serious difficulties. In conferences of this type, *your* skills in human relations are given the supreme test. How would you go about talking to a student concerning gross lack of tact in meeting others, or promiscuously giving his opinion of practices observed in the school? Can you do it without seriously damaging the student's ego, his relationships with you, or his attitudes toward teaching? If you can do this as he is getting acquainted, you can get him off to a much better start than would otherwise be possible.

One teacher used a procedure that would be effective for any of us. She and the student attempted to isolate the problem and then considered procedures that might be effectively used. For example, her student was sympathetic toward boys who had been suspended from basketball because of late hours at a home party during the week. Statements made by the student got back to the coach, who reviewed the problem with the teacher. In the next conference period the problem was discussed, but the student was not reprimanded. The treatment was objective. The teacher reviewed the conditions of the case and the results— strained relations between student and coach. Next, they discussed other procedures that might have been followed by the student; that might be followed by any teacher in a similar situation. The teacher, through patience, understanding, and knowledge of procedures in good working relationships within a school, was able to help the student without the student losing confidence and security. Most of us are not born with some sort of sense that tells us how to proceed effectively in all sorts of situations involving human relations. We have to learn.

INTELLECTUAL AND PROFESSIONAL ENERGY

This involves an individual's mental and physical vigor, his creative imagination, and his general level of personal and professional accomplishment. A person who is strong in this area would have lots of drive and would exhibit traits of initiative, perseverance, and dynamic energy. He would have a habit of overcoming obstacles, taking on challenging tasks, organizing them well, and carrying them through to completion. Some people can only meet bare minimum requirements, while others are challenged to unusual effort by problems which seem difficult or impossible of solution. Strength in this area comes from good work habits built up over the years.

Work habits and general drive show up quickly. The student's materials are not organized, he can't find his notes from the last conference, he forgot to write the autobiography you asked for, he has seen nothing all day that he would like to ask about, and he isn't sure that he could get ready in time to attend the PTA meeting. You've no doubt heard thousands of others if you've worked long with student teachers.

A student lacking intellectual and professional energy needs your attention immediately. Again, you are exhibit A. The student cannot be expected to exhibit characteristics that you do not hold essential for yourself. Also, your energy may function at such a high level that you may hold standards *too high* for the student who naturally operates in a much lower gear. More difficult in some ways is the student who operates on an extremely high level of drive and efficiency, especially if your level of operation is slower, calmer, and less vibrant. The last mentioned type of student would have to learn not to overstimulate pupils, not to drive them too hard, and not to be too impulsive and directing. You are working toward a happy medium and therefore may have to slow down the high-geared and pep up the low-geared.

Regardless of the tempo of the student's operation, he must learn that certain basic habits are essential for success in teaching. He should start discovering these immediately, and you should insist upon their observance. Some of these are:

Be prompt in attending to details—when natural light is obscured by clouds, artificial light should be turned on immediately, not for the next class.

Be thoroughly ready for each teaching-learning situation—the loss of time because the teacher is not ready for class is always suffered by the learners.

See what needs to be done and do it *when* it needs to be done —not "I'll get at it some day."

Use the criteria "What is best for the pupils?"—not "What will require least work?"

There is no more effective procedure in working with a student than to do yourself the things you expect of him, to work with each other on this basis. No issue need be made of the situation, it can be accepted as a matter of fact. You should not accept flimsy excuses, evasions, or poor workmanship. This understanding between you must be operative from the first day.

Guiding a student involves your ability to determine readiness and to judge what experience might be provided next to assure continued growth. To determine student readiness for the next step in any type of teacher activity, such as parent relationships, requires close observation, discerning judgment, and a degree of chance. You cannot expect to be a good judge in your first experience with a student. Evaluation of your judgment as you guide students should reduce error in moving students too fast or too slowly up the scale of responsibility. Your judgment is also tested in determining next steps in cases in which the student demonstrates lack of readiness for given experiences. Regardless of degree of readiness at the moment, all experiences should be designed to provide for growth in readiness for activities that require greater teaching skill, are more complex in nature, and enable the student to assume more complete responsibility for the major types of teacher activities.

SUGGESTED REFERENCES

Off-Campus Student Teaching, Thirtieth Yearbook. Lock Haven, Pa.: Association for Student Teaching, 1951. Chapter III, "Readiness for Student Teaching," prepared by Charlotte Junge, gives a review of research in readiness and its implications for the student teacher.

6

Motivating the Learner

NOWHERE IN THE WHOLE RANGE OF THE TEACHER'S work is there greater mystery than in the question, "Why does Teacher A stimulate pupils to such great accomplishment, when Teacher B can't get a thing out of the same group?" You know that there is no simple answer to that question. Herein lies a good reason why you so often hear the statement, "Teachers are born, not made!" Today we accept the idea that most able young people with good minds and well-developed personalities can be guided, through experience, into becoming successful teachers. For the student or the beginning teacher, the key to that growth is the development of his ability to stimulate boys and girls to learn.

During the time that the student is observing and assisting under your guidance, he is studying the procedures that you and other teachers use in stimulating pupil learning. He notes the different attitudes that pupils in any class have toward the learning experiences in which they are engaged. He also notes differences in attitudes between classes, how some classes are generally enthusiastic about their work and others are not. As he observes and assists, he is trying to decide what he would do in one situation after another. He may be making mental or written notes of what you did, so that he will be prepared if such situations arise while he is teaching. He is anxious to succeed, he sees that your procedures are successful, and, there-fore, wants to teach like you. This is natural, but you must help him develop his own way of teaching. You can be successful in this task by helping the student understand motivation and by helping him apply his understanding to actual situations.

Students may have less trouble in getting pupils interested than in contributing to the development of pupil purposes. The latter, of course, is the real function of motivation. Although it should not be so, the difference between interest and purpose may be very great. For example, you may have seen a student keep pupils well entertained, but they had no inclination to do anything for themselves. You may have had a student who over-sold himself to motivate pupils or at least to get pupil support, again, with no important outcome.

How can you help your student see what motivation really is and what good motivation can accomplish? Then, how can you help your student learn to use effective motivation procedures? We are suggesting specific helps under the following headings:

Studying motivation procedures.

Use of extrinsic motivation.

Using motivation in assisting activities.

Building motivation skills while teaching.

STUDYING MOTIVATION PROCEDURES

We have emphasized before that observation should be spe-cifically directed. Here, the student is directed to study the motivation used by you. You might direct him as follows:

In class today, I want to get the pupils to see a need for writing good business letters (pupil purpose). I'll try by stressing our need for the information concerning the control of red spiders on the cedar trees on our school grounds before we write the letters to the County Agricultural Agent (method of motivation). Notice very care-fully the reactions of the pupils (direction to student).

In our unit on the problem, "Why does the United States Govern-ment regulate interstate commerce?" I want the pupils to focus their thinking and later their questions on major reasons for such regulations, not upon how interstate commerce is regulated (purpose). I'm going to start out by describing briefly a few major difficulties that have arisen (method of motivation). As you observe, try to decide how much interest the stories created and whether or not the pupils were stimulated in their thinking. You can tell by the questions they raise to guide our later study and discussion (direction to student).

In the above type of preparation the student is observing closely the motivation you use, the way you use it, and the results upon the pupils. In order that he may study motivation systematically, however, you might want to use the suggestions given below in working with him.

DIRECT HIS STUDY OF THE RELATIONSHIP OF MOTIVATION TO PURPOSE

Demonstrate motivation to develop purpose. Call his attention to the purpose you hope the pupils will develop as a result of the motivation you use. Ask him to determine whether or not the motivation you used resulted in the pupils wanting to do what you wanted. Some examples might be: "Today I'll attempt to get the pupils concerned enough about their handwriting so that they will really want to improve." "I'm going to try to get the pupils thinking about ways to improve the appearance of their room." "During literature period tomorrow, I'll try to develop a procedure for making book reviews that the pupils will like. We'll work on it during most of the period."

Have student help determine purposes. The student next should participate *with you* in determining purposes to be worked toward in *your* teaching. You might approach him thus: "In planning for the excursion to the foundry, what purposes should I attempt to motivate?" "The pupils must develop better attitudes toward the care of the shop. How might I go about getting better attitudes?" "The pupils showed evidence of some loss of interest yesterday in their unit on Community Responsibilities of Citizens. How might I go about building up their interests so that they will want to go ahead with the study?"

Have the student differentiate between teacher and pupil purposes. The student should be growing in his ability to select purposes that are basic and to think of them in terms of pupil purposes. This might help him to recognize the difference between the way in which you state the purpose and the way in which it may be stated by pupils. For example, you may have stated the purpose in this way, "To keep the chemistry shelves in good order." However, in talking with pupils, one of them put it this way, "What we better do is to be sure that everything is back in place before we leave the room. We'll probably have to stop work a little sooner each day, but that will be better than never being able to find anything." The student should learn early to recognize the value of such clear-cut statements of purpose given by pupils and to note that you never try to put your wording of purpose in their mouths. Even though written on the board or recorded in outlines for pupil use, the wording of pupils is always used. Again, the student must never forget that the function of motivation is to contribute to the development of *pupil* purpose.

It is imperative, in this connection, that the student be able to see the difference between purposes the teacher has in mind for a given lesson and the purposes that the pupils may have in mind. In fact, they may have all sorts of purposes, none approximating those of the teacher! Also, there may be many with no purposes whatsoever. Students are generally surprised that pupils don't catch purposes as the teacher tosses them about at the beginning of the lesson. You might suggest one reason that would impress the need for consistently good motivation. Pupils in fourth grade with twelve class periods daily are motivated at least sixty times each week while at school! Another would be that the teacher assumes pupil understanding and purpose without checking.

You can demonstrate this situation quite well by asking each member of the class, if in upper elementary grades or high school, to explain why he has been doing the classwork in which he was engaged. The student will be surprised at the variety!

Help the student determine pupil purposes for specific experiences. The most difficult part of motivation for the student may be in becoming sensitive to the procedures most effective in stimulating desired pupil purposes in particular situations. For example, the teacher who wants the pupils to learn to take helpful notes from reference reading in high school social studies may spend one or two periods explaining and working with the pupils in discovering how notes are taken, how they are organized for use in discussion, and their value to a class in working out solutions to problems being studied. The teacher is emphasizing the value of note taking for a particular situation. He hopes that pupil purpose will be to take notes so that they are ready to contribute effectively in class discussion.

The same teacher, in preparing a class for an excursion to a court hearing, may use quite a different type of motivation. In this case, he may concentrate on the matter of getting specific information concerning the procedures used in court hearings. There may be no problem in getting the pupils interested in taking the excursion. In fact, his motivation may have to be directed partially toward toning down the enthusiasm for the general experience. This he may do by working with them in setting of standards of conduct for the experience. Thus, he hopes that pupils have two purposes: one, to get specific information from the hearing, and two, to conduct themselves in an approved manner.

You might use some of the following suggestions in helping him to develop judgment in how to select motivation procedures:

1. Discuss the desired purposes for your lesson and possible approaches in motivating the lesson. Which does he think might be better?

2. Ask him to explain the difference between the motivation used in an arithmetic class and in a physical education class; a music class and a spelling class; a class period in which corrections were made on first drafts of a business letter and a class period in which the pupils were preparing for an assembly

program; a class period in which you were preparing for an excursion and one in which the pupils worked on handwriting.

3. Ask him to explain the difference between the motivation used at the beginning of the lesson and that used at the end of the lesson in making the assignment for next day.

4. Ask him to record apparent individual reactions to the motivation used in a particular class. This could be done on a sheet with the names typed down the left side. Did the motivation seem effective for some but not for others?

DIRECT HIS STUDY OF THE RELATIONSHIP OF MOTIVATION TO THE PARTICULAR CLASS AND/OR INDIVIDUALS

The student observes you using all sorts of motivating procedures and should come to recognize which seem to be most effective with particular groups or individuals. He may observe that a particular pupil never seems to be motivated other than by direct command. There may be others who show no animation whatsoever but proceed to do a fair job in following the class. Thus, the student becomes aware of the individual differences even in motivation.

He needs to study carefully the reactions of your class as a whole and of the individuals in your class. By so doing, he should develop some ability in predicting what may work with your class and what may not. It is extremely important that he be able to anticipate probable pupil response to particular types of motivation. Eventually he must be able to size up a group of pupils quickly and be able to select regularly the motivation procedures that produce desired results. For example, a student teacher was asked what differences he found between working with fifth- and sixth-grade pupils and seventh- and eighth-grade pupils. His response was that he "had to be more formal with the seventh and eighth grades." This was a difference he found between two different groups, not a difference between pupils generally at those two levels.

There are several things you can do to help the student become acquainted with pupils so that he can understand their responses to motivation.

1. Become acquainted with each pupil through direct association with him in the classroom and in other school situations. You can set a good example of brief, friendly conversations with pupils in nonclass situations. Give the student some specific procedures for getting started. Point out the value of speaking cordially to a pupil, making some friendly comment or compliment, if one happens to be appropriate, and breaking off the conversation quickly. If your student is in the school all day you can give him all sorts of opportunities to become acquainted.

2. Have your student begin to give "elbow" assistance to the pupils as soon as you think he is ready. The combination of close working contact in class and informal conversations outside of class time should give your student ample opportunity to get acquainted with pupils.

3. Have the student observe the same pupils in other classes and in other activities in the school. He may find that the pupils' responses, attitudes, and habits are very different as he goes from class to class and as he observes them in other activities.

As the student observes the reaction of pupils to motivation, he is in a much better position to work with you and to use motivation procedures in bit teaching. Now he has a better background for understanding when you say:

"We'll have to remember that John doesn't need all of this motivation so we might let him go to town and get the can of paint," and he will know why you're so confident.

"We'll have to try a different way to get Jill to work in dissection this afternoon."

"But how are we going to get Earl interested in learning his multiplication facts?"

The student should more and more recognize motivation as an individual matter. One doesn't think of the class when planning motivation, but of ways to stimulate each pupil. The additional suggestions given below may help you further:

1. Ask the student to jot down the ways by which you tried to motivate individual pupils during the class period. Also ask him to evaluate the effectiveness of each instance observed.

2. Ask him to jot down situations in which it seemed that individuals needed motivation and suggest what motivation he thinks might have been effective.

DIRECT HIS STUDY OF THE RELATIONSHIP OF MOTIVATION TO THE MATERIALS OF INSTRUCTION

A student in fifth grade had planned using a film as the major motivating procedure for the beginning of a unit on the *Conservation of Natural Resources*. The film depicted the tremendous waste of forests, soil, minerals, and other resources. He expected the pupils to "rise up in arms" when they saw the film and literally strike out on their own to put a stop to the business. Instead, they blinked when the lights came on and waited patiently for the next move by the student. Perplexed, he asked, "After seeing the film, what do you think 'conservation' means?" One boy spoke up quickly, "Conservation means waste. Why do we have to study that? We've already seen it."

Students learn quickly that the use of films, slides, excursions, materials brought to the classroom, and demonstrations are not sure-fire motivating procedures. It is much less *what* materials one uses than it is *how* the materials are used. This is the emphasis you need to give all students.

Again, you and the student work together in planning the use of materials to motivate your teaching. Through repeated selection of materials or activities, he develops judgment concerning their use. We are suggesting ways by which you can help the student to become sensitive to this problem and to use good judgment in meeting it effectively.

1. Each time that materials or activities may be used in motivating desirable pupil purposes, list those possible to use. For example, most pupils should be able to write a good business letter by the time they are in sixth grade. But what type of situation might prove successful in getting them to *want* to write

35302

a good business letter? You and the student might list possible situations you see forthcoming, situations that would give the pupils good reason. You select one in which they must write for information not available in the school. The above illustration represents the functional approach to motivation, an approach that the student will soon identify as being as near foolproof as any if properly used. Pupils can generally be interested in and want to do things if they can see that the activity is of real value to them.

2. Help the student select activities on the basis of definite criteria. Activities selected on the basis of the criteria given below are generally successful if properly used:

The activity should be real, not make believe.

Examples: Making soap while studying American History, making a formal dress in home economics, making a rock collection in second grade.

The activity should result in something of tangible value.

Examples: A radio made in science class, flower vases made in art class, a potholder made in first grade.

The activity should be appropriate for the age planned.

Examples: Arc welding in senior high school, tree planting in junior high, gardening in elementary.

3. Be sure that the activity or material has not been overused with the pupils. For example, pupils literally become immune to sound films. In one school, income tax blanks were used for motivation in three different classes! This is a situation in which you have opportunity to work intensively with the student on imagination. If he can develop some feeling for variety and the unusual during student teaching, you will have done much to make motivation for him successful in later teaching.

4. When using materials or activities, help the student to see how you plan for their use. You might even demonstrate poor use of materials to show that pupils may look them over lightly and relax. In another situation, demonstrate good use of the

same type of materials. Be sure he sees that the *way* you use illustrative materials really makes a difference.

DIRECT HIS STUDY OF THE RELATIONSHIP OF MOTIVATION TO PUPIL CONTROL OR DISCIPLINE

The importance of pupil motivation in relation to discipline is repeatedly called to our attention by studies of the causes for failure of beginning teachers. No matter when, where, or on what data these studies are made, one cause for failure is always found near the top, if not actually first on the list. Usually, the studies just report it as discipline or failure of the teacher to obtain pupil control. However it may be labeled, it still means that the young teacher does not have the personality, the skill, or the judgment to stimulate real interests of boys and girls in the curricular experiences at hand.

Thus far in this chapter we have considered motivation as contributing to pupil desire to do that which the teaching-learning situation requires. You know of this type of motivation as intrinsic. That is, the teacher, or something in the teaching-learning situation, stimulates direction from within the pupil because of values for himself that he may see or anticipate in the experiences. The value may be simply that he has a very real desire to please the teacher. Those teachers who are successful in the use of intrinsic motivation rarely have to resort to the use of motivation from without. The latter you recognize as extrinsic motivation. It is characterized by such things as prizes for the pupil who misses the fewest words in spelling during the year, stars on the chart showing correct arithmetic papers, staying in after school to study if the pupils misbehave in class, and honor roll for pupils making grades of B or above. Also included are the punishments that will happen "if."

Most student teachers have to use some form of extrinsic motivation. This may be due to many factors, such as:

1. The degree to which *you* have been successful in stimulating desirable attitudes toward behavior standards in your group or groups. Students are very much aware of the situations they

find. Several described the way they felt about the situation in which they started teaching as follows:

> I started out in an environment with good previous control.
>
> The class had an excellent attitude and was under excellent control when I took over.
>
> The teacher seemed to go out of his way to make it easy for the student teachers to slip into the class. The pupils respect the teacher and that helps.
>
> The most important thing in student teaching is to get a good start.
>
> My teacher didn't have the class as well under control as he should have, which made it hard for me to take over.
>
> Discipline was weak; so it was hard to take over from there.

Such judgments may not always be sound, but there is no mistaking the attitudes and feelings of the students. Certainly those attitudes would have a lot to do with the self-confidence students gain in the early stages of their teaching with you.

2. General attitudes of the pupils in the school toward educational experiences.

3. Lack of personal appeal on the part of the student.

4. Inability of the student to apply understanding of motivation to learning experiences.

5. Attempt on the part of the student to direct a type of discipline unlike that used by you, that is, more formal or more informal.

6. Slow development of skill in use of desirable motivation procedures.

7. Lack of imagination in use of a variety of motivation procedures.

8. Lack of security or confidence in ability.

USE OF EXTRINSIC MOTIVATION

Because you face basic reality, you must instruct most students in the use of extrinsic motivation no matter how distasteful it may be to you. We don't like it either, but since there is no alternative for you or us, we make the following suggestions:

DIRECT STUDENT STUDY OF THE USE OF EXTRINSIC MOTIVATION

First, demonstrate to the student the wholesome atmosphere existing in the use of pupil control as discussed above. Most will want the same atmosphere in their own teaching.

Next, with the student, study carefully situations in which you have resorted to a sharp command, definite directions arbitrarily given, or threat of consequences (no more excursions unless we can use better judgment in conducting ourselves). Try to analyze each situation with the student. You might consider such questions as:

Why was it necessary for me to say or do what you observed?
What had I not done well?
What had I failed to take into account in planning the motivation procedures?
How might the need for my action have been prevented?
What was the attitude of the group or pupil toward my action?
Could I have done something at the moment that would have been better?
What will be the effect of my action?
Will it contribute to the type of pupil control that we want?

This type of procedure repeated many times should gradually result in student sensitivity concerning what to do if and when such situations arise while he is teaching.

MAKE THE STUDENT RESPONSIBLE FOR WHATEVER MOTIVATION IS NECESSARY AS HE STARTS ASSISTING YOU IN TEACHER-LEARNING PROCESSES

The student should not be placed in situations in which he would be unable to direct learning. For example, you would not ask the student to help a pupil who would defy even you if he thought he could. You would be sure that he would cause a beginning student trouble. Also, the above recommendation has to be somewhat qualified because of the policies in particular schools concerning the degree of responsibility that a student may assume. Suppose one pupil took a swing at another pupil in a committee project or a kindergarten pupil mashed an object that another was molding in clay and then ran, what responsibility could the student assume in your school? This must be known to the student and also the pupils.

Have you taught in a school in which the pupils had developed the idea that they could get by with anything when they were under the supervision of students? The major problem is not so much the degree of responsibility that the student can assume in your school but rather getting the student to assume the responsibility that he has been given. Perhaps you've worked with a student who could not bring himself to get an orderly teaching-learning situation. Even though necessary for learning, he could not hold pupils to definite standards although he could speak lucidly about them. In situations of this kind, move the student back to assisting activities which require less courage and do not move him into situations that might be more difficult until he does show courage. The reasons for such decision on your part should be made clear to the student.

USING MOTIVATION IN ASSISTING ACTIVITIES

Perhaps the student will not understand how motivation really works until he tries it. At least, the test for him is in using motivation to achieve desired goals in working with pupils. He first needs practice in situations including one or a few pupils in brief activities. Review motivation possibilities with the student, have him select a procedure that sounds good, and let him try it. After he has tried the procedure, discuss results. The following examples illustrate situations in which the above approach might be used:

1. The pupils are not discriminating in selecting pictures for the bulletin board.

2. You would like for a pupil in science class to report on a new treatment for the common cold.

3. A kindergarten child needs to report to the school nurse, but does not want to leave the group.

4. A fifth-grade boy in physical education does not want to go swimming with the other pupils.

5. A girl in home economics is careless in her cooking procedures.

6. A first-grade child wants to dominate class discussion.

7. A group working on a skit for assembly is not serious about the task.

He can advance no farther in the use of motivation until he can successfully cope with this type of situation. There are several principles we would like to emphasize here concerning student growth in use of motivation:

1. Start with situations in which you are relatively sure of student success.

2. Start with situations in which there is only one child or at most two or three.

3. Give the student a variety of experiences in motivation before you present real problems such as 3, 4, 6, and 7 above.

4. Give the student difficult individual and small group problems in motivation before moving him to motivation of the total group.

5. The student should not be given responsibility for the motivation of the total group until he has achieved success and confidence in small groups.

6. Review motivation procedures with student before their use.

7. Review results of motivation procedure following use.

BUILDING MOTIVATION SKILLS WHILE TEACHING

Suggestions will be made here of activities which should help your student develop skill, understanding, and professional judgment in several areas. You have your own way of solving certain types of classroom problems and, with study, can develop many additional activities for your students.

GETTING AND HOLDING THE ATTENTION OF PUPILS

Example is your most effective tool. You can demonstrate procedures that stimulate your pupils to an intense interest in learning and to show the real thrill that comes to them with successful achievement. A student reported enthusiastically on his observation of foreign language teaching as follows:

Miss L. uses a great deal of animation in her presentation. At first I felt she was overdoing it, but soon the class caught her fire and the response was the best I have ever seen. Frustration on the part of the pupils seemed to be at a minimum or nonexistent. It was a pleasant sight to watch.

When books are finally put into the hands of these pupils they will go hog-wild. They are amazed at this point that they can understand simple sentences spoken in a tongue so different from ours and even more astounded when they can speak for themselves.

She accomplished this by her cheerful approach, by her simple presentation in simple words, and by the repeated act of letting the class participate to the hilt in solving this mystery of a new language. Her praise of all their effort, be it good or bad, catches on, holds fast, and pulls ever forward.

Unfortunately, to understand this performance is one thing, but to duplicate it is quite another. You will find that you have to help students acquire many minor skills before these skills can be put together into a truly artistic classroom performance. By close observation, careful analysis, and much study you can identify some of the minor skills which your student needs to develop. Guiding his learning until he masters some of these will give him a great sense of accomplishment and increase his self-confidence and enthusiasm. The following are examples of skills with which he may need help.

Kick-off procedures. Help the student select a number of appropriate procedures and encourage him to try them out. You must also caution him to avoid overuse of certain types of interest-arrestors. Variety is one sound basis for selection.

Good kick-off procedures must aid in establishing a center of interest, and the less artificial the interest created the more valuable the procedure. Encourage your students to select procedures which will contribute directly to the purpose of the learning activity. Demonstration, use of the blackboard, pupil presentations, pupil activities of an unusual nature, and the use of objects are samples of activities which can be used as functional kick-off media. Stress the point that an attention-arrestor needs to be chosen which fits in well with the other activities that may develop immediately afterward.

Getting the range. Students can be expected to begin teaching by shooting over the heads of the pupil or by talking down to them. The student, with guidance, can sharpen his aim as he goes along.

You can suggest ways of judging the effectiveness of a presentation, while it is going on, by watching the faces of the pupils, and noting especially the reactions of certain pupils who seem to be good barometers of class receptance. Performance activities and test scores are a good index of effectiveness, but the results come some time after the initial presentation. If you sense that your student is not successful in getting the range, you can set up specific test situations in which he can get data for himself. This is much better than merely telling him that he is shooting too high or too low.

Having a very able group or a very poor group may leave the student with a problem of adjustment when he goes out on the job. Here is the way a beginning teacher analyzed her situation:

Perhaps my major problem was that my standards were too high. I had an exceptional group when I did my student teaching. The students had high IQ's; were well mannered; did their homework; and their parents cooperated with the teachers. Now I assign very little homework, because the majority of the pupils don't do it and letters to the parents seem to accomplish very little. Therefore, I have tried to make every minute count in each teaching period so that each student has had a chance to learn every minute of class time.

Your student must understand the peculiarities of the group with which he is working and see where this group fits into the range one may find in public schools. Observation and analysis of other classes and other schools and study of comparative standards are necessary to give a broad outlook and a readiness for what may come.

Using the real-life interests of the pupils. This procedure can often be brought to a higher level when a student is present. Two people can usually discover more about a group than can one teacher working alone. Many remarkable tales of pupil improvement can be traced directly to the efforts of students. Your job is two-fold: encourage him to discover real life interests of pupils and demonstrate how these interests can be put to effective use. Your well-directed efforts bring dual satisfactions in seeing pupils learn and seeing students get the thrill of successful teaching.

Very often a student discovers out of school interests that you did not know about. The student may have some hobbies which help him to capitalize on the pupil's interests. Aviation, radio, sports, collecting, and other hobby activities can serve a student well, if he has a creative imagination and can follow the leads he uncovers.

THE EFFECT OF THE STUDENT'S PERSONALITY UPON THE CLASS

In discussing discipline with a student, a teacher observed, "When a teacher is having disciplinary trouble he should give himself a good going over and he might find some of the troubles within. Eight hours of sleep and a good disposition may cut disciplinary problems in half." You may not find it easy to get this idea across to the student unless he remembers some specific teacher in his own experience. By planning his activities wisely, and especially his observations, you can increase his understanding of the effect of the teacher himself on pupils. Aspects of the student's personal relationships with pupils that may need your special help are:

General physical presence. Students are usually cautioned about dress, posture, grooming, and mannerisms, but they may not realize that these personal matters really affect pupils, and especially pupil control.

There is no law against teaching while seated at the desk, and experienced teachers can do it successfully. However, during the early stages student teachers should stand whenever they are leading group activity, except in the lower grades and with small groups. This is especially true for students who are short and particularly youthful in appearance. Many college students have made a habit of not showing outwardly the emotions they actually feel. You will need to encourage them to show more zest while working with a group and to speed up the tempo of their speech and action as a means of holding attention.

Frequently you direct group work without occupying the center of attention. This may be difficult for your student, however, and you should demonstrate and discuss with the student the great influence that the physical proximity of the teacher can have on pupils who may be inattentive.

Eye-control. Eye-control by the skillful teacher is a most effective tool for maintaining class activity at a high level. Point out to students the peculiar problems that exist and the amount of actual visual observation they can and must maintain. In such classes as home economics and industrial arts, for example, the teacher needs to have as much of the class in view as possible all of the time.

In the beginning stages, students may be preoccupied with many things and may fail even to look at most of the pupils. Some tend to develop funnel-shaped vision—just looking at those readily in view within a narrow angle. Others habitually look at only one side of the room, around the edges, sometimes even over the heads of most pupils, or at an individual or a small group. Have the student work at this skill consciously until he can keep most of the group in view most of the time. Show him how to use eye-control to hold the attention of some pupils whose minds might otherwise be wandering, and, with practice on this and physical proximity, he will be pleased with the results.

A sense of humor and a wholesome attitude toward life. These can work wonders in maintaining good working conditions in the classroom. Students tend to become tense and rather formal when they start teaching. Since they are afraid of making mistakes and of inability to answer questions, they may tighten up and put on a pretty serious exterior. The "hail fellow well met" individual can actually overdo it, while "old sobersides" may lose his group for the opposite reason.

The overly serious student may have to develop his display of a sense of humor through several stages. Students should be able to tell a funny story or amusing incident, laugh at it heartily with the pupils, and still return quickly to a serious attack on the job at hand. Before student teaching days are over most students should be able to let youngsters laugh freely at the funny things that come up and still bring them along quickly to the regular activities of the day. The real test for a relaxed teacher is to be able to laugh at his own mistakes or tell a joke on himself.

Impartial treatment of pupils. Pupils want students to be good fellows and square shooters. Helping students attain this status and still maintain complete respect requires that they be interested in boys and girls and show this interest sincerely. You can give them cues to show their interest, ways and times for talking with individuals and suggestions for making sincere and effective responses. Also, you can suggest procedures that will help them avoid the suspicion of partiality and unfairness. By watching them at work with the pupils you can spot practices that can be improved and additional activities to try out. A combination of good example, cooperative discussion of the problems, and actual instruction of the student is necessary, as these student comments point out:

My teacher was extremely interested in everything of interest to his pupils. An interest in their families and their activities, such as tumbling, art and stamp collecting as well as their parties, helped the relationships.

Many of the teachers talked to their kids after school about non-school affairs in order to establish better rapport.

Always told us why he did certain things to maintain relationships.

My teacher taught me how to gain the respect and still hold the friendship of pupils.

Some of the teachers gave good suggestions, but others gave none at all.

I wish that my teacher could have told me more little things on how to work with my pupils.

Spontaneous responses. Teachers and students alike need to recognize clearly that little things can cause big negative reactions on the part of pupils. Comments containing sarcasm or showing disinterest, impatience, prejudice, lack of sincerity, or excess ego can cause a lot of tension in a classroom.

Students must learn that harsh and unfair treatment of pupils will have effects which are anything but helpful. Punishing and bawling out pupils indiscriminately is bound to stir up resentment. A wise teacher put it this way, "You can't teach a person after you condemn him." The following example was reported by a student:

I was the witness of a very sad episode that I will long remember. A girl made a very low score on a standardized test. In reading the grade the teacher said, "I guess you know that makes you the dumbest kid in the class." Later I learned from this "dumb kid," with a tear-stained face at this point, that the test reviewed the work of the previous year. She had not attended this school and had no background whatever for the test. This episode gave a picture of how wrong a teacher can be in making snap decisions when he does not have all the facts of a situation.

As teachers we must all watch our own procedures and be sure that we are not setting some bad examples of pupil-teacher relations.

BUILDING AND MAINTAINING A GOOD CLASSROOM ATMOSPHERE

Developing a "we" feeling with pupils in a classroom is possible and very much worth doing. Few students do it naturally and far too many experienced teachers fail to do the simple things that will help. Students with a background of question-answer and lecture procedures through elementary school, secondary school and college may be expected to say "I" every time they speak to the pupils. "I want you to do this for tomorrow." "Tell me!" "I am going to have you do this." "I did that." "Can you give me the answer?" "Please speak so I can hear."

Using the first person plural pronouns, "we" and "us" and emphasizing the group is not hard to do. The whole atmosphere seems so much more warm and friendly when we say, "We are going to do that for tomorrow." "Let's take up the next topic now." "Tell the class what you think." "Should we do this or that first?"

A democratic classroom atmosphere. A teacher-dominated classroom tends to repress pupils' natural drives and self-expression. A complete *laissez-faire* attitude by the teacher may touch off anarchy if allowed to go far enough. A truly democratic class atmosphere is not always easy to develop, but does hold out promise of stimulating pupil self-direction. Can you demonstrate for your student what is meant by these three approaches, and help him analyze their strengths and weaknesses? Can you help him build skill in getting pupils ready for self-direction? He will need thorough competence backed by experience in these skills if he is to be successful in most situations into which beginning teachers go.

Student vocabulary, speech habits, and personal mannerisms. Improvement in these areas is often very necessary. You may have to help a student reduce his vocabulary burden in talking with the group. Sometimes this means suggesting that a student consciously reorganize material so that it is in a form and language which the pupils can understand. Less commonly, students may use baby talk, excessive slang, or colloquialisms; all of which may need conscious effort toward reduction. Sometimes pupils will make fun of a student behind his back or even openly disrupt the class out of lack of respect, making some improvement a necessity. In extreme cases you will have to help the student work out conscious substitutes and see that he practices them in an empty room before trying to work with a group again. Less frequent and more serious are the actions of occasional students who are guilty of over-familiarity with pupils. Handle these cases on a thoroughly professional basis by trying to point out to the student the dangers in such actions.

Group standards. Using the standards of the group as a basis for setting expected levels of behavior is a sound approach psychologically but difficult to accomplish. Help your student understand that extensive preparation and excellent rapport with a group is necessary before he can use group standards very effectively.

Another side of this problem is in adjusting his actions in handling pupil behavior in groups of different ages. A student had this experience:

I found out that I could not handle the discipline situations in the first grade. I did not know whether to be stern with the children or to be lenient with them. I decided to be stern, but not too stern. One boy was acting up and I told him if he did not stop I would make him sit on my lap. His remark was, "But teacher, I want to sit on your lap."

Mores of school and community. Adapting standards to the mores of the school and community may be very difficult for your student. His own school experience may have been in an entirely different environment. He may have to adjust considerably to carry on successfully in the sort of school atmosphere that you have built and desire to maintain. You need to talk over with each new student the whole matter of school and community standards so that they will have a background on which to build. This is very important because every beginning teacher has the same assessment to make as he goes into a new community. Simple matters such as the manner of address in and out of classes, the use or non-use of nicknames, the extent of formality in the pupils' approach to teachers, hall conduct, or the amount of freedom pupils have to go to library, laboratory, workroom, or other special place sometimes pose real problems for the beginner. You should help your student make his adjustment easily in your situation and prepare him well for different types of situations later.

In summary, student growth in learning to motivate pupils is focused upon the following points of emphasis:

1. Ways by which motivation can be used to stimulate pupil development of desired purposes.

2. Determining specific motivation to be used, such as:

Procedures effective with a particular group

Procedures effective with particular individuals

Procedures considered to hold most promise in contributing to pupil development of desired purposes in specific situations

Personnel and facilities available for use

Procedures which can be most effectively used by particular students.

3. Student development of effective personal characteristics in motivation.

4. The effectiveness of motivation and the development of pupil purpose upon pupil control or discipline.

5. The relative effectiveness of extrinsic and intrinsic motivation in the development of pupil purpose.

SUGGESTED REFERENCES

Grim, Paul, and John Michaelis, *The Student Teacher in the Secondary School.* New York: Prentice-Hall, Inc., 1953. Chapter III "Planning Your Work" gives explicit suggestions to help students motivate desirable pupil learning experiences.

Michaelis, John, and Paul Grim, *The Student Teacher in the Elementary School.* New York: Prentice-Hall, Inc., 1953. Chapters V "Planning the Unit of Work" and VII "Using Group Processes" review procedures to use in contributing to the development of pupil purpose in learning.

Schorling, Raleigh, and Max Wingo, *Elementary School Student Teaching.* New York: McGraw-Hill Book Company, Inc., 1950. Chapter IX, "A More Interesting and Challenging School Day" pp. 207-227, treats in detail many aspects of pupil motivation.

7

Learning to Plan

THE STUDENT LEARNS UNDER YOUR GUIDANCE
that the premium in planning is placed upon both *effectiveness*
and *efficiency*. Your responsibility to the student is, therefore,
twofold: (1) to help him learn to plan so that his plans work
effectively, and (2) to help him improve in efficiency so that he
can plan adequately for all of his daily activities as a teacher.
He sees you planning for responsibilities which may include
several classes; some extra-class activities such as a club, student council, study hall, assemblies or school newspaper; faculty committee concerned with some phase of school improvement; guidance or counselling activities; parent contacts; community activities; and professional growth.

Most students have had some experience with planning preceding student teaching, but you can never know how much.
Neither do you know how much previous experiences with
planning have helped or hindered them in getting ready for
planning on their own. Your best bet is to start the student with
very simplified plans in connection with participation and assisting activities and move toward more complex plans in relation
to the student's readiness to progress. The following progression
will be reviewed in order in this chapter:

Planning in participation and assisting activities.

Lesson planning.
Unit planning.
Planning for other activities.

PLANNING IN PARTICIPATION AND ASSISTING ACTIVITIES

Student planning other than lesson and unit planning is often overlooked. Readiness for lesson or unit planning may be developed to best advantage during the time the student is assisting you with your many activities as a teacher. Actually, the assisting stage of the students' work continues until he has learned to plan and execute plans effectively. You can have no confidence in student planning for the teaching-learning activities of a class or the activities of an extra-class organization unless the student can plan and use plans effectively in assisting you. Neither can you have confidence in the ability of the student to assume responsibility in other teacher activities until he can plan and function successfully while assisting you.

Characteristics of plans used when assisting are the same as those used when assuming full responsibility, with one exception: they are concerned with only a few pupils, a part of the total lesson or unit, a part of the total activity, or a part of the total approach in working with parents, administration, or faculty. For example, in talking with the principal of the school concerning need for reference materials in seventh grade science there is a definite purpose, definite procedures to be used in achieving the purpose, and evaluation of the results of the plans. The student has specific responsibilities, such as preparing and presenting a list of the books now available giving date, reading level, and quality. He might also prepare and present a list of the reading levels of the members of the class.

In a club activity such as ceramics, the student working with a particular pupil would have to determine specifically how he planned to proceed. These plans would be carefully reviewed with you, revised if necessary, and evaluated after the club period. The student often objects to this type of planning at first and has to learn from practice that specific plans help. One student objected seriously to plan-making when he was asked to assume responsibilities with individuals and groups. He was not forced to make plans but was soon coming to his teacher with questions: "Should I have let Joe start on another experiment in science club after he finished the first?" "Was it all right for me to let the committee change the plans for the display table?" "How come the parents didn't like what I said about their child's reactions to his home?" "What should I have done when the pupil didn't pick up the food he spilled at lunch?" The teacher soon had sufficient evidence to support her idea that foresight was much more helpful in meeting situations than hindsight.

You probably are not in the habit of making detailed plans for all of your activities, but some should be written while the student is with you. If you expect the student to make plans for specific participation and assisting activities, you should have samples to show him. Suppose you are going to work with a committee of pupils, you could make plans and give the student a carbon. He could see specifically how *you* make and use plans. An art teacher made the plan reported below in preparing to work with a group responsible for a ceramics display in the library:

PLANS FOR CERAMICS COMMITTEE
November 15

1. Get pupils to formulate purposes for which display is made. Possible purposes:
   To acquaint other pupils with ceramics work of fellow pupils
   To provide artistic atmosphere in library
   To stimulate interest of other pupils in art.
2. Get pupils to plan display to realize objectives. Consider:
   Arrangement, color, quality of work, variety in types of pieces, number of pupils whose work is represented, the setting in which the display is made.

3. Get pupils to share responsibilities for preparing display.
4. Arrange time for pupils to finish display.
5. Get pupils to plan for care of exhibit.

Examples of this type make the student aware of the need for the teacher to have thought through his work with pupils, regardless of how minor the activity is. Also, the student sees how plans are followed through and can recognize the results.

Your next step is to ask him to plan for his participating and assisting activities. The following examples should suggest many other procedures that you can use:

Ask the student to make plans for work with individuals. He might be asked to help a pitcher at baseball practice, assist a certain kindergarten child in learning to use the jungle gym, work with a pupil in use of the turning lathe, or work with a first-grade pupil in manuscript writing. Go over the plans with him carefully and, if necessary, have him revise them until you approve. Note his use of the plans and mutually evaluate the effectiveness of his plans. Ask him to assist in another activity and follow the same procedure. His ability to make plans and to use plans in assisting activities with individuals or groups may be the best evidence you have of the student's readiness to assume major responsibility.

Ask the student to plan for a ten minute review of the news to be given at the beginning of class next day. Discuss the nature of such a review with him. How many news items might be considered? Who might start the discussion? What maps, globes, or other illustrative material might contribute if used? How might one get pupils to participate instead of just sitting? How might the discussion be summarized or closed? Observe his review carefully and make mental notes concerning ways in which he might improve. Talk with him after class, if possible, concerning his review. Ask for his evaluation and respond frankly to questions he asks you. *Most students are eager to learn and really want your suggestions.*

Ask the student to plan to work with pupils in preparing a bulletin board. Discuss the need of the teacher to be guide and advisor, not authority and director. Also, review problems which may arise concerning getting needed materials, reaching agreements, dividing work among members of committee, keeping pupils on the subject, holding to standards in arrangement, and determining color and design. Observe working relationships existing between pupils and student; attitudes and reactions of student to suggestions, disagreements, and attitudes of pupils; availability of materials needed for bulletin board; student knowledge of material to be displayed and possible methods of display; attitudes of pupils and student toward the working relationships that existed and toward the completed task.

Next, the student may be given two or three more general questions such as: "What difficulties showed up in the summary which indicated that the pupils had been verbalizing during the discussion. How might this have been prevented?" "What problems appeared in homeroom that were not resolved satisfactorily? How might I have helped the chairman?"

If the student is to be able eventually to evaluate and improve his own plans, he must attempt to determine why plans did not work as expected. Therefore, you might ask him to determine why pupils showed lack of interest, why less was accomplished in Lettermen's Club than anticipated, or why the pupils in study hall were restless.

As you observe the student in his initial planning activities such as the types above, there are several major questions which you should keep in mind. These questions will help you determine (1) whether or not the student is ready for major planning and increased responsibility, (2) what difficulties persist in preventing successful planning, and (3) what further steps may be necessary in getting him ready for major planning. The following questions may help you:

1. Does he have the purpose of the learning situation clearly in mind?

2. Is he willing to put forth the effort to get plans and materials ready for the learning experience?

3. Has he provided for appeal to all pupils in the class or only a few?

4. Do his plans indicate teacher domination or pupil-teacher planning?

5. What provision is made for individual differences in pupil needs, interest, and abilities?

6. Does he follow his plans to the letter or does he follow them flexibly and yet stay on the subject?

7. Does he run out of plans before the end of the period and find himself at a loss?

8. Does he maintain poise and sense of direction even though his plans seem not to be working?

9. Is he able to alter his plans when he sees them not working?

10. Do his plans show an understanding of the age-group with which he is working?

11. Can he determine wherein his plans failed or succeeded?

12. Is he willing to take your suggestions and try them?

13. Does he understand your suggestions and is he able to adapt your suggestions in revising plans, or in planning for other learning experiences?

14. Is he able to make application to other specific situations after generalizations or principles have been developed from specific situations?

15. Are the activities planned so that they may run smoothly?

16. Are his plans for evaluation or summary designed to evaluate the ability of pupils to apply what they have learned?

Student experiences in preparing brief, definite plans and in following and evaluating such plans where not so much is at stake provide excellent background for later lesson and unit planning. In cases where the student starts planning for full responsibility but is not ready, you might revert to the types of planning discussed above. The following examples of what other teachers have done may help you:

1. A student in social studies could not talk with his class but kept his eyes on his plans most of the time. The plans were very well prepared but the student lacked assurance when he

could not see them. The teacher decided to retrace steps and ask the student to plan for very brief responsibilities. He was asked to lead a five-minute "News of the Day" period without using written plans. During the first few days he was quite nervous and at times seemed not to be sure what they were talking about. No doubt he was trying to recall previously-made mental notes. By the end of the second week he spoke with enthusiasm. He brought related bits of news from the past to bear on the present topics. He had an interesting and well-ordered discussion and "didn't have nearly enough time."

He then moved to responsibility for a lesson plan for a full class period (forty minutes). He was again glued to his plans before the period was half over. He was made responsible for the lesson next day, but deprived of his written plans. This was worse than the day before. What next? He was then asked to enlarge the "News of the Day" period to fifteen minutes one day each week, and then thirty minutes one day each week. He made careful plans, but they were not in his hands while teaching. Steady progress was observed and he was judged ready for the preparation of a unit. The unit, as in previous planning, was well prepared, but he resorted to his notes too frequently even yet. His growth in self-confidence was slow but definite progress was made.

2. A fourth-grade student couldn't get his science unit set up so that his teacher could tell just what activities were going to be used or how they were going to be used. The teacher decided to have him present a brief science experiment each day in connection with the unit being taught. The student wrote a description of the experiment and the steps to be followed with the class. Again the classroom procedure was hazy. Following the experiment, however, he was asked to write what had taken place. This he did quite well. In the discussion that followed, he began to catch an idea of what was meant by "planning the procedures to be followed in an activity." Several experiences like the one above during the next two weeks enabled the student to write a detailed, clear-cut unit.

LESSON PLANNING

The student must be informed specifically concerning the types of lesson plans that you expect him to make. This can be done in several ways:

Show him samples of the kinds of plans used in your school. You no doubt have plans you have prepared or that students have prepared while teaching in your room or class. These you can go over carefully with the student to be sure that he understands each part and the purpose of each part. A sixth-grade teacher and her student studied the plan reproduced below. It was the kind she expected her student to make.

MAP READING LESSON PLAN

Miss Joan Smith, *January 12*

Pupil Purpose: To learn to estimate distances on a map.

Materials for Instruction: Map of Missouri, yardstick.

Instructional Procedures:

Motivation: On a wall map of Missouri, ask the pupils to locate the following cities in relation to their home town (Kirksville, Missouri): St. Louis, Kansas City, Springfield, and Columbia. Ask pupils (3 or 4 for each location) to estimate distance from home town to cities mentioned. Ask different pupil to measure each distance to check relative accuracy of estimates. Discuss with pupils the advantage of having reference points on a map in order to estimate distances between other points. Illustrate using the known distance between Kansas City and Kirksville and estimating the distance between Kirksville and St. Joseph. If time permits, try Macon and Memphis.

Assignment: Explain to the pupils that they are going to be given a chance to see how well they can estimate distances. On a sheet of paper, they are to write the estimated distances between Kirksville and the other cities to be written on the board. The wall map will be left up for their use.

Study, activity, etc.: Write names on board:

Maryville, Moberly, Sedalia, Hannibal, Cape Girardeau, Rolla,

Mountain Grove, and Joplin. Have different pupil locate each place on map. Allow pupils to return to map if they forget location.

Evaluation: Get range of estimates for each distance and have pupil check accuracy for each.

Summary or conclusions: (Suggested) One must have points of reference. One must practice estimating. Changing size of map might be confusing.

If a form similar to the one above is used, how detailed do you want him to make his plans in following the outline? In how much detail should he describe the step-by-step procedure of the lesson? Should all instructional materials be listed? The student may not have planned before, may have seen only a few unexplained lesson plans, and, therefore, must be told or shown *how* to make plans following an outline you give him. He may be even more lost if you give him no outline to follow.

If you require only very brief plans, another danger arises; that is, he may not be required to think through his planning to the point where he can see clearly what he is going to do. *One of the major functions of all planning is to visualize just how the teacher and class are going to proceed.* Here again, the student may have trouble. Little experience in working with pupils makes it difficult for him to *anticipate pupil reactions* and the problems that arise in connection with pupil learning.

No matter whether you ask him to prepare daily lesson plans or units, follow the plan of the textbook or manual, or use units previously prepared and in the file, the student must know exactly what planning is expected from him.

Use the same kinds of lesson plans in your teaching that you expect the student to use. The student can follow these plans as you teach. He will be helped by a discussion of your use of the plans as soon as possible after the lesson. Encourage him to be perfectly frank in his questions concerning use of the plans.

Let the student use sample plans while he makes his own plans. One danger in this procedure is that he may follow the plans exactly instead of using initiative in setting up the plans to fit his particular situation. For example, the details of lesson plans concerning the business letter might not be suitable for his lesson. The major parts would fit exactly, of course, but the kind of approach used, the reasons for writing the letter, and the specific type of business letter might be different. The student, with your help, needs to learn to adapt the details of the lesson to the major parts of the lesson plan. Initiative in adapting details to the several outlines of types of plans is another very important teacher competency that the student must develop.

In fields or classes such as physical education, music, art, spelling, reading, or arithmetic, where large instructional units may not be used, the same specificity referred to above should be followed in preparing daily plans, and the plans should be made several days in advance. Plans should be reviewed and approved or revised and approved before they are used. Some teachers never let a student use plans without approval. We heartily endorse this procedure.

You may require no written lesson plan but may, for example, expect the student to follow exactly the lesson outlined specifically in the manual for the Reading Series. In such case, you would want the student to have the lesson so clearly in mind that he could go over it in detail with you at least one day before teaching. Also, in science, social studies, arithmetic, or any school subject, you may expect your student to follow the text with or without the accompanying manual. If so, you should require the student to go over the plans with you so that you are sure the student understands the plans and has the step-by-step procedure clearly in mind before he teaches.

UNIT PLANNING

The first task is to determine the unit that will be used by the student in his teaching. This should be determined on the basis of student background, interests, special abilities, and sequence in the schedule for the year or season.

The student must know what he is to teach well in advance of the teaching date. The way in which you decide what he is to teach is not so important. He may choose what he is to teach, you may tell him, or you may work it out together. He should have at least one week to plan a unit. This would give you time to go over his plans with him. He would then have time to revise the plans so that you could go over them with him again if necessary. He would still have time to get materials ready. The student may learn more than you realize by your patient, understanding helpfulness in going over plans carefully before teaching.

After he knows what he is going to teach, he must see the unit in relation to the work which has preceded and the work that is to follow. For example, if he is teaching a history unit, he must see that the pupils are constantly relating the understandings of this unit with those which preceded. Also, he should keep in mind next units and definitely prepare the pupils for the learnings which follow *his* teaching. In teaching units, however, the unit taught by the student might not be directly related to the units immediately preceding and following. A unit in seventh grade general science, home economics, English, or industrial arts might not be directly related in content to the units that precede or follow. In typing or shorthand, however, they may be sequential; that is, each follows the other in the development of certain understandings and skills. He needs to understand these relationships in making his plans.

It is also important for the student to see the relationship of the particular subject he is teaching to other subjects in the pupil's curriculum. If he is teaching arithmetic or mathematics, he may be able to relate something being studied in science and, as a result, stimulate more interest and understanding in both. A student in fourth-grade used spelling words in sentences, each sentence about something being studied in another class. If the student is in your elementary class all day, he will be able to see these relationships, but if his student teaching assignment is only one or two hours or a half day, you will have to supply the

information concerning some or all of the other classes. A student in the secondary school is generally least acquainted with
the pupil's total school program. He should have opportunity to
visit in other classes so that he can discover at first hand what
the pupil's program is in other fields. Again, if his assignment is
less than a full day, you will need to provide much of the information second hand.

THE UNIT OUTLINE

You may want the student to follow the unit structure that
you use, or you may have several samples from which the student may choose. In any event, you and the student should
agree upon the structure he is to follow. One teacher asks her
students to follow the outline below:

    I. Statement of problem. (Title of unit.)

    II. Pupil objectives.

    III. Statement of subproblems. (Includes outline of content
under each subproblem.)

    IV. Development of purpose. (Includes motivation procedures
designed to stimulate pupil development of purpose; raising of problem and subproblems; formation of skills, habits, attitudes, etc.)

    V. Sources. (Includes references, textbook, films, maps, graphs,
bulletins, models, equipment and supplies for experiments, play
equipment, personnel, etc.)

    VI. Learning experiences. (Includes provision for study, excur-
sions, experiments, games, demonstrations, committee projects, discussion, special reports, use of sources, assembly, displays, etc.)

    VII. Conclusions or generalizations.

    VIII. Use of learning. (Includes assembly, newspaper articles,
school display, projects in school or community, preparation of
permanent record materials for group or individuals, presentations to
school and community groups.)

    IX. Evaluation. (Includes oral informal evaluation of procedures,
material used, use of learning; and written tests to evaluate specific
pupil growth in understandings, skills, etc.)

Making specific plans within the unit can be deadening
drudgery or a stimulating experience, depending upon such

factors as your interest in the unit, the student's interest in the unit, the variety of learning experiences available, the variety of instructional materials available, the inherent worth of the unit, and the extent to which you insist upon tedious specificity to meet your standards. This is the opportunity for the student to demonstrate competence in independent planning.

USING MOTIVATION PROCEDURES

We are re-emphasizing the cruciality of this aspect of unit instruction. Stimulation of pupil drive is absolutely necessary in obtaining potential pupil growth. At this stage of unit instruction, motivation should be planned to stimulate sufficient pupil interest to get the unit problem and subproblems stated. Also, statements of general and specific objectives concerned with such things as understandings, skills, and habits should result. The latter, however, also may be isolated and recorded as the unit progresses.

Motivation is a continuous process through the unit. Pupils do not reach a high degree of drive and maintain the same level. Again, motivation is individualized. One pupil may need motivation to keep going, another to regain focus, another to improve skills, another to share materials, and so on. These aspects are not completely discernible preceding the teaching of the unit, but many can be determined by the characteristics demonstrated by pupils in all or some of their activities. For example, in planning a unit on social dancing, preparation can be made for the pupil who is handicapped physically.

The climax of initial motivation is the statement of the problem. In planning this aspect, the student should recognize that he must think of the problem in terms understandable to the pupils. For instance, the student in fourth grade might state the problem as follows, "How has the industrial revolution changed the basic activities of modern man?" The problem would be more meaningful and might become interesting for fourth-grade pupils if he said, "How have factories changed the way we live?" The student must see that pupil learning depends largely upon interest and desire to learn. Problems, therefore, must be stated in such a way that they are *real problems* to pupils. Many plans may be revised before the student is able to predict possible problem wordings that click with pupils.

A still more difficult situation faces the student in planning to raise the problem with the pupils. He may have set down a tentative problem, but in the process the pupils might give it a different twist or might not be sufficiently interested to participate in isolating it. The student, therefore, must plan in detail the exact procedure he thinks will be effective in getting the problem set up. Specific motivating devices, such as pictures, concrete materials, stories, information, and questions, designed to stimulate and focus thought upon the intended problem should be set down explicitly. A student in biology class planned raising the following problem, "How does diet affect bodily functions?" The effect of diet upon tooth decay arose, an argument precipitated, and only a subproblem was raised! In analyzing the situation later in conference, the student recognized one peril in problem-raising; that of getting off the track. Specific plans were made to strengthen the approach next day.

PLANNING LEARNING EXPERIENCES

Units usually are not set up indicating day-by-day procedures and, therefore, the student will need to prepare specific plans for each day. You may have seen students try to follow a unit without daily lesson plans. They need a much better marked course to steer by. Planning the daily activities in advance is not easy for you, but it is much more difficult for the students because they have insufficient experience to predict. They should make specific plans for several days in advance and then revise plans as needed. A student in social studies made specific plans for the first week. Monday and Tuesday were set aside for problem-raising and the last three days for selecting informational materials and gathering data. The class was ready to start selecting information by the middle of the period on Tuesday, however, and he did not have the materials ready on the shelves and tables. He improvised badly during the remainder of the period and gave the pupils a chance to lose much of the enthusiasm they had generated in raising the problem. Daily plans must be sufficiently elastic to enable the student to move through several days of plans in one day if he has predicted poorly.

Within the daily lesson, the student should have provision for carry-over from the preceding day; that is, a brief review of the work of the previous day. For example, he might ask the pupils, "What were we doing yesterday? How far had we gotten? Then where do we start today?" The same sort of thing should be planned at the end of the period. He might say, "Let's see what we have accomplished today. What do we have yet to get done? Where do we start tomorrow?"

His lesson plan should outline specific pupil activities for each day. If a film is to be used, the exact procedure should be included in the plan. The film introduction, directions to pupils before or while seeing the film, and method of discussing the film should be given. Use of excursions, slides, community personnel or resources, experiments, and demonstrations, should also be explained specifically. All of this detail in planning is necessary for you and the student. You have an opportunity to counsel with him before the lesson and thus may prevent many problems that he cannot foresee. You need to know specifically what his plans are and he needs to have your expressed confidence in his plans. Also, you can assist the student in revising plans for the days ahead in terms of progress and problems arising.

Notations should be made in the unit as work progresses, as you and the student evaluate and revise daily lesson plans, and as you see where previous procedures might have been improved. The student can then have the valuable experience of revising the unit after using it.

Selecting Materials of Instruction

Each student needs to go through the process of locating materials available for his teaching. He also needs to decide which materials will contribute most to learning. The following are examples of ways you can help him:

Provide bibliographies of available materials kept up-to-date. These may be lists of textbooks, references (books, booklets, pamphlets, magazine articles, newspaper clippings), maps, graphs, tables, charts, films, slides, filmstrips, pictures for opaque projector, samples, and displays. Again, the above types of materials may be listed in previously developed units. Such lists will let him know what is available but it will be necessary for him to locate and determine the way in which the materials can best be used.

Explain your system of filing instructional materials. He needs to know the organization of your filing system, not just where to find materials. He is always responsible for putting materials away after they are used. The student may collect materials which can be added to the present file. The importance of having a well-organized file for the use of students cannot be over-emphasized. You are helping him to maintain and add to your files and also helping him to develop a very important teacher competency, that of learning to collect and file materials for use in connection with teaching and extra-class activities. When the student starts using instructional materials, you have an excellent opportunity to emphasize the importance of a well-organized file of instructional materials. If possible, provide space so that he may start his file where he uses it and where you can give him the help needed.

Encourage the student to seek materials not included on available lists. As pointed out earlier, one danger in referring the student to previously prepared plans is that he may follow them too closely. You will need to encourage him to use initiative in seeking materials which might contribute to pupil learning. It is well to work with him to a certain extent in looking for materials, but make sure that he doesn't become dependent upon you. Going with him to other staff members, school employees, and members of the community gives you a chance to make introductions and contributes to the partner relationships referred to in Chapter 12.

Help him select materials for specific purposes. An energetic student will ordinarily find many more materials than can be used in his teaching. It then becomes necessary for you to help him decide what to use. Suppose your student is teaching a section of American history entitled "The Settlement of the Great Plains." This may be a teacher-developed unit or it may be several sequential chapters in a textbook. He must learn to select materials that will best contribute to learning because, since no pupil can read all of the books, books must be selected that the different children can read. The following criteria will be helpful to him as a student and in subsequent teaching:

1. The material gives specific information.
2. The information is pertinent.
3. The information is authentic.
4. The context is understandable for a pupil at a certain reading level.
5. The information presents both sides of issues. (For example, in the struggle between the sheep and cattle ranchers.)

In selecting reading materials he will also need to be concerned with the explanation of new words and new terms, style of presentation, and size of type. He already knows the reading level for each pupil in the class, but he will probably need your help in determining the suitability of reading material for particular pupils. He may thus be prepared to provide reading materials (books, bulletins, booklets, pamphlets, and magazine articles) which each pupil can read with satisfaction.

Since illustrative materials may be available in quantity greater than can be used, these must also be evaluated and those selected which contribute most. This can be done when materials are on hand. When materials such as films have to be ordered on a rental basis without opportunity to preview, the selections can only be made with your guidance. You are probably already familiar with rental materials and can review for him the strong and weak points of each and help him make the selections.

Problems repeatedly arise in the student's selection of material because of his inability to predict pupil interest or understanding. This results from lack of experience in observing or working with pupils in learning situations. In working with concepts in fractions, would it be better to have cardboard units cut into fractional parts for each pupil or to use one flannel board at the front of the room? In demonstrating the three types of levers, would it be better to use actual objects or to show pictures using the opaque projector? In studying methods of preserving wood surfaces, would it be better to apply wood preservatives according to directions, to observe wood which has had preservatives applied, or to see a film strip showing the different methods? These are problems that cause the student trouble when he begins planning the selection of instructional materials.

Help the student become independent in judgment. Your help in making selections is necessary at first, but care should be taken that he does not become dependent upon you. As he continues planning and selecting materials, ask for his judgment first. If you find his choice not to be good, you can suggest another choice and explain why it is better. Your responsibility, therefore, is to *guide the student to become independent of you in the choice of instructional materials.* However, you do not want the student to become so independent that he does not seek the judgment of others. *A teacher in a classroom can become too self-sufficient.* Teachers need to be mutually dependent within a school and yet not helplessly dependent. Such a happy medium is not easy to attain.

USING INSTRUCTIONAL MATERIALS

Following selection of the materials, or sometimes in the process of selection, the student plans how the materials are to be used. He is again faced with the same pitfall: lack of experience in using or seeing materials used by pupils. He has little or no basis for predicting effectiveness. Suppose the student has selected a certain film for use. Should it be shown as a motivating device, as a source of information during study, or as a summary device? He may be at a loss because he may never have seen a film used with pupils, or he may have seen them used only as summary devices. Your good judgment in the early stages of the student's planning may be absolutely necessary.

A student wanted to show his fifth-grade pupils that the shortest distance between San Francisco and Tokyo was not as it appeared on the map hanging at the front of the room. He decided to use an eighteen-inch globe placed on a table at the front of the room. This decision was made contrary to the suggestion of the teacher that he use individual six-inch globes. The pupils at the back of the room could not see and started edging toward the front of the room. Their view thus obstructed, others rose from their seats and started moving forward. Soon they were collected around the globe struggling to see. The teacher opened the cupboard and started setting the six-inch globes on the nearest desks. The student noticed what his partner was doing, quickly asked all pupils to return to their seats, and gave each a globe to use. He also used the long slip of paper she handed him and suggested that the pupils use the same thing in measuring distance. Thus, before the period was over each pupil was discovering for himself; exactly the suggestion made by his teacher when the lesson was planned.

Little harm was done the pupils in the lesson referred to above and the student learned something of the value of practical suggestions from his teacher. Needless confusion can result from serious mistakes made in pupil planning. You want this to occur as rarely as possible, because you are responsible for maximum growth of each pupil in your class. It is sometimes necessary for you to be arbitrary in a nice way if the student cannot see why instructional materials should not be used as he has planned. Occasional minor mistakes which you foresee may, and in some cases should, be permitted to impress upon the student the values of critical judgment gained through experience.

USE OF SCHOOL AND COMMUNITY RESOURCES

There is so much red tape with which the student must become familiar. He not only has to discover what facilities are available, from you, from the school handbook, or from other staff members, but he must also learn how to make arrangements for the use of facilities. Perhaps he wants to take a class on an excursion and needs to use a school bus. First he must get your permission to proceed with plans, then he must clear with another teacher because the pupils will be gone two periods. His next stop is the principal's or superintendent's office. The bus is busy on the day he wants to go, and the day finally chosen is not fit for the trip because of rain. He must then start over. This time another teacher has planned a special program in his room on the day selected, so alternate days are proposed. One of the days is suitable to all staff members but he discovers from the principal that the local garage is scheduled to replace the clutch on the bus that day. Again he starts over!

Teachers accept similar experiences as routine. Students must face such conditions in any busy school system. Your encouragement and sense of humor will be most helpful. Each student needs the experience of working out such situations for himself. Some students become discouraged more quickly than others and need more push. Some will avoid using facilities outside the classroom because of scheduling problems, attitudes of other staff members, or timidity. You can be most helpful by being sensitive to each student's need for suggestions, encouragement, and moral support. Help the student when he needs help but don't permit him to learn to lean on you. He must become independent.

You may have to insist that the student use facilities outside the classroom even though you have demonstrated to him the advantages of using such facilities. You may have situations in your school which require that different teachers use the same room, and you may have to operate very carefully to keep peace. In such cases, it is well not to tell the student that some staff members are very particular about the condition in which a room is left. They have no basis for judgment and may think **you** unprofessional. Discuss with them the courtesies that one should observe in using a room that another uses. If someone is also using the room used by you and the student, you have a good illustration to offer. You can help the student build excellent attitudes toward joint use of facilities. The student also gains insight concerning how he can work effectively with staff members.

The routine of scheduling use of facilities may cause the student some uneasiness. Awkward situations arise, such as planning with the pupils to use the auditorium for play practice only to discover that it has been scheduled by the band director. You have a responsibility to inform the student concerning the process of scheduling the movie projector, the auditorium, the radio, the home economics kitchen, and so on.

Planning for use of community resources also involves intensive planning away from school. Before an excursion is taken, the student should go through the process of visiting the persons from whom permission must be obtained, giving information concerning age of group, number in group, desired time for excursion, purposes of excursion, and function of personnel at the site in contributing to the success of the excursion. The student should also study the place to be visited or take a committee of pupils with him so that specific plans for the excursion can be set up with the group making the excursion. Follow-up of the excursion requires plans that are just as specific.

In case materials are brought to the school, plans must be made with the parties from whom the materials are obtained concerning how they are to be used, when they are wanted, and when they are to be returned. At the beginning of the student's experiences in the use of school and community resources, you should go through the processes or routine with him to be sure he understands each step. This assistance should stop as soon as you are sure that he knows how to schedule facilities.

School and community personnel

The student should become acquainted with personnel who may contribute to the effectiveness of his teaching very early in his experiences. The high school science teacher may be of great help to the elementary teacher in clarifying concepts; locating references, materials for experiments, samples, and sources of materials not on hand; checking accuracy or authenticity of information; suggesting methods or procedures; and suggesting possibilities for excursions. The English teacher, the art teacher, and the music teacher may all be able to give the student assistance in his teaching of a social studies unit. Students learn by your example and guidance that any other member of the staff may be a consultant—another step in the development of good working relations. The situation can also be reversed. Teachers in a building can give students further experiences in the value of working together by consulting them for information, materials, and judgments.

Special consultants in the areas of guidance, reading, speech, curriculum, or children's books (librarian) can further emphasize the values of using all personnel available for assistance. If such consultants are available, students should meet them early and be informed concerning the services they can provide. Special consultants operate differently in different schools, but in most places the room teacher is responsible for remedial procedures in the classroom following diagnosis and decisions concerning treatment. Ordinarily the consultant has forms available to be filled out by the room teacher for cases to be referred to him. The diagnosis is then made by the consultant, or with assistance from the teacher, and decisions are reached concerning treatment. The teacher follows through and refers back to the consultant. Continuing plans are made as they proceed.

Drawing conclusions and generalizations

During a unit on how to entertain small groups in the home a group of seventh-grade boys and girls had a series of experiences in types of appropriate entertainment. Committees studied the problem and the pupils of each group invited their parents and a few teachers to an informal party. Following the series of committee parties, the pupils listed six suggestions that they thought would be especially helpful to others. The list was published in the school paper.

You can give many other illustrations of the procedures you have used, depending upon the particular situation. The student must understand that there must be purpose in drawing conclusions and generalizations. Sometimes there is general use that can be made of conclusions or the results of the study. At other times, the pupils summarize with future use in mind; for example, so that the group or grade next year can profit from our experiences. One group, following an excursion to Chicago for definite purposes, prepared recommendations that would be helpful to the corresponding group that would be making the trip next year.

Using the learning resulting from the unit

Students often have trouble with this aspect of unit instruction. To be sure, the growth the pupils have made will contribute to future learning experiences. Skills, attitudes, habits, and understandings will have become a part of each pupil. The student must plan ways by which the pupils can recognize such growth. For example he might say to a pupil, "Using all of these references has certainly helped you in finding information." "Don't you think making the special report has made you feel surer of yourself?" "As carefully as you are learning to use the lathe, why don't you make something really worth while for your room at home?"

The student recognizes the value of the unit study to the pupils, but plans must be made to help the pupils recognize those values.

Less personal uses are also important and must be included in the student's plans. Uses such as those below are illustrative:

A fifth grade has studied the flora characteristic of a forest area in Iowa unmolested by human activities and domestic animals. Following the study, the pupils decided to replant an eroded hillside on their school grounds with flora that, insofar as they could discover, would be typical of the natural flora of similar steep hillsides in Iowa.

Another fifth grade had studied ways by which people can protect their yard trees from disease and other damage. Following the study, they prepared a list of suggestions with illustrations and had the material published in the local paper.

Following a sewing unit, a seventh-grade home economics class asked permission to make curtains for the windows of a corridor connecting two buildings. They selected the material, made the curtains, and asked the custodian to help with installation.

Plans for teaching-learning situations are made primarily to facilitate *pupil* growth. Therefore, the student needs to know and understand the abilities, interests, progress, needs, habits, and attitudes of the pupils for whom the plans are made. This presents a difficult problem because students often have only six weeks to a semester while you are still discovering helpful information to guide your planning by the end of the year. We can easily expect too much of students in this respect, especially if they have had little experience with boys and girls.

PLANNING FOR OTHER TEACHER ACTIVITIES

A conference with parents, a meeting of the arithmetic committee, or playground supervision must be thought through ahead of time. Planning for the development of good professional relations and for worth-while extraclass activities is as necessary for success as planning for lesson or unit teaching. While the student is learning to plan for these responsibilities, his plans should be submitted to you for approval. Also, when he is assisting you, plans should be mutually prepared, evaluated, and revised. We know of no other way to make sure that the student will learn to prepare for all teacher activities and to recognize the importance of such preparation. Since planning is so necessary to student success, you should not only require that plans be written out but also that they be well thought through.

Specific applications of planning to building professional relations and to extraclass activities are treated in Chapters IX and XII respectively.

Planning is time-consuming and often tedious, especially with students who grow slowly. The effort and time are necessary if the student is to learn to think through and to prepare thoroughly for the activities of the teacher. The plans in themselves are not so important; the real values come in the student learning how to make plans that provide wholesome learning experiences for all the pupils, to evaluate use of plans, and to revise plans to remove imperfections.

SUGGESTED REFERENCES

Burr, James B., Lowry W. Harding, and Leland B. Jacobs, *Student Teaching in the Elementary School.* New York: Appleton-Century-Crofts, Inc., 1950. Chapter IV, "Planning Your Work."

Grim, Paul, and John Michaelis, *The Student Teacher in the Secondary School.* New York: Prentice-Hall, Inc., 1953. Chapter III, "Planning Your Work."

Michaelis, John, and Paul Grim, *The Student Teacher in the Elementary School.* New York: Prentice-Hall, Inc., 1953. Chapter IV, "Making Plans for Teaching," and Chapter V, "Planning the Unit of Work."

Schorling, Raleigh, and Max Wingo, *Elementary School Student Teaching.* New York: McGraw-Hill Book Company, Inc., 1950. Chapter VII, "Teacher and Pupils Plan Together," and Chapter VIII, "The Broader Concept of Method."

8

Your Student Assumes a Teacher's Role

THIS IS A CRITICAL STAGE FOR THE STUDENT, THE pupils, and you. The student has probably looked forward to the time when he could take over the class, the club, or the parent conference. You have studied the student and have guided his growth to the best of your ability. The greatest impact of the experience, however, will be felt by the pupils for whose growth you are responsible.

You have made as sure as possible that the student is ready for this step for three reasons:

1. You want nothing to jeopardize the instructional program of the boys and girls.

2. You want nothing to jeopardize the student's opportunity for maximum growth. For the student to assume responsibility before he is ready may seriously impede his growth.

3. You are responsible to the college for the growth of the student.

The decision may have been reached cooperatively with the student by using the list of competencies in Appendix F, another list of competencies (perhaps your own), or the list of readiness factors in Chapter 5. You may have asked the supervisor to help in analyzing the situation. Regardless of the process, you are the one who will have to judge the wisdom of the decision and, if trouble arises, determine, perhaps on the spot, what should be done.

The student has *progressed* toward this stage. Even now, he does not suddenly assume the role of teacher but progresses through the stage, assuming more and more of the responsibilities of teachers. It is with your guidance of the student through this stage of expanding responsibility that this chapter is concerned. Five aspects will be reviewed:

The student is ready to assume a teacher's role.

The student's first major responsibilities.

The student moves toward completely assuming the role of teacher.

Student-teacher relationships as the student assumes the role of teacher.

Observing student reaction in the role of teacher.

THE STUDENT IS READY TO ASSUME A TEACHER'S ROLE

In classroom instruction

The student has been assisting you in all or most of the areas of teacher activity. You have observed him closely as he assisted. He and you have evaluated his work, found him needing additional experiences in particular areas, and found him quite successful in experiences in other areas. In each class or activity he made plans and then worked with you in assisting activities or bit teaching. He has moved through a progression of experiences, each requiring more planning, more skill in motivation and direction of experiences, and more sensitiveness to immediate and basic needs of pupils in learning. For example, a student in first grade progressed in reading class by types of experiences as follows (this does not refer to consecutive days):

Assisted teacher by having books ready for each reading group.

Assisted teacher in planning lesson for each reading group.

Assisted teacher by writing (manuscript) new words for each group on chalk board.

Worked individually with several pupils who had been absent several days.

Worked several days with new pupil who had started in a different reading series.

Worked with three pupils who needed additional readiness experiences before starting to read.

Worked with four advanced pupils who wanted to make an experience chart concerning a trip they had made to a bakery with one of their parents.

Worked with the second reading group one day without teacher assistance.

Worked with fourth reading group one day without teacher assistance.

Worked with third reading group two days without teacher assistance.

Worked with first reading group three days without teacher assistance.

The teacher observed the student's ability to follow plans, to develop good working relationships with pupils, to motivate pupil interest, to meet spontaneous situations effectively, to sense individual problems in learning, and to relate immediate learning to preceding experiences. She judged the student to be effective in directing learning experiences in reading and asked the student to make plans to take over with full responsibility her choice of the reading groups. The student chose the second reading group and started making plans for the first week. When plans were completed, they were reviewed by student and teacher, also using the manual accompanying the reading series. Revisions were suggested, made, and again reviewed—this time approved. The next day she started assuming responsibility for this aspect of the instructional program. This was her start in assuming the role of teacher.

A student, teaching in music, had the following experiences with the orchestra before he was judged to be ready to start assuming the role of teacher:

Checked to be sure the music was in place and available to the pupils responsible for distributing it.

Gave pupil individual help with his viola.

Assisted individuals during practice.

Assisted individuals with instrumentation after school, before school, and during noon hour.

Worked with French horn players several days during sectional rehearsals.

Worked with cello players during several after-school sessions.

Worked several times with cornet player on solo part.

Worked with violin players during several sectional rehearsals.

Directed number which orchestra had played for first time at previous rehearsal.

Directed same number as above and directed concentration on two passages with which the pupils were having difficulty.

Again, the student was having the same types of experiences in chorus, band, and elementary music. With all groups he was assuming increasingly more responsibility as the teacher judged him ready to progress.

The experiences provided for the student in fourth grade, shown in Fig. 1, illustrate characteristics typical of most students. You will note that the student moved into more responsible activities in music, literature, and physical education before she did in other areas. Her special interests and abilities seemed to be in those areas. Music was the field in which she first assumed complete responsibility, literature next, and physical education next. Assisting and bit teaching were continued in the other curricular areas.

Another student might have shown most readiness in language arts, arithmetic, or any of the other areas. The points we wish to emphasize in this connection are:

1. Students are moved as rapidly toward responsibility as a teacher as they show readiness to progress.

2. Students assume the role of teacher first in the field or area in which they show readiness to assume such responsibility.

FIGURE 1. TYPES OF PROGRESSIVE EXPERIENCES PROVIDED FOR A STUDENT IN FOURTH GRADE. THE STUDENT TAUGHT FULL-TIME IN AN OFF-CAMPUS SCHOOL.

Physical Education	Science	Music	Social Studies	Arithmetic	Language Arts	Literature	Art
Play as member of one squad	Assist committee to prepare lever demonstration	Sing with pupils	Participate in discussion	Observe pupil procedures in solving problems	Help pupil locate spelling of word in dictionary	Observe books pupils select in library	Help pupil with raffia and reed weaving
Play piano for rhythms	Assist pupils to present lever demonstration	Move from pupil to pupil giving help as needed	Help pupil use index to find information	Listen to individual pupil explanation of method each used in solving problems	Help pupil obtain information from reference to present in science discussion	Interview pupils to discover their reading interests	———— same ————
Assist one squad in tumbling	Assist pupils in locating crickets for observation under magnifying glasses	Give special attention to two pupils during music period	Guide pupil in selection of book to use as reference	Work with pupil who missed several days	Work with pupils on index skills	Check records to see which books pupils have read during the year	
Work with pupil in corrective exercises	Assist pupils in finding information on feeding and other habits of crickets	Play piano for assembly	Work with pupils during study period, helping pupils as need arises	Try to discover why pupil is having trouble with fraction concepts	Help several pupils with handwriting problems	Read poem to pupils on "favorite poem day"	
Work with low coordination group in ball handling skills	Help pupils in use of references as needed	Work with quartet to sing at assembly	Work with committee preparing graph for use with opaque projector	Work with committee preparing fraction demonstration using felt board	Assist pupils in writing thank you letters	Give brief review of new book added to room library	Help pupils who ask for assistance in use of water colors
Assist one foursome in learning folk dance	Help committee preview film on harmful insects and make preparation for showing film in class	Work with pupils learning to play instruments	Work with committee to give special report using film strip	Help pupils present above demonstration	Work with group preparing a skit on English usage	Direct class period during which pupils discuss books they have read and liked	
Demonstrate folk dance with three pupils		Direct class in singing two of their favorite songs	Talk with total group about a news event of general interest (**five** minutes)		Help individuals prepare story for local newspaper		Help pupils who ask assistance in clay modeling
		Help pupils learn a new song					
		Teach music during entire period					

3. Students increasingly assume the role of teacher in these fields or areas as they show readiness to assume such responsibility.

4. Students assume the role of teacher in other fields or areas as they demonstrate ability to assume additional responsibilities.

We should review briefly a problem that you may have in a secondary field such as science. Suppose you have tentatively planned that the student will teach in chemistry and ninth grade general science in his major field and geometry in his minor field. You teach chemistry and general science but geometry is taught by another teacher. The student starts participating and assisting in the three classes but soon you discover that he has personal relationship problems with pupils that indicate a struggle ahead. You and the other teacher will need to coordinate your work with the student. Perhaps you may want to withdraw him from the geometry class where he shows practically no growth in working with the pupils. Instead of the geometry class, you might ask him to spend time observing other teachers working with the pupils with whom he is working in chemistry and ninth grade general science.

By mid-term he may have progressed to the point that you feel safe in trying him with bit teaching in the small chemistry class. If this seems successful, you may permit him to proceed with a short unit. You should carefully evaluate his work in the small unit before permitting him to move beyond assisting and bit teaching in the general science class. He might progress well enough so that you would want to move him back into the geometry class for assisting and bit teaching even though he might never assume a teacher's role in the geometry class or even the ninth-grade general science class.

In other teacher activities

The student also should be provided with opportunities for growth in ability to assume responsibility in areas other than classroom instruction. For example, he may participate in a particular club, in the student council, at school parties, in parent-teacher conferences, and in preparing reports for the school administration. Later, he may assist in such activities by assuming more responsibility, as for the decorations committee for the school party. You should observe many features of his relationships in such activities; for example, the pupils' respect for his judgment, his ability to keep the activity moving, his sensitiveness to and ability to meet effectively the many spontaneous situations that arise, and his ability to challenge and motivate the pupils.

As in classroom instruction, you should decide what responsibility he might first assume in the role of teacher. Observe the results of his first try, and, if successful, you may decide to let him continue assuming responsibility for the particular activity, perhaps a school club.

THE STUDENT'S FIRST MAJOR RESPONSIBILITIES

Each student's first major responsibility is the one for which you think him to be most ready and, therefore, the one which offers most assurance of success. There can be no putting the students through the same mill. Perhaps you have heard such expressions as:

I always have the students help me the first week and then put them on their own.

I have my students prepare their units before student teaching starts, then they're ready to start right off.

I always start my students right out with their units. That way they get plenty of experience.

The above procedures cannot be used if we believe that individuals grow at different rates, that they have variety in interests, and that there is a wide range of ability among students. If you've had six or eight student teachers at one time, you may have observed that no two are ready to start assuming major responsibility at the same time and neither are any two ready to start assuming responsibility in the same area of instruction. The best assurance you have that the student will succeed in directing complex teaching-learning situations or in extra-instructional activities is to assess the student's growth in the variety of experiences provided and select the type in which you have most confidence in his success.

In determining first major responsibility, therefore, you have choices to make as you study the growth of each student. Six possible choices are given below:

FOR CLASSROOM ACTIVITIES OR OTHER ACTIVITIES

You may have a student comparable to the one in physical education who had had experience as an assistant manager in a local store. He was a good organizer and thrived on responsibility for and organization of equipment and materials. His first responsibility was to plan for a more effective organization, distribution, and inventory of materials and equipment used in physical education classes and athletics. His enthusiasm and ability were such that he effected excellent procedures, which the teachers adopted; however, one admitted on the side that "we got ourselves into a lot of work."

Wrongly, we too often think that the first major responsibility must be in directing teaching-learning processes. The physical education student referred to above quickly demonstrated readiness to assume major responsibility in an area outside directing teaching-learning processes. Other types of activities first assumed by students are illustrated by the following:

The student who was in charge of make-up for college plays first assumed that responsibility for a three-act play in the high school.

The student who served as assistant editor of the college newspaper first assumed major responsibility for the high school newspaper.

The student who was especially interested in testing and guidance first assumed responsibility for the preparation of results from the annual test of educational development to present to the parents of ninth-grade pupils. He made the presentation and answered questions.

The student who had spent several summers in youth camps first assumed major responsibility for recreation and entertainment at the one-week camp for the seventh grade.

The student who had several leadership positions in high school first assumed responsibility for guiding the assembly committee in planning an appropriate Easter program.

That the student experience success in assuming responsibility is of major importance, not the curriculum area or field or the extracurricular area in which he assumes responsibility.

FOR A PART OR ALL OF THE CLASS

You may not feel too sure that your student is ready to have responsibility for the entire class. The six-week student teaching period is one-half over, however, and he should start assuming the role of teacher soon. You might try giving him responsibility for one of the reading groups, one of the committees in science, the high jumpers in track practice, one unit kitchen in home economics, the first violin players in sectional rehearsals of orchestra, or the boys working on a particular project in vocational agriculture. His plans would be prepared and approved by you preceding the lesson each day.

As you observe the student assuming the role of teacher with a part of the class, you can determine the degree of success and determine whether or not he is ready to continue with that much responsibility. Your decision may be that he is not ready to teach without your constant assistance, or you may decide that he is ready to assume responsibility for the larger group. In the former case, he should revert to assignments in which he has fewer pupils and somewhat less responsibility. For example, he might help two pupils from a reading group who missed several reading periods, work with one or two pupils on science projects, help two boys refine their timing and skill in baton passing, etc. You should watch for evidence of readiness to assume major responsibility and again try him with a committee or particular segment of the class or group.

In case you start him with the total group and discover after one or two days that he is not ready, you should move him back one step, that is, to responsibility for a part of the group. You observe his demonstration of competency with less responsibility and when you think him to be ready, try him again with the total group.

FOR A PART OR ALL OF THE PERIOD

You may prefer to start no student with the total group for a full class period; for example, assigning the student responsibility for the arithmetic class, French class, physical education class, or science class for a full period. There are always possibilities for student responsibility for a part of the class period. The following are illustrative:

In contemporary affairs class, the student writes on the chalkboard the name of a new political figure in the news. At the beginning of class, he helps the class to identify the individual and the significance of his activities.

In chorus, the student directs a number that the pupils know fairly well and calls attention to one passage in which the tenors are fuzzy.

In literature period (sixth grade), the student reads a short story and reviews one part of the story with the pupils.

In Latin I, the student reads a news item concerning findings of a current archeological expedition in Italy. She relates the findings to a class discussion a few days earlier.

In first grade physical education, the student directed a game that the pupils already knew how to play.

You may have sufficient confidence in a student to let him assume responsibility for the total class for the full period. However, we doubt that there are many who should be moved so quickly from assisting activities to full responsibility. Our observation, however, indicates that this practice is too frequently followed. The procedure seems to be somewhat as follows: The student observes and assists the teacher for several days or a week or more. Meanwhile, he is preparing his unit and/or lessons and on a predetermined day "takes over the class." We do not recommend such a procedure no matter how much the student wants it that way. We stress this point because of our concern for the welfare of both pupils and student.

FOR A LESSON OR UNIT

Again, in fairness to the pupils and student, we recommend that in all but rare instances the student start with no more than a lesson for one day, whether it be with all or part of the class. By such a procedure, the student does not lose face with the group if he is found not to be ready for major responsibility. Also, pupil progress is not jeopardized during a two- or three-week unit in which the student provides a poor learning climate. Through assisting and bit teaching you can build the student up for another lesson if he does poorly in the first. We are not saying, however, that this procedure will exclude all chances that you will not have to remove a student after he does start teaching a unit or assumes responsibility for an extended series of lessons.

FOR HIGHLY DIRECTED OR COOPERATIVE ACTIVITIES

In most cases, the student should start in the least complex activities. In industrial arts, for example, the student would assume responsibility for supervision of pupils working in a particular area rather than in all areas at the same time. Perhaps he would supervise the pupils working in printing but not, at the same time, the pupils working with plastics, welding, lapidary, radio, and photography. Other examples might be:

Dictating spelling words in elementary grades rather than conducting a class in which there is much discussion.

Directing a number in band which the pupils already know fairly well rather than starting with a new number.

Reading a story to kindergarten pupils rather than talking with them about what they had seen at the greenhouse.

Presenting several problems for solution individually and

observing individual work rather than teaching a lesson which is largely discussion.

Each type of experience listed above enables the student to avoid a large amount of oral communication, cooperative planning, informal discussion, and chances of pupils getting him confused. Some of the most complex teaching-learning experiences to avoid are informal discussions in which pupils and students are trying to assemble a variety of essential information regarding a problem; individual activities in various stages of progress, as in art, industrial arts, home economics, vocational home economics, agriculture, vocational agriculture, and science; a new and difficult number in orchestra, band, or chorus; a club in which pupils are pursuing individual interests; and any class which involves a high degree of pupil cooperative activity.

In conclusion, we urge you to assess the student's ability and growth carefully and determine initial major responsibilities for him that will give greatest assurance of success.

THE STUDENT MOVES TOWARD COMPLETELY ASSUMING THE ROLE OF TEACHER

We have emphasized the gradual progress of the student through participation, assisting, bit teaching, and initial major responsibilities. The remainder of the time that he is with you, his sphere of responsibility will expand gradually as his readiness and as the welfare of the pupils permit. It is much more important that he make real growth as he progresses and that he is really ready for additional responsibility than that he have a wide range of responsibilities. In the latter case, the student frequently flounders under the load, real growth stops, or he becomes soured on the whole business of teaching. By the time your student gets to this stage in his development, you should be sufficiently familiar with his rate of growth so that you can predict rather well how fast and how far he can move in assuming the role of teacher. Also, the suggestions under the topics below may be of help to you.

THE NATURE OF PROGRESSION IN ASSUMING ADDITIONAL
RESPONSIBILITIES

If you are a first-grade teacher, you may wonder whether
or not your student can successfully assume responsiblity for
all of the learning experiences over a period of time. It is not
often that one can predict. Perhaps we should return to the
progression of experiences listed for the student in fourth
grade (p. 166). He was ready to assume major responsibility
first in physical education, music and literature. He started in
music, planning for each day separately. On the third day, he
did so well that he was asked to start making preparations for
literature, also each day separately. Again his general competency was rated high and he was asked to prepare for the
physical education class. The teacher noted, as is often the
case, that up to this point the student assumed each new experience more effectively than the last. Why? There were probably
several reasons:

1. He was getting the feel of teaching.

2. Success in each responsibility contributed to confidence,
poise, and assurance as he approached each new responsibility.

3. His successful work with pupils contributed to their confidence in him.

4. He liked to teach.

To follow the fourth-grade student further, he continued in
assisting activities in other areas as he assumed major responsibility in the above three. He now asked to assume responsibility for art and arithmetic. He was given permission
and was also asked to start preparing a unit for science and a
unit for social studies. Before starting to teach either unit, however, something happened. The teacher suddenly realized that
the student exhibited a nervousness not noticeable before, that
he was losing patience easily, and that the lessons were highly
teacher-directed although the plans showed pupil-student cooperative planning. The situation was discussed in conference
and both decided that responsibility was increasing too rapidly.
It had been three weeks since he first assumed major responsi-

bility in music and three weeks remained (nine-week period, full-time student teaching).

They faced the problem objectively and considered several alternatives:

The student would continue assuming responsibility for music, physical education, literature, art, and arithmetic and would continue assisting and bit teaching in the other areas.

The student would continue assuming responsibility for music, physical education, and literature and would assist in the other areas.

The student would continue assuming responsibility for music, physical education, literature, art, and arithmetic and would not participate or assist in other areas.

The student would assume responsibility for a science unit and participate and assist in other areas.

The third alternative was selected to be followed for one week. The situation was appraised at the end of the week and both agreed that the student had regained composure, so he was permitted to assume responsibility for a short social studies unit. He was fairly successful with the additional responsibility and resumed assisting in the language arts and science areas during the remainder of the period.

The experiences of the above student outside classroom instruction should be noted also. At the beginning of the student teaching period, he started participating with the teacher in playground supervision, lunch-hour supervision, School Patrol supervision, health check, parent contacts, administrative responsibilities, and community contacts. By the middle of the period, he was assisting in all of the above activities, but, because of growth problems in classroom instruction, he had assumed major responsibility only in playground supervision, lunch hour supervision, and administrative responsibilities.

The student teaching in music (referred to on p. 165) offers another illustration of quality versus quantity in student teaching. The student first assumed major responsibility in orchestra and assisted or participated in other music groups, both elementary and secondary. His first major responsibility in orchestra was to introduce a new composition and to spend about fifteen minutes working through it with the pupils. He demonstrated sufficient hesitancy so that the pupils did not follow his suggestion, analyses, and directing. They objected and offered counter suggestions and analyses, continued playing when he rapped for attention, and continued talking when they were directed to start playing. Obviously the situation was too much for the student. What next?

Following a conference, the student and teacher decided that the next step should be a return to less complex situations in assisting and bit teaching until the student felt that he could hold a larger group together. Meanwhile, he continued assisting in the other activities. In about two weeks he worked with the total orchestra again but this time directed their playing of two numbers that they could play fairly well. They worked on two parts of each number as agreed previously by student and teacher in conference. There was definite improvement, so next day he directed work on the number that he had previously introduced. He recognized that the pupils responded well to his self-assurance. This seemed to relieve tension and more pleasant interrelationships resulted. It was agreed that he should direct the orchestra during the remainder of the term (six more sessions).

Three weeks were left in the term and he had not assumed major responsibility in any other music activities. To be certificated to teach music in this state, he had to teach in both elementary and secondary; therefore, he was asked to prepare a lesson for the fifth grade in which he had been assisting. His plans were well prepared but, in teaching, he found meeting the spontaneous reactions of pupils disconcerting. He tried next day and showed enough improvement in effecting good pupil-teacher relationships that he was permitted to continue to the end of the term. He assumed no other major responsibilities for classroom instruction, his teacher feeling that it was wiser for him to concentrate on the two.

The music student also was assuming responsibility for a vocal trio and was participating in and assisting with administrative responsibilities, party supervision, parent-teacher contacts, and community contacts (accompanied vocal trio to Rotary Club). Of these, the student finally assumed major responsibility for party supervision and community contacts.

You might conclude that the music student was weak generally or that teacher standards for student performance were too high. Knowing the particular situation, we could not agree with either conclusion. The teacher in question had definite policies which he observed in working with students and with which we heartily concur:

1. A student must be able to carry major responsibility to the extent that potential pupil growth is not jeopardized. Otherwise, permitting him to continue to try to assume the particular major responsibility cannot be justified.

2. A student must not be assigned an additional major responsibility until he has demonstrated that he can carry effectively the one or several already assigned.

3. It is better for a student to learn to carry a few major responsibilities well than to attempt to carry a wide variety of responsibilities.

4. It is better for the student who can carry only a few responsibilities to have as much variety as possible; for example, not all responsibilities in classroom instruction.

5. We must not take advantage of pupils to "get students ready for their first jobs."

THE STUDENT WHO PROGRESSES RAPIDLY

Some students are able to move rapidly from one responsibility to another and, before the end of the student teaching period, may have assumed effectively the major responsibilities of the teachers to whom they are assigned. For example, a student teaching in elementary school may acquire a high degree of efficiency in assuming the instructional and other responsibilities of his teacher. Some students may progress to this point and still have time on their hands, but it is not fair to the student to let this happen. There are many things you can do to keep these students growing at top speed. We suggest the following as examples:

1. Plan and carry out procedures to provide for individual differences in interests, abilities, and needs. For example, making available a wider range of activities in kindergarten, including those that challenge both the gifted and the mentally retarded.

2. Plan for and learn how to use a wider variety of instructional procedures for the class and individuals. For example, try a variety of procedures in motivation, and, with individuals who are not interested, try all possible ways to capture interest.

3. Make special studies of particular pupils and prepare summary copies of each for pupil cumulative folders.

4. Make an analysis of some aspect of the school program or practices and, from results, make recommendations to the faculty. Examples might be: Effectiveness of home assignments; relationship between pupil grades and achievement or academic aptitude; pupils' out-of-school activities; reading range of pupils in a particular class or classes and availability of reference materials to provide for discovered range; or parent attitudes toward pupil curriculum and recommendations for changes.

5. Prepare an article for publication or distribution to parents on some aspect of the school. Examples might be: the counselling system, experiences for gifted pupils, extraclass opportunities for pupils, parent-teacher cooperation, or school-community cooperation.

Experiences as suggested above must be worth while for the student, must provide for the growth of which he is capable. There may be all sorts of jobs needing to be done in your school, but for a particular student they may be of little value. Each experience must be judged on its merit for a particular student, his interests, needs, abilities, and future plans.

THE STUDENT WHO PROGRESSES SLOWLY

This presents real problems because (1) you have to determine his basic difficulties in order to help him, (2) you have to decide upon types and areas of responsibility in which most success may be realized, (3) you have to decide what procedures may contribute most to his growth, and (4) you have to protect the pupil while trying to provide opportunities for student growth. Your efforts with such students may pay large dividends, because most of them are not weak in mentality, personality, or background of understanding. Rather, they may lack interest or maturity, or they may be slow in growing into any kind of work. We certainly do not want to imply that all students who progress slowly are generally weak candidates for the teaching profession.

We are offering several suggestions that you should keep in mind when working with a student who progresses slowly:

1. Do your best to isolate types of experiences in participation, assisting, bit teaching and responsibility that will contribute most to student development of confidence, poise, assurance, feeling of success, and pupil-student satisfaction in working together.

2. Explore types of procedures that you can use to stimulate him to face his problems seriously and try to do something about them. Examples might be withholding the student from responsible teaching longer than he thinks you should, removing the student from responsible teaching, or having a three-way conference with student and supervisor.

3. Start the student in responsible teaching with a part of the class, with the total class for a small part of the period, with the total class for a larger part of the period, and, finally, with the total class for an entire period.

4. Do not let the student start teaching a unit unless you feel quite sure that he has more than a fifty-fifty chance to succeed.

5. Do not feel that you have to give the student a variety of experiences in responsible teaching, whether or not he is ready

for the responsibilities, just to get him ready for his first job.

6. Move the student progressively through more complex and more responsible teaching experiences as he shows readiness to move with success.

THE STUDENT'S MINIMUM PROGRAM OF RESPONSIBILITY

To set a standard for all students is not possible if we recognize individual differences. But to determine minimum standards of achievement in terms of recommendation for certification is another matter. This problem you should review thoroughly with the supervisor so that you have some idea of what to expect from a student. Also, understanding of such requirements might give some students added incentive; for others it might increase tensions.

You may have students who cannot assume the role of teacher beyond a few lessons, who do not progress far enough to assume responsibility for a unit or for any teaching extended over a period of a week or two. Your student in elementary grades may not be able to assume responsibility for more than two or three areas, such as spelling, arithmetic, and music. In other areas he may only have assisted. You have to consider not only his level of development but the rate at which he is growing at the end of the student teaching period. Perhaps he has just caught on and is now developing rapidly. If the latter situation is true, your recommendation certainly would be unlike the one you might make for a student who has not yet caught on at the end of the student teaching period.

In the secondary school, what responsibilities might be considered minimum if the student is to be recommended for certification? If he is a full-time student teacher, would you expect that he should develop to the point where he can assume responsibility for a unit in two subjects in the major field and one in a minor field, besides responsibilities in other areas of teacher activity in public schools? You might keep such a standard in mind but move each student as far toward or as far beyond it as he is capable of moving. Always, the student should be moved no farther than he can move successfully.

STUDENT-TEACHER RELATIONSHIPS AS THE STUDENT ASSUMES THE ROLE OF TEACHER

How should you conduct yourself as the teacher when the student first assumes major responsibility? Your decision should always be made in terms of greatest assurance of a desirable learning situation for the pupils and success for the student. You can adopt no particular practice for all students. We suggest several types of procedures which you might follow. Most likely you will need to use several procedures or many variations of any one of the procedures suggested.

PARTICIPATING AS THE STUDENT TEACHES

The student participated in teaching-learning experiences while you taught. This arrangement was accepted by the pupils and we suspect they liked it because they had two teachers instead of one. Now, when the student assumes the role of teacher, you can place yourself in the position of participant. In planning for the student to assume some major responsibility as discussed in the preceding section, you and the student can plan *your* participating activities. For example, you might agree that you would participate in the discussion, the game, the singing, the sewing class, or the mathematics class, much as one of the pupils.

The success of this type of arrangement depends upon the degree of mutual confidence and trust that has developed in your working relationship as the student participated while you were responsible. We have emphasized the *we* relationship, and this should continue until the student assumes the role of teacher. Even now, you should continue to say *we*. The student, however, at this point, should say *I* to establish the fact with himself and with the pupils that he is the responsible teacher.

There are several advantages in your participation as a member of the group:

The student may feel more secure in taking over if you stay in the group so that you can quickly lend support. If the student is overconfident, you may feel that it is necessary for you to stand by to protect the pupils.

You may want to stay in a position that enables you to take over in case the student gets into trouble.

Your school may be one in which there are many students observing and you need to remain in the teaching-learning activities to protect both pupils and student.

The chief danger here is that the student will not develop confidence while you assist. You may have the problem of weaning the student from your support, and this procedure may only contribute to his dependence. If this occurs, you and the student may decide that the best procedure would be for you to cease participating. This move should not be made, however, if, in your judgment there is likelihood that the teaching-learning situation may go to pieces. Your alternative would be to provide for student growth in independence by assigning him assisting and bit teaching activities.

ASSISTING AS THE STUDENT TEACHES

This procedure is much like the above, but here you are assuming a part of the responsibility as for one reading group, one committee, one squad in physical education, one section in orchestra rehearsal, or one area in art class. Thus, you are assuming a transition status between teacher and participant. Your next step may be either to shift from assisting to participation or observer on the one hand, or to remove the student from his assigned responsibility on the other hand.

The student should be given time to prove himself, that is, he should have several days, not necessarily consecutively, to demonstrate his ability to assume responsibility. In case he does not demonstrate readiness for a particular responsibility, another type could be provided with approximately the same degree of responsibility. For example, if he shows inability to work effectively with the industrial arts group working in photography, he might be shifted to another group and then to another. Thus, you are providing a variety of opportunities for him to demonstrate competency to assume the role of teacher. If he is unable to assume the responsibility assigned after a variety of attempts, you have no choice but to return him, for the time being, to assisting activities and bit teaching. He should recognize this as a logical procedure.

Placing yourself in the position of assistant also enables you to move into the situation gradually and to take over if the learning experience is collapsing. Serving as an assistant enables you to relieve the student of major responsibility without the procedure being too obvious to pupils. We hope that you judge student readiness carefully enough so that you rarely have to take the class from the student and also that you do not make such a move unless absolutely necessary.

CONTINUING TEACHER RESPONSIBILITY

It can hardly be said that the student is assuming the role of teacher if you retain any significant part of the total responsibility, but in some cases you may want to start your student this way. For example, you may ask the student to assume responsibility for some aspect of your unit such as the showing of a film, including preparation for the showing and discussion following the showing. Another illustration would be for the student to talk with the class about additional references and illustrative material that had been added to the resource table.

Other types of situations might include:

Retaining responsibility for discipline or pupil control while the student is in charge (in some schools, this is necessary).

Retaining responsibility for a problem pupil until the student demonstrates that he can meet problems effectively.

Retaining responsibility for some aspects of the teaching-learning environment such as light, ventilation, arrangements with administration, and scheduling use of equipment.

Arrangements such as the above should be used only when you are very skeptical of student ability. You may have a student for whom any teaching-learning experience seems too complex. If so, the above procedures may be the only way you can get him started. From this type of relationship, you might be able to shift to assistant, then participant, and finally place him completely on his own.

GIVING THE STUDENT COMPLETE RESPONSIBILITY

"Complete" responsibility must not be construed as meaning the same responsibility for all students in all schools. All students cannot assume the same degree of responsibiilty. Also, the extent to which a student may assume responsibility in a particular school depends upon the policy of the school administration or board of education. For example, in some schools, the student has no authority in matters of discipline. In others, the student assumes no responsibility in parent contacts.

There may be situations in which you consider it wise to start the student in situations in which he assumes complete responsibility. Your student may be unusually dependent and you may have tried other procedures to help him develop independence. In desperation, you may place him strictly on his own and make it impossible for him to fall back on you. Sometimes students have to face the bitter truth. You and the supervisor might decide to talk with the student and explain clearly that independence must be developed before he can be considered to have done satisfactory work in student teaching. This should be followed by opportunities such as the responsibilities reviewed in the preceding section. He should not start out with a unit, or any other responsibility with the total class that will extend over a period of days. Your task is to find types of situations that will contribute to his development of independence.

Most often, complete responsibility will be given the student who seems to achieve maximum success in any responsibility he assumes. This is the unusual situation, however, and therefore you will start few students out with no strings attached.

INFRINGING UPON STUDENT RESPONSIBILITY

The responsibilities of student and teacher are specifically defined while the teacher is responsible and the student assisting. The same is true when the student starts assuming responsibility and the teacher assists or observes. When responsibilities are assigned, the student must understand that you do not infringe upon his rights to learn to assume responsibility. Every student, before entering the profession, has a right to establish his personality as a teacher.

The student must know that you will not overrule his decision in front of the pupils. By overruling student action, mutual understanding already established is bound to deteriorate. There may be situations in which you would like to correct the student's statement, point to an obvious error in his thinking, or call his bluff, but this must wait until conference time. Incidents similar to the one reported below have been observed too frequently and reveal what a teacher can do, without thinking, to create an impossible learning climate for students.

A student was teaching volleyball to a group of junior high school boys and girls. The teacher observed from the side of the room until the school superintendent came in. Admittedly, the student was responsible for an activity that seemed too much for her but conditions were no worse after the superintendent came than they were before. Nevertheless, the teacher started giving explanations, correcting pupils, telling the student what she should do, and finally stopped the game to explain the rules and to demonstrate. The student had started the period with poise and assurance but, in the face of such a breach of professional ethics, faded over to the side of the gymnasium and stayed until the end of the period. Fortunately, the superintendent recognized the real problem and talked with the teacher concerning the rights of student teachers.

OBSERVING STUDENT REACTION IN THE ROLE OF TEACHER

As the student starts to assume the role of teacher and as his responsibilities increase, you need to be especially sensitive to reactions that may seriously jeopardize his progress. A particular type of response or reaction may appear consistently. You may have difficulty in determining why a learning situation is not clicking or why personal relationships are not good. After determining the reaction that is causing or may cause undesirable conditions, you and the student will need to apply therapeutic measures immediately. We are calling attention to several reactions in the form of questions and suggesting procedures to use in removing or alleviating the causes.

Pupils sense very quickly the student's real attitudes toward them. One seventh-grade boy reported of a student, "The teacher wasn't in the room so the student didn't have to be nice to us, but she was. She smiled once." Whether the student's problem was tension, disinterest in the experience she was directing, or lack of feeling for working with pupils, she was not gaining the respect of the pupils. Your student may be unable to unbend enough so that he commands warm respect from the pupils, although a stand-off respect may be present. If enough of the latter exists to hold the group together in teaching-learning situations, the student may be ready to proceed. Otherwise, he should be placed in situations in which there is a minimum of activity requiring a cooperative relationship with the total group.

Does he make effective responses to spontaneous situations that arise?

Does he tighten up when a visitor enters the room; when a pupil does something in class that is unexpected and discourteous; when the pupils, for some unknown reason, have not prepared the lesson of the day; when the expected film for the day's lesson does not arrive; when the pupil asked a question which he did not anticipate and which he was not prepared to answer; or when the parent he was visiting became excited and angry about something that happened at school?

Students may get along quite well while the class follows planned procedures with little variation, but problems arise when the student is suddenly faced with an unexpected situation. Those of you who have seen students falter when pupils ask certain questions, when the experiment doesn't work, when a parent asks for information concerning his neighbor's child, when a parent questions the school's philosophy of reading instruction in first grade, or when the pupils in the club want to do just opposite to what the student had thought he could get them to do, recognize the problem as serious.

To develop facility in meeting such problems, students should have extensive experience in the types of situations in which they show difficulty. A given student may have extreme difficulty in learning to meet parent criticisms effectively. If so, he needs to have contact with more parents. You should be sure, however, that he has *more* contacts with those less critical, or he may get the wrong impression of parents in general. Another student may have difficulty in adapting to an unexpected turn of events in the classroom. Perhaps he has not had sufficient experience with committees in which the pupils are thinking through plans and making decisions. He needs to be in situations with pupils in which the unexpected may arise with less dire consequences than when all eyes of the class are upon him.

DOES HE FUNCTION WITH SENSITIVITY TO THE NEEDS OR REQUIREMENTS OF THE SITUATION AT THE MOMENT?

Does he overlook or stifle a pupil's interest by answering a question hastily and moving on or by ignoring an interesting lead suggested by a pupil? The following are illustrative:

The pupils in a third grade were discussing Indian mounds found in the state. One child volunteered that his family had visited the mounds last summer. To this, the student responded, "That's nice," and went on to *cover the material in the lesson she had planned!*

A student, using the opaque projector, had shown pictures of the type of clothing worn during the early days of the community. A girl in the group said she had some large pictures that were taken of people at the time of a centennial in a community where they had lived and asked, "Could I bring them to school to show?" The student responded, "The difficulty with pictures of that kind is that they are not authentic!" This would have been an excellent chance to have capitalized upon pupil initiative and to have given the pupils experience in determining authenticity.

The knack of immediately detecting specific difficulties of pupils in understanding the concepts being considered in a lesson is slow to develop for any teacher. Even though the student detects difficulty in pupil development of concepts, what does he do about it at the moment? If he does nothing, the remainder of the period may be lost for the pupil. If you help the student, what will the other pupils in the class be doing? These are only examples of the many problems that face a student in much greater complexity than they face you.

The only help we have to suggest is experience, followed by conference with the student. Help him to recall specific situations and to consider possible types of teacher responses. Watch him teach and again discuss specific situations with him. The values of discussing specific situations and at the same time considering specific types of responses cannot be overemphasized.

DOES HE EXHIBIT A SENSITIVITY FOR THE FUNCTION OF THE TEACHER IN THE SCHOOL AND COMMUNITY?

The student is not a bird in a cage; he is identified with both the school and community. Communities do not like "suitcase teachers" or teachers who confine their activities to the school alone, or, worse yet, identify themselves only with their classes in the high school or grade rooms in the elementary school. Does your student demonstrate such characteristics? The two illustrations given below might help the student to understand the significance of such sensitivity.

The student who proclaimed himself a scholar and who saw no point in association with patrons or with the community in general may be used as an example. He literally set himself apart from society. In school he functioned only in class, thinking that the many other school activities were irrelevant and degrading to the mind! He did not realize that guiding pupil growth is not bounded by the four walls of the classroom.

Another student in the same school and in the same subject field was discovered to be coming to his rooming house each Sunday morning about seven-thirty. He was well dressed, as if he had just come from church. At PTA meeting one evening, a parent was overheard to express appreciation for his community service. It seems that this student had been concerned that boys delivering papers Sunday morning didn't get to Sunday School. Unknown to his teacher, he had arranged with a local restaurant owner to open early so that the boys might have breakfast and Sunday School before starting their paper routes. He was the Sunday School teacher and consistently attracted most of the boys to the breakfast and Sunday School. He had a feeling for the function of a teacher.

Do tensions appear or persist which may jeopardize his success?

For the student to continue to assume the role of teacher if serious tensions appear is neither fair to the pupils nor to him. Example: A student in a physics class was hounded by a fear of pupil questions. He had not been able to get the idea of pupil-teacher cooperative study of a problem in which the teacher didn't need to know all of the answers. The penetrating questions asked by the pupils terrified him. His day-by-day observation and work with individuals and groups convinced him that the pupils were too sharp for him. He decided he would rather work with junior high. A short time later, in eighth grade science, he was alarmed to find the pupils the same way except even more unpredictable concerning what questions they might raise! He never overcame the fear and thus never assumed the role of teacher.

The seriousness of the tension, the likelihood of the tension's becoming more serious, and the effect upon the pupils should help determine whether or not he is to assume the role of teacher. It is a matter of judgment. After working with many students, your judgment will improve. You are concerned with success of pupil and student, but always the welfare of the pupil comes first. The nature of the tension must also be considered. Some tensions may not affect the pupils, only the student. Such tensions as anxiety over student teaching grade, worry about ability to maintain home responsibilities during student teaching, fear of pupils in informal out-of-class activities, sensitiveness concerning real or imagined physical handicaps, or concern over social insecurity with adults, may cause the student sleepless nights but might not affect the pupils.

Other tensions may be more serious for the pupils than for the student. Examples might be fear of pupil questions or comments, feeling of insecurity in subject background, feeling that he does not understand the psychological background of pupils with whom he is working, feeling of inferiority in English usage, fear of temper, fear of blushing and overt emotional frustration, fear of becoming too serious in trying situations, fear of pupil displeasure, or fear of pupil disinterest. Any of the latter may be serious enough to prevent your allowing the student to teach because of your concern for the welfare of pupils. However, if tension is not too obvious, you may discover that assuming the role of teacher tends to reduce tension. After a few trying days in the role of teacher, he may find that his imagination had been working overtime.

Suppose that the tension becomes more obvious and serious. You must then determine at what point the tension becomes critical enough so that the student should be removed from role of teacher and returned to the stage of induction. This has to be done in such a way that the student does not lose face with the pupils. There are several procedures you might follow, decided mutually by you and the student:

1. The student is absent from school two or three days while you get things back under control and take over the unit. Explain to the pupils that he isn't well. (He really isn't.)

2. You and the student exchange places for a few days; he becomes your helper whereas you have been his helper.

3. The student visits some other part of the school system.

4. The student with small committee of pupils takes a few days to make a survey of community resources which might be helpful in teaching of unit under way.

5. The student concentrates on work in school with a small committee of pupils while you take over class.

6. The student shifts concentration to another group or class with which you think he might more likely succeed. Explain to pupils that he is going to be working most of the time now with the other group or class although he will be back to work with us.

7. The student might be shifted to another school. This suggestion might be used if the seriousness of the situation warranted and the term were less than half over. Explain to pupils that he is finished in this school and will be working during the remainder of the term in the other school.

8. The student might drop student teaching for the term and start again next term. He might spend time visiting in the campus laboratory school or, if he goes to his home, he might visit in the home school. You could also make a satisfactory explanation to the pupils in this case.

In case any student is removed from role of teacher, you are confronted with the problem of rebuilding him through another induction program. A planned procedure is worked out with the student. Example: A student in fifth grade was trying to get a unit on Alaska set up with the pupils but could not get beyond the problem-raising stage. He could not get the pupils focused upon the problem; they literally rode off in all directions. By the third day, the pupils were almost entirely out of control.

He did not return to the room for the next three weeks but spent his time helping the fourth grade. The teacher explained that he would be in the fourth grade helping with a unit on air transportation because he was a pilot during World War II and would have a lot of valuable information and interesting stories to give the boys and girls. She thought the fourth grade was very fortunate. She also reminded them that she was sorry that they had not seemed to want him to stay with them, considering that he was stationed in Alaska during a part of the time that he was in the Air Force. The fourth grade had shown that they did want him so he would spend his time with them.

The student had spent a part of his time each day participating in the fourth grade so continued in this capacity. (This illustrates an advantage of having a student working in more than one room.) He worked with groups, took charge of the day's activities frequently, contributed information and illustrative stories from his experiences, and was placed in all possible situations that would build his stature with the pupils and himself. It worked. He completely took over the class before the end of the term and had found himself as a teacher.

Tensions that persist should be investigated to find the causes. The causes may be quite difficult to determine and to eliminate, or they may be ridiculously simple. A student in science invariably became quite flustered when pupils asked a question which required explanation. He finally admitted to his teacher that he couldn't give clear explanations. Why not? A former teacher had told him so! He was asked to demonstrate and supplement with description some interesting bit of scientific phenomenon the first thing each morning. The interest of the pupils gave him courage and he was amazed that they could understand the explanations of the phenomenon. He was then asked to describe without the use of demonstration, objects, or pictures. Even then he was understood and thoroughly appreciated. No more tension.

You and the college supervisor may be at your wits end more than once, but don't give up too quickly. Many excellent future teachers have been saved by patient, understanding, resourceful teachers and college supervisors.

If tensions are serious and persist, the student should be withheld from assuming the role of teacher. However, it may be a case of slow development, one in which induction should continue for at least one term and perhaps continue on into the next. In some colleges, student teaching must be completed in one quarter or semester and there is no chance for the student to continue into a second quarter or semester. In such case, you and the supervisor are not justified in recommending the person for a teaching certificate. The final responsibility, in most cases, rests with the college authorities.

In this chapter, we have tried to emphasize several basic policies that should be followed in helping any student progress in assuming the role of teacher. Briefly stated:

The first major responsibilities are those which offer greatest assurance of student success. These may be in instructional areas or fields, in extracurricular teacher activities, a part of one lesson, a part of a class or other group, a lesson for the class period, or a unit.

The student's major responsibilities expand in a particular area or field and/or into other areas or fields as he demonstrates *definite* success in responsibilities presently assumed.

The student meets no standards in number or breadth of experiences, but progresses according to his ability to progress.

The student assumes the role of teacher insofar as possible in as many areas of teacher responsibility as possible.

The student is not given responsibility in a variety of teacher activities regardless of readiness just to prepare him for his first job. The welfare of the pupils is given first consideration in determining whether or not a student should attempt to assume a particular responsibility.

We suspect that students generally would assume the role of teacher to a much lesser degree than at present if the above policies were followed. Further, we believe that such a change would benefit students, pupils, teachers and the teaching profession. After all, during a student teaching period of six to twelve weeks, it is hardly reasonable to expect students to develop a high degree of competency in the major areas of teacher responsibility.

9

Directing Teaching-Learning Processes

THERE IS NO WAY THAT WE CAN GIVE YOU SPECIFIC suggestions that will solve a particular student teacher's problem. Each student has his own particular problems. Perhaps you can recall one who said, "Yes, I know that I'm repeating the responses given by the pupils. I'll get out of the habit." Next day was the same, and on through the semester there was little improvement. He could hear perfectly well, repeat after you, but could not change. You may never have another like him.

During the time that the student is made responsible for complex learning experiences, your guidance continues to be a critical factor in his growth. He is not yet a teacher, but we hope that this is a stage in which competencies are refined and that his success reaches a level which will give you confidence in recommending him for teaching.

In this chapter we are suggesting (1) ways by which you can help him with particular aspects of teaching or problems that arise, and (2) procedures by which you can help him achieve independence in directing teaching-learning processes.[1]

[1] Herbert Walter Wey, "A Study of the Difficulties of Student Teachers and Beginning Teachers in the Secondary Schools as a Basis for the Improvement of Teacher Education with Special Reference to Appalachian State Teachers College" (Doctoral dissertation, Indiana University, 1950). An intensive survey of specific problems of student teachers and beginning teachers with well considered suggestions for removal of problems.

HELPING THE STUDENT WITH
PARTICULAR ASPECTS OF TEACHING

We are suggesting below specific helps in areas in which students frequently need special guidance. They may give you courage and more insights concerning how you can meet student problems effectively.

STUDENT IMAGINATION IN TEACHING

For many students, successful use of a few procedures is inclined to stereotype their teaching, and you may have difficulty in getting them into new approaches. The following suggestions may be used to help them. With proper adaptations these procedures can be used from kindergarten through twelfth grade.

1. Have at least three major activities during any one period. Examples are: silent or oral reading, discussion, writing, demonstrations by teacher or pupils, work at the board, a game, work with objects, a film, group buzz sessions, free play, construction, practice on fundamental skills, and individual projects. Any group of pupils should be able to list 25-50 different useful activities for any particular subject.

2. Have five or six minor changes of activity each period. Two or three brief discussion sessions can be held in a 40 to 60 minute period without losing the group if other activities are inserted between them.

3. Provide a change of pace in intensity of activity, tone and volume of teacher's voice, humor and seriousness, shifts from pupil-centered to teacher-centered activity, and vice versa.

4. Plan transitions from one activity to another very carefully.

5. Provide variety through illustrative materials.

6. Provide variety in each of the major aspects of instruction: preparation, presentation of material to be learned, assimilation-application, and evaluation and testing.

STUDENT USE OF INITIATIVE IN TEACHING

Although we may try hard to encourage creative thinking,

we are always inclined to balance the students' ideas off against our own plans for the group. Here is another relationship which requires that we maintain a delicate balance. Frequently you need to stand off and look at your own attitudes and manner of handling your students. We must preserve the enthusiasm and initiative of the college student at all costs. He will need it on the job. Students have very strong feelings on this point, as the following comments indicate:

The best part of my experience was being allowed to develop my own materials and ideas.

He could have helped by allowing me to use my own initiative more.

My teacher broke up some of my over-all plans because he didn't see what I was getting at. He should have asked for my ideas before attempting to suggest a different plan of attack. He was fairly good at accepting suggestions if he allowed me to explain my reasons.

The initiative of a student can be damaged irreparably by too much criticism of his teaching and too little recognition of creativity. Here are some ways by which you may encourage him to give variety to his teaching:

1. In going over the lesson you taught, call attention to the fact that "this was the third way that we have organized the class for gym period. Can you think of other ways that we might try?"

2. Call his attention to the variety of activities you used in your general science class. Suggest others that you might have used.

3. In going over plans, always pose the question, "Are these the procedures that we can expect to contribute most to the learning we want in this particular situation?" For example, the student may think of the sound movie as the final word in contributing to understanding. It may be in a particular situation, but it may be far from the best procedure in many other situations. *The student must learn that a particular learning aid or method is best in particular learning experiences, not in all experiences.*

4. In going over plans, accept some procedures that you

think may not be the best. Much of his learning that certain procedures may work and others may not will result from experience. This is better than to check him too closely and stymie initiative. Also you can ask him to change some procedures that you think may be detrimental to pupil welfare.

ANALYSIS OF TEACHING-LEARNING PROBLEMS

As indicated earlier, this should start with assisting activities. First you and he should analyze problems occurring in your teaching. This tends to throw the focus of attention from him to you, and you don't mind being evaluated. Then he may be less on the defensive when his teaching is analyzed.

We must give students a sensible, sound basis for analyzing teaching-learning problems. Stripped to its essentials, it is our old friend the scientific method, adapted to a special type of situation. Let us take a quick review of the basic steps one might use with students in trying to solve teaching-learning problems.

1. *Locate the difficulty* by discovering the real issue or the core of the problem.

2. *Get new information* by studying: the pupils—their backgrounds, behavior, and needs; the subject matter—its relationships and application to real life; the possible teaching procedures—their potentialities and limitations; and yourself—your strengths, limitations, and attitudes.

3. *Propose many different methods of attack* which might be applied to this particular problem. This is the place to give creative imagination full sway.

4. *Consider the proposed procedures critically* by projecting the likely outcomes. Estimate the probable effect on individual pupils and on the group. Professional judgment can come into its own here, and the value of experience is clearly evident.

5. *Select and try out the proposal that seems most promising.* The decision must take into account the previous experiences of the pupils and the total climate of the school. Apply the new proposal with open-minded enthusiasm.

6. *Check the results* by securing the reactions of all parties

concerned, including the pupils. A cooperative analysis is much sounder than the judgment of any one person.

7. *Revise the procedure and repeat* the attack on the problem. The best results often come from modifying our first efforts.

The rapidity with which students can learn to carry on this process independently depends on the individual student. Their rate of growth varies widely. Some are anxious to be on their own very soon, as these expressed preferences indicate:

Letting us plan teaching work rather than telling us what to do.

Giving us full responsibility and having us tell them what we planned to do about certain things, and then having them discuss with us why it wouldn't work, or why it was a good idea.

Provision for individual differences

There are few areas of teaching that are more challenging and yet more baffling to the student teacher than that of adaptation to individual differences. Throughout your association together you will have many opportunities to demonstrate sound procedures. Getting a thorough acquaintance with just a few of the common types of deviates and even a good introduction into the problems of normal children is a task too huge to be completed in any period of student teaching. You must capitalize on the opportunities you have around you for raising your student's perception through observation and participation in the work with individual pupils.

Regardless of your situation there are two minimum essentials of experience which all student teachers should have:

1. They should have an opportunity to work with one pupil who needs special assistance in reading, social adjustment, emotional adjustment, speech, or the like. They should be responsible for studying the child and discovering, if they can, some of his deficiencies and abilities. Then, if circumstances permit, they should be guided in developing some remedial procedures and applying them. Working with this type of child gives your student an opportunity to consult with a person who

has special preparation in a particular area, such as reading, if such personnel are available in your school system or at the college. The student may also need to confer with a doctor, a scout leader, a juvenile officer, or a pastor. This is a desirable experience for the student to have in preparation to meet possible problems in the field later. First-hand experience plus study of some practical articles in the field will be about as far as a student can go during student teaching. In addition, however, you should be sure to help him discover that slow pupils really can learn, and that it takes about the same processes as for average or bright pupils. The only major difference is that the teaching must be slower and better. Students must be led to realize that there are many ways of allowing pupils to progress at their own rate. Some of the newer processes adaptable to unit planning and group work make adjusted assignments entirely reasonable and possible, although certainly not easy.

2. All students should have contact with some of the brighter pupils and should have an opportunity to realize that the key to their development is enrichment. This can come in experiences, activities, materials, or responsibilities, but it is absolutely essential. There is no better situation in which a student can realize the value of well-selected learning materials than in trying to stimulate a strong pupil to work at top capacity. Student teaching is an excellent time to start a collection of materials and to learn how to hang the juicy carrots of new adventures in learning just far enough ahead of the noses of these pupils to stimulate them to maximum achievement.

Teachers often ask, "How can students help me most with my job?" Parents also wonder, "What good are student teachers anyway?" If you organize your work properly, the presence of a student can be made to mean the addition of an extra teacher. Regularly, student teachers sense some pupil learning problems that escape you, hit upon some solutions you never thought of, and stimulate some pupils to sharply increased achievement. Capitalize on these possibilities and you can make your classes a richer learning experience for pupils of all abilities.

ASSIGNMENTS IN DIRECTED LEARNING

Students need much help in gaining facility and confidence in making assignments. As we have said before, determining the purpose is the first prerequisite. Also, acquaintance with the pupils and their backgrounds, thorough knowledge of the materials to be used, and provisions for study all have to be considered by the student. Have your student analyze his own performance in the light of these suggestions:

1. Select assignments which are reasonable and possible of attainment.

2. Determine pupil readiness or provide for its development before specific tasks are assigned.

3. Differentiate the assignment so that each pupil can succeed.

4. Relate previous activities and long-range objectives to each major new activity.

5. Give directions which are brief, direct, and clear to all of the pupils.

6. Use more than just the auditory sense to insure understanding in giving assignments and directions. Include other senses by a preview of the material itself, items on the board, duplicated or written instructions, organized lists of procedures, and pupil-developed plans for insuring pupil understanding of the tasks ahead.

7. Check the vocabulary used to be sure that it is clear to pupils.

8. Organize the assignment into logical parts.

9. Make a quick check of the pupils' understanding. Note their facial expressions. Sometimes ask individuals to repeat the directions to the group. Answer the necessary and reasonable questions.

10. Include enough activity to challenge the best pupils throughout the desired period, and enough alternatives to give even the poorest something they can do.

11. Include adequate attention to the "How" and "What

for" in giving directions. Avoid concentrating only on the "What to do." Leave out "What will happen to you if you don't."

Directing learning through study

Students may think of supervised study as that portion of the period when pupils study their lessons for the next day. They need to discover that supervised study is another learning experience in which pupils need direction. This becomes clear when they begin to direct all sorts of formal, informal, individual, or group work activities as a part of responsible teaching.

Here is a list of steps that illustrates what might be done. Have your student try them out. He will find that some are too formal to be followed exactly and some are not always necessary. With adaptations to the particular job at hand they may prove very effective.

1. Be sure the pupils are properly prepared for the work they are to do.

2. Give brief, clear directions for going to work. What should they do? With what materials? When? Where? For how long?

3. Make a quick visual survey of the entire group, checking to see that all have their materials and are starting to work.

4. Take a minute or two to make a quick tour of the group. Check to see that all have started to work and seem to know what they are to do. Do not tarry long with individual pupils. Stimulate them to try to solve their own problems.

5. Make a more leisurely tour of the group, checking to see that they are making progress. Answer brief questions, and try to get each pupil to put forth real effort on this own. One problem most students have is an inclination to give the pupils too much help. In such cases they may be hindering pupil growth.

6. Work as time permits to help the slow pupils and others having real difficulty, but not too long with any one pupil.

7. If several pupils are having similar problems get the attention of this group (or the class, if that seems wiser) and try to lead a group attack on the problem.

8. Watch for students of superior ability who need stimulation and materials to go on to greater achievement.

9. Make another swing about the group and obtain a reasonable estimate of progress made, both in quantity and quality.

10. Give pupils a little warning, thus allowing them to finish up *before the close* of the period, the beginning of discussion or other activity.

QUESTIONING TO STIMULATE LEARNING

Students often experience great difficulty in formulating good questions in teaching and want help in perfecting their skill. The following suggestions may be helpful to you in working with this problem:

1. Ask questions which stimulate thought, require the development of an idea, the presentation of an opinion, or the development of relationships.

2. Use questions that require the use of knowledge rather than the mere recitation of facts.

3. Try to avoid questions which may be answered by "yes" or "no," a word or simple fact.

4. Use questions that draw out opinions or judgments and thus stimulate pupil responses.

5. Confine questions to brief sentences. Present needed background first and then ask the question in the simplest form.

6. Avoid trying to memorize questions in planning a given lesson. This practice is impossible on a regular job, and leads to a mechanical approach rather than the desired emphasis on thought content.

7. Refrain from referring to lists of questions except perhaps in drill or review lessons. Infrequently, a key question can be written down for use in a specific situation.

8. Concentrate on the idea involved in a question rather than on its exact wording.

9. To gain facility in questioning, practice writing out good questions, destroy the lists, and try again repeatedly. Francis Bacon said, "Reading maketh a full man . . . writing maketh an exact man."

In an early conference, give your student an overview of your school's general policies on testing and grading. Help him accept that policy as a frame of reference in which to work as a student, but recognize that he may take a job in a school that has an entirely different philosophy and pattern. Allow students much freedom to propose procedures and prepare tests, but take time to review their efforts carefully before the instruments are used. Be open-minded about allowing students to try out their own ideas, but reserve the right to reject the results if the evidence shows that the instrument was very faulty. Sometimes you will be pleasantly surprised. The following suggestions may be used in working with your student on this problem.

1. Use a variety of testing and evaluation procedures carefully chosen to produce the results that are desired.

2. Use evaluation as a means of measuring pupil growth and needs, rather than as a tool for promoting control and extrinsic motivation.

3. Emphasize important items of learning. Avoid using many minute and inconsequential details to get a greater range of scores, or to prepare trick test items.

4. Emphasize the use of tests as teaching devices. Plan for the use of test results and the discussion of test items as carefully as any other lesson.

5. Use special types of tests to develop specific abilities. Essay questions, for instance, give pupils experience in organizing their thoughts. Avoid excessive use of tests presented orally by the teacher; their ease of administration is far outweighed by their ineffectiveness for either testing or learning.

6. Develop procedures to use in evaluating the ability of pupils to use learning in practical situations.

7. Use evaluation procedures frequently enough to keep a close check on the efficiency of the teaching-learning process.

8. Develop a policy for determining the formal, periodic grades for your pupils. Be sure that they are within the over-all

school policy and also follow as far as possible accepted standards and principles in evaluation of pupil growth.

9. Explore the effectiveness of subjective judgments by comparing the ratings made by all the different persons competent to judge the development of the group. Also, compare general subjective judgment against the objective evidence.

10. Exercise the greatest caution to maintain the standards of fairness which all pupils believe proper for teachers. Whether working with groups or individuals, use sound guidance procedures designed to promote good attitudes toward learning and good mental health.

GETTING DESIRABLE TYPES OF RESPONSES FROM PUPILS

Establishing desirable patterns of response is very difficult for most student teachers. The more freedom your pupils have been accustomed to, the more attention you must give your student in preparing him for the situations that may arise. The problem is accentuated sharply if the student does not know the pupils' names and has to resort to pointing or nodding.

When starting with a new group many teachers tend to set the acceptable mode of response themselves. A student teacher should have in mind the types of response that would be most desirable in particular learning experiences and should be prepared to direct the pupils' responses consciously if it seems at all necessary. Often, the teacher should tell the pupils quietly but firmly, "Direct your question to Miss Jones, she is your teacher just now."

1. When speaking to a group, direct the pupils to the acceptable mode of response by a positive suggestion: "May I see hands of those who have something to share this morning— who want to be on the panel?" "Those who agree raise your hands." "Wait until you are recognized before starting to talk." Avoid the unwieldy oral clamor which results when one says, "Who knows? Who wants to comment? Who sees an error?"

2. Discover classroom control necessary to maintain good

working conditions for a particular group. Devise ways to keep responses well within the necessary limits.

3. Develop the habit of using multiple response procedures and through them provide learning activity for every pupil as much of the time as possible. Set up conditions under which every pupil has a job to do, a responsibility to fulfill, and a re-action to make, rather than just the one pupil who may be responding or performing.

4. Use a variety of recitation procedures designed on the multiple response basis. Creative students can devise scores of ways of promoting learning activity for each pupil, rather than having the whole class wait, as when each pupil in turn uses one piece of apparatus. In discussion, such directions as: "Those who agree hold up their hands," can be varied with "Those who disagree show hands," thus forcing a conscious mental process. These patterns can be adapted to either teacher- or pupil-initiated activities, and to almost any type of learning activity.

5. Generally keep the balance of teacher-pupil activity very high in favor of the pupils. Avoid monopolizing class time, except temporarily for a well-considered reason. Talk less and direct learning more.

6. Direct pupils to speak to the group, and loudly enough so all can hear. Constant positive direction both by word and hand motions is needed to maintain good conversational conditions in large groups. Run your eyes over the whole class while pupils are speaking; say, "Mary, give your ideas to the class," "John, what is your reaction to June's comment," and, "Susan, you should give your ideas to the group only after the other person has finished speaking."

7. Refrain from repeating answers and comments of pupils, whether heard by all the class or not. When necessary, have pupils repeat answers, directions, and other information needing clarity and emphasis. Ordinarily, teachers should repeat pupil comments under just two conditions: first, when a minor error can be cleared up quickly and does not deserve the time required for development by pupil responses; and, sec-

ond, when the teacher can amplify an idea quickly and thus enable the discussion to proceed toward the main objective without delay.

8. Avoid the classroom tete-a-tete like the plague; that is, all pupil responses directed to the teacher, or a private teacher-pupil conversation while the class waits. Normal reaction when conversing with another is to come closer together and look directly at each other. Students must consciously learn the opposite pattern in the classroom. Call on a pupil, look at him until he starts to speak, then turn your head and run your eyes over the whole group, incline your head toward the speaker, and continue using "eye-control" on the whole class. This technique helps to develop pupil-group and pupil-pupil verbal and social contacts and thus reduces teacher dominance. Try it, perfect it, and use it when you need to achieve these special results.

9. Use competitive activities only after careful study of the purposes to be achieved and probable pupil reaction. Emphasize the competition of the individual with himself in bettering his own record, or competition between groups. Games and group competition must be organized specifically to further real learning objectives. Care must be taken to keep the rules simple and clear, to avoid lengthy arguments over rules and their application. Student teachers often devise new competitive devices, some of which give every pupil a learning responsibility all the time.

Let us take an actual case of a student teacher in trouble and see how the above list could be used. Jim Olson was an All-American guard who had succeeded rather well in his regular student teaching in physical education. He decided he wanted some experience teaching in a classroom setting, so he was assigned to a seventh-grade boys' health class. Unfortunately, his teacher had to be called out of town on the first day he planned to teach, and he started by himself. A supervisor was alerted and did visit the class during the middle of the period. Absolute anarchy reigned. The boys were all talking at once and moving about the room, no one paid any attention to Jim, and any pupil who tried to recite or discuss the lesson was never even heard. To make matters worse the teacher would not be back for the next lesson either. What to do?

The symptoms were clear—there was no pattern of response which the pupils used habitually and the student was unable to provide one which worked. Surely drastic action was needed. In conference, Jim and the supervisor recognized the problem and decided that Jim must establish an acceptable mode of response and see to it that it was followed. No half-hearted approach would swing the tide. The pupils were not mean, nor did they dislike Jim. In fact, they probably didn't know much about him, but would follow him as readily as anyone else if he knew what he wanted done and how he was going to get it done. Finally it was agreed that since Jim would be alone with the group he would resort to the most formal approach possible, just for emphasis.

He planned to enter the classroom, stand, and in a business-like and serious manner wait for the group to arrive and come to attention. He discussed the previous session just briefly enough to point out that they all lost out because working conditions were unsatisfactory. Then he gave brief, simple instructions for the procedure that day, and did it as if he really meant it. Pupils were told that he would wait to ask questions until he had the attention of the entire group, then he would state the topic and question just once, and call on a boy. The boys were to stand to respond and wait until they had the attention of everyone before beginning to speak. At the close of each contribution the boy would sit down and the same standards would be used before other pupils could add comments, or ask questions. The recitation lesson went off as smoothly and profitably as any of that nature ever could. The contrast with the previous period was probably as great an improvement as any student teacher ever achieved.

"But," you may complain, "was that good teaching?" Of course, it was formality in the extreme, but it was an acceptable lesson of the type the supervising teacher had directed. In another period or two the student moved away from the stilted procedure and soon had a successful and informal atmosphere. He broke several commonly held principles in the process, but he solved his own teaching-learning problem successfully in one period. You will find that he used several of the suggestions given in the list on acceptable modes of behavior. Other methods could have been used, but Jim wanted to go from failure to sucess with the same lesson in one move, and he did.

Few students will ever solve their problems as suddenly and dramatically as Jim did, but his experience illustrates the point that an able student teacher can often be guided into success. The job takes three essential ingredients: a careful analysis of the problem, a clear picture of the result desired, and enough ingenuity to devise a way to get there. Teachers seldom get a greater thrill than watching a student lick a tough problem with a first-class solution.

DEVELOPING INDEPENDENCE IN
DIRECTING TEACHING-LEARNING PROCESSES

We have already emphasized the development of the "we" or partnership in your relations with your student teacher. This is absolutely necessary in the beginning, but it must be tapered off gradually as the student demonstrates confidence and success in directing teaching-learning processes. It is true that some will not progress far enough so that complete independence from the teacher can be realized. You hope for the student who can shoulder the whole job before his term of student teaching ends. As one teacher expressed the situation, "Before she had taught very long I realized that this was going to be a very rich experience for the pupils. I just got out of the way so that I wouldn't unwittingly interfere with her progress. She used me as a consultant."

INTERVENTION BY THE TEACHER

When to interrupt a student for the good of the class and

when not to is a question that plagues the best of teachers. There are no certain clear-cut rules to follow, but it is obvious that the less you take over pupil control while he is teaching the better. A bulletin to teachers gives this suggestion:

The student should be assisted with control by your on-the-spot intervention only until he is on his feet instructionally. After that he should be allowed to control the class without interference. Suggestions for improvement and handling special problems should be given privately and after class.

This is another type of situation about which students feel very strongly. Here are the comments some of them have made on both sides of this point:

Sometimes my teacher spoke out in class when pupils were noisy, making me think I didn't have to face the problem of discipline and not giving me too much experience with pupil control.

My teacher interceded too often.

Teacher often made control difficult by scolding a pupil for inattention while I was working with them.

I felt I had the complete support of the teacher and he helped by not overruling me.

I was given complete control of the students in the classroom.

My teacher at no time increased my troubles by any action.

Many students describe how they have been elevated to the status of responsible teacher in the eyes of the pupils. Sometimes the teachers have done this before the student arrived, sometimes by specific directions to the pupils and sometimes more by their manner. Typical comments are:

The teachers told the class I was as much in control as they were.

My teacher informed the pupils that they should respect the student teacher as they did him.

My teacher tried to build me up to the class as well as have the pupils respect my direction.

Pupils did not feel that they need respect the student teachers as much as the teachers.

She would correct us in front of the children, making us lose some pupil control.

Children considered us as friends and weren't instructed otherwise. More emphasis should have been put on the fact that we were also teachers.

Illustrations such as these make it perfectly clear that in guiding student teachers in the classroom there are a whole series of issues on which you must continually exercise professional judgment. You must begin by respecting the personal integrity and the day-to-day needs of student teachers and pupils alike. You must decide on the objectives you want to achieve, and the basic procedures you will follow. With your plan of operation carefully thought through, you still have many decisions to make from day to day. Often the choices are not easy, but the importance of the decisions in influencing the learning of both pupils and students makes the work of the teacher a real challenge, and the rewards in student growth can be most gratifying.

ABSENCE OF THE TEACHER FROM THE CLASS

Until the student has developed confidence in directing learning activities, he should not be left alone with the pupils. You can begin leaving occasionally for a few minutes at a time according to plans made with the student after he demonstrates ability to direct learning activities successfully. You might find it convenient to go to the office for your mail, on an errand to the library, or carry on some other perfectly normal activity. Sometimes it is better at first not to leave just before the end of a period or a session, or to be gone at the beginning of a class. If you leave in a casual manner, the student may not even be aware that you are gone. Coming back in five or ten minutes, you can enter the room as unconcernedly as if you had been there all the time.

Soon you will sense the student's reaction to your absence, and usually you can get a good idea of the pupils' behavior as you return. If all goes well, the time of absence can be varied and the length increased. Sometimes you can tell the student that you may be gone when dismissal time comes, but to go right ahead and complete the class just as if you were there. When you feel sure the student is ready you can prepare him the day before by saying, "I'll probably not be back before the bell rings tomorrow for class to begin." It may reassure you the first time to come in ten or fifteen minutes late, just to be sure all is well.

Practices in schools vary concerning the amount of time that a teacher supervising students may be absent from the classroom. In some places, a rule of thumb standard is set: "The teacher should be present with the student teacher 80% of the regular class time." Also, students differ in their readiness for teaching alone, but some time without you is desirable for the students' development of independence. If the student is weak in control you may want to wait until late in the term, and then to make the periods short. Even in those cases, a carefully planned approach to this problem helps you to carry both your legal responsibility to the community and your professional responsibility to the student. In some cases, your student may be so weak that you cannot risk leaving him alone with the pupils. One of the very real advantages to you in having a student teacher is the opportunity it provides for you to be absent occasionally for committee meetings, conferences, visitation, and the like.

Students' opinions as to what they would like the teacher to do vary greatly in this matter as in most others. The case for more supervision and more independence is put this way by four students in several different areas:

The teacher should stay in the classroom full time for the first few days.

He could have been more helpful by observing my teaching more and making constructive criticism.

The best part of my experience was the actual classroom teaching without the supervisor present. If he or she is there, it gives the pupils the idea that he is a watchdog, and the student teacher can't do anything by himself.

I would have liked it better if she had let me take the class more on my own and really made an experience of it. Many mistakes could be seen better.

SUBSTITUTE TEACHING

Substitute teaching by your student in your classes or in those of another teacher can become a real problem if not handled carefully. If you know that you are to be away, and you feel sure that the student is ready to carry on successfully alone, substituting provides a good experience. There are three special cautions that should be considered before permitting a student to substitute. Does the student have enough skill and self-confidence? Does the student have time to prepare adequately? Will the school provide backing and assistance if the student finds his control inadequate? If you feel sure that you can answer all three questions in the affirmative, then the chances are that it will be a good experience for him.

Unfortunately, opportunities to substitute may come at the very beginning of the term. At that time, it is usually wise to have a regular substitute teacher come and have the student do just what he would have done if you had been there. If this is not feasible, two student teachers sometimes share the responsibilities of a teacher rather successfully for a day or two. Detailed planning with a careful selection of activities for the particular circumstances is an important way of helping them prepare. Although there are many arguments against it, many student teachers do substitute under very unfavorable conditions. One way to give them a greater feeling of security is to tell them that some other teacher, the principal, or the college supervisor will drop in on them to be sure they are getting along all right. It gives the students a good feeling if this other person comes in very unconcernedly and stays only briefly if things are going reasonably well. Generally two or three short visits are better than one long one.

Despite its undesirability students are sometimes called upon to take over on the spur of the moment when emergencies arise. If the student has reasonable self-confidence and a strong background for the work, this may be a valuable experience. This type of substituting is often less dangerous than planned substituting because the student doesn't have time to get scared. The pupils usually know that an emergency exists and accept the situation for what it is. Planned substituting in a situation known to be very difficult may give the student time to become so tense that successful work is virtually impossible, unless he has help and the backing of some other teacher.

It would be most helpful in your future work with student teachers if you were to list procedures that you have found successful with students having particular problems. The list in this chapter is limited, but it should suggest a much more comprehensive list that you could make. Perhaps there are others in your school who would like to share this bit of creative work with you.

SUGGESTED REFERENCES

Burr, James B., Lowry W. Harding, and Leland B. Jacobs, *Student Teaching in the Elementary School.* New York: Appleton-Century-Crofts, Inc., 1950. Chapter V, "Integrating Experiences for Children"; Chapter VI, "Guiding Children in Self-Discipline"; Chapter VII, "Developing an Educative Classroom Environment"; Chapter IX, "Critizing Learning Materials with Children"; Chapter X, "Guiding Group Work"; Chapter XI, "Utilizing Community Resources."

Grim, Paul and John Michaelis, *The Student Teacher in the Secondary School.* New York: Prentice-Hall, Inc., 1953. Chapter IV, "Working with Individual Pupils"; Chapter V, "Using Group-Process Techniques in Your Student Teaching."

Michaelis, John and Paul Grim, *The Student Teacher in the Elementary School.* New York: Prentice-Hall, Inc., 1953. Chapter VII, "Using Group Processes."

Schorling, Raleigh and Max Wingo, *Elementary School Student Teaching.* New York: McGraw-Hill Book Co., Inc., 1950. Chapter IX, "A More Interesting and Challenging School Day."

10

Directing Extraclass Activities

THERE ARE SO MANY TEACHER ACTIVITIES IN WHICH the student should develop proficiency during student teaching and so little time to get things done. Besides classroom experiences, he should have experience with school-sponsored pupil activities outside the classroom. These will be a part of his program in the public school. Questionnaires returned by beginning teachers in the field consistently show that most of them, both elementary and secondary, have responsibilities with pupils in extraclass activities such as clubs, drama, athletics, music, homeroom assemblies, lunchroom duty, study hall, hall duty, and bus duty. We have definite obligations to (1) prepare each student to assume responsibility in some extraclass activity before he goes into the public schools as a teacher and (2) to guide the student in assuming responsibility for extraclass activities. This chapter is designed to help you meet these two obligations.

PREPARING THE STUDENT TO ASSUME RESPONSIBILITIES IN EXTRACLASS ACTIVITIES

ACQUAINTING THE STUDENT WITH THE EXTRACLASS PROGRAM

By this time, the student has undoubtedly visited several extraclass activities; he now must prepare himself for participation and responsibility in one or more. You have talked with him about the activities, but he should also talk with sponsors of clubs or other activities in which he is especially interested. Perhaps you would like to sit in on some of these discussions so that you can keep informed for student orientation to follow. Continued observation and discussion with students and spon-- sors should follow until the student decides in which activities he wishes to concentrate.

The student will soon recognize that working with pupils in extraclass activities may be quite unlike teaching classes. He may recognize certain restraints in classes that are much less evident in extraclass activities. He may see a period pass before the club reaches a decision. The things he sees may make sense to him and they may not; therefore, existing differences should be carefully reviewed with each student following observations of and assistance in extraclass activities. Success in assisting with and assuming responsibility for extraclass activities depends first upon his understanding of their purposes, organization, and program as compared with classroom teaching.

Characteristics of extraclass activities which students should observe and plan intensively to meet effectively are:

Informal setting and procedures. Student problems may be in direct proportion to the freedom of movement and communication and variety of activities. Practices vary greatly among schools; in your school activities may be largely organized and directed by pupils. They see pupils move from teacher-dominated classes to pupil-directed clubs with no problems arising in pupil control. Why? Probably because of two reasons: first, careful teacher-pupil planning to make sure that each pupil knows upon arrival what his activity will be; second, pupil understanding of conduct acceptable during the activity. The latter is most difficult for the student to bring about. Also, pupil-student and/or student planning is as important and even more critical than in classroom teaching. You may have seen a student and pupils work out standards of conduct which the student could not bring himself to uphold. We cannot expect pupils to honor standards if the student ignores them.

Elective pupil participation. Pupils may elect to participate in an organization because of interests in the activities, social impulses, dislike for other activities, or home influence. It is false to assume that pupil presence in an organization denotes sincere interest. The big job, therefore, is to help the student develop a program with the pupils that will create and maintain sufficient interest to replace the impelling influence of grades, credits, assignments, and the magic four walls of the classroom. The student should see how this condition is met in the organization in your school.

Variety of pupil interests. Interests are perhaps no greater in extraclass activities than in classes, but fortunately they have greater opportunity for expression and development. In a science club, perhaps no two pupils are working on the same project. The student's problem here arises in giving sufficient guidance to each pupil so that no pupil loses time having to wait. The student will probably require specific, time-consuming counseling in learning to work effectively with fifteen members of a photography club, each intent upon a particular interest.

Spontaneous incidents in large-group or all-group activities. In most schools, teachers have responsibilities for informal activities, such as lunchroom, corridors, playground, parties, pep meetings, and dances. There is over-all planning and organization as in small group activities, but often the pupils assume most responsibility. The spontaneous incidents requiring on-the-spot action or decisions present real problems for students. They must be well acquainted with established routine, administrative policy, and pupil nature, and must have extensive experience in observing and assisting before assuming complete responsibility.

Lack of continuity. Activities which meet only once per week or on alternate weeks break continuity. Interest may be difficult to maintain. Pupils literally may have to start over each time. You may have developed a system whereby you remind pupils and discuss their projects with them between meetings. This takes time, and students in the school less than the full day are seriously handicapped.

Pupil planning and directing. In some schools, the homeroom meets one hour each week. Officers are elected at the beginning of the year and the program is largely planned and directed by the pupils. The teacher counsels with the executive or planning committee and unobtrusively assists in conducting the meetings. This procedure requires excellent rapport with pupils and a helping rather than directing approach.

DETERMINING STUDENT READINESS TO GUIDE PUPILS IN EXTRACLASS
  ACTIVITIES

The student may have participated extensively in extraclass activities as a high school student, or athletics and music may have been the only activities provided. He may also have participated and assumed leadership in several activities in college, or he may not have been a member of such organizations. His participation in high school or college may have been only in competitive activities, whereas in your school there are also a variety of noncompetitive activities. You need to know what his experiences have been with extraclass activities, what his attitudes are toward them, and in which he feels greatest proficiency.

As he becomes acquainted with the activities through observation and discussion, you need to note carefully his reactions or the feeling he develops toward the activities. He may question the purposes, policies, practices, and pupil attitudes toward or concern for the activities in your school. He may indicate some concern for and fear of the informal nature, the competitive spirit, the indifference, or the informal nature of the activities. To his great surprise, this may not correspond at all to the ideas he developed while studying extraclass activities in college classes. His adjustment to the basic philosophy of extraclass activities in *your* school, the policies and practices of pupil membership, the financial support, and the degree of teacher direction may cause him some uncertainty in anticipating working directly with them. He may even want to argue with you. Some of his points may be good and applicable to the situation. If they are, give him a chance later to apply them. Whatever the situation, you have the task of explaining the school's philosophy and practice in extraclass activities. In your school, for example, the chorus may be a select group. He recalls that in college class the discussion favored providing chorus for those who want it. You will need to explain the reasons for the policy in your school.

As the student becomes acquainted, he also starts assisting you or whoever is sponsoring the extraclass activities. In photography club, he might work with a group in evaluating the quality of pictures taken of the same subject in the same setting at the same time by different pupils using different equipment. In track, he might work with the pole vaulters. The student should be observed, to note pupil attitudes toward him, his attitudes and manner of working with pupils, and the apparent presence or lack of good working relationships. At the same time, you or other teachers should attempt to determine causes for presence or absence of wholesome relationships between student and pupils.

You may note any one of many difficulties. Perhaps he is too dictatorial and definite in his statements, instead of saying, for example, "Maybe you were using too much light. Where did you have the shutter opening set? What might have prevented you from getting insufficient detail?" The student may be too much concerned with getting pupils to like him rather than concentrating on getting the pupils interested in doing something. Or, he may be doing too much for the students rather than getting them to do for themselves. As stated earlier, much time will need to be spent during the early part of the student's work with pupils in helping him to establish good rapport with them.

As you or other teachers observe the student while he assumes responsibility, you may note certain clues to the student's readiness to assume a teacher's role in the activities. For example, suppose you note him operating a rigid lunch hour with the elementary pupils. You have noted him to be pleasant and informal in the classroom. Why such a change? He may be afraid outside the classroom or he may have seen pupils take advantage of students and teachers in previous lunchroom situations. Initial shock is also a possibility. You may feel sure that he is not ready to take over. But you may be wrong. Perhaps the only way in which he can become ready to do a good job is through practice. He needs to discover that pupils are often more bark than bite.

On the other hand, you are responsible for the well-being of one or more groups of children. You have worked toward pupil development of certain attitudes, habits, and skills. You note that the student isn't ready to assume the responsibility essential to maintain continued growth in these attitudes, habits, and skills. What are you going to do? This is a constant problem in all student teaching programs. Shall the potential growth of pupils be jeopardized by permitting students to assume responsibility with varying degrees of readiness?

CONTRIBUTING TO STUDENT DEVELOPMENT OF READINESS

There are a number of things you can do to help the student get ready to assume responsibility for extraclass activities. The suggestions given below may help you to think of still others that have helped particular students.

Your attitude toward extraclass activities. If the student notes that you are interested in the extraclass activities of the pupils, he is more likely to look upon these activities as really important. You can indicate the importance of pupils participating in activities in your conversations with the student. Enthusiasm is catching. If the student does not recognize the effect of your enthusiasm for and attitudes toward extraclass activities upon your relationships with pupils, the condition should be pointed out to him.

Your participation in extraclass activities. The student observing you and others wholeheartedly engaged in extraclass activities with pupils can help more than anything you say. Again, what you say, you must be able to do. Thus the student builds confidence in you and the things you believe. Your ability to work effectively in the classroom is not enough. He must also see how you and others talk to pupils in informal situations, as in a science club or on the elementary playground. He must see how standards of group social and work relationships are maintained. Classes demand a certain type of teacher-pupil control and clubs require quite a different type, because classroom restrictions are not operative.

Your information concerning the student's background of special interests and abilities. The student generally has most confidence and can demand most respect from the pupils if he starts in extraclass activities in which he has most interest and ability. The student who is especially interested in photography and has achieved considerable skill in the field might start with a club such as photography or audio-visual. The social studies student who has participated in sports may decide that intramurals offer him the best chances for success. The student in elementary school who is talented in drama may want to have a little theatre club for those interested. Thus the student gets a feeling for pupil extraclass activities by participating in those in which he already has personal confidence and skill. One problem—ability in the activity—is therefore removed. He has only to find time to concentrate upon pupil interrelationships, pupil-teacher interrelationships, pupil attitudes, and pupil growth!

Student observation of activities outside previous experience. Perhaps there was no student council in the elementary school which he attended. Several observations may give him sufficient feeling for the group so that he is ready and eager to sit and participate with them. A student who has never seen a high school policies and practices committee, composed of pupils and teachers, would need to observe such a group in action to study the secrets to the success of its operation. You can be a great help to the student by observing with him and helping him to understand the purposes, procedures, and values of the activities. Also, you should keep in mind that observation in several activities does not mean that the student will participate in or assume responsibility for any. However, he may select one or two in which he would like to concentrate.

Breadth of observation enables the student to study many types of extraclass activities in an attempt to determine why they click. He will probably see them operating equally effectively, although following many different procedures. Even though he assumes responsibility in only one and assists in another, the feeling he develops for the direction and guidance of extraclass activities in general will be invaluable for his work in the field.

Student assisting in chosen activities. The student selects those activities in which he wants to assist. This may give him the advantage of familiarity with the activity because of past experience, of having the desirable skills, and of having confidence essential to assure success.

Assisting activities might start with the student contributing only in discussion, as in student council, or by assisting you, as in the audio-visual club. If you notice his understanding of the work and eagerness to participate, you might ask him to work with a pupil, with a committee, or to participate freely in the discussion, depending upon the activity. As rapidly as possible, he should become a working partner with you or whoever is sponsoring the group. This may involve securing the cooperation of teachers not responsible for supervising students.

Student-teacher planning. Planning for observing and assisting in extraclass activities is no less important than in classroom teaching. The student's observations are planned; that is, you may ask him to list the ways by which you or the other teacher helped the class chairman keep the homeroom program moving, kept all pupils progressing in their projects during club period, or met problems of thoughtless conduct in the lunchroom. During conference the student's report can be carefully studied. The student should assist in no capacity without first planning the activities with you. Again, the effectiveness of the plans and his participation should be considered critically in a follow-up conference. The student should also participate in pupil-teacher planning with you or other teachers.

PROVIDING FOR STUDENT RESPONSIBILITY FOR EXTRACLASS ACTIVITIES

We may have lead you to believe that students can observe or participate freely in all extraclass activities. Experienced teachers know that such conditions are exceptional.

You may face any one of a number of problems in getting students into extraclass activities. These problems may seem insurmountable to you at first, but there are usually ways to work them out.

The student is assigned for one hour per day and there are no extraclass activities during that period. The student's schedule, however, reveals a number of vacant periods during the day. Some of these come during the period or periods when the clubs, school newspaper staff, annual staff, student government, or intramural activities meet. He may also have free periods during the time used for music, athletics, and drama. Unless he is working for board or eating at a set time in a boarding house or dormitory, he will most likely have the lunch hour free and can take part in the lunch-hour program.

The student may have no free periods during the day other than the noon hour. Perhaps he can participate in no activities other than the lunch hour, but he wants to see how several of them operate. This may be overcome in several ways:

1. Contact the supervisor and ask him to see whether or not the student can be excused from class on specific days in order to see and work with the activities in which he is interested. Be sure to keep the supervisor informed concerning the days he meets with the club.

2. Contact the supervisor and you and the student go over the problem with him. Perhaps he and the student can make the contacts with the other college teachers and clear the way.

3. Expect the student to use some of his "allowed cuts" in college classes to take part in extraclass activities. In colleges

where attendance is not compulsory, this problem is especially easy to meet.

4. If no other way can be worked out, you might ask the sponsors of the extraclass activities in which the student is interested to meet their groups at the convenience of the student. This procedure should be used only as a last resort because both the teachers' and pupils' schedules may be seriously disrupted.

5. Suggest to the student that he visit the school in his home town, if vacation periods are not the same as those in the college. He can have a report sent back to you by the home town superintendent or principal.

6. Ask the student to return the following term to visit and participate in extraclass activities if his schedule permits. If his schedule the quarter following student teaching does not permit, try the following term. Keep trying until the student graduates. (You might have to be a good salesman to get him back, however.)

7. Work with the supervisor in all of your attempts to get the student into extraclass activities.

You do not sponsor any extraclass activity. Some teachers have major responsibilities other than sponsorship of extraclass activities; for instance, administrative, supervisory, public relations, night classes, college classes, extension classes, research, or major staff committee. In such cases you and the student will have to arrange for the student to visit activities, to participate in them, or to assume responsibility for them. The teachers in the building can mutually arrange to supervise students in activities sponsored by them even though the students are not assigned to them. Good working relationships thus enable you to give the student a better teaching experience than if you each assumed complete responsibility for your own students. The type of experience for the student in another teacher's activity may range from observation to complete responsibility. The student should understand this fact.

You are the only supervising teacher in the building. The possibilities for the student to have extraclass experiences other than those you direct depends upon good working relationships within the staff. In off-campus centers, in which only one or a few staff members are assigned students, many or all of the other staff members are glad to assist in any way possible. Nevertheless, your task is to acquaint your student with the extraclass activities in the school and to give him opportunity to see the extraclass program in operation and to participate and assume responsibility in those activities in which he wants and needs experience.

There are few extraclass activities in the school. Many schools have only athletics and music. These should not even be called extraclass in many instances, because athletics may be accepted for credit in lieu of physical education, and a credit or two may be allowed for music. In case there are no assemblies, clubs, student council, or lunch-hour activities, there is still hope. As suggested above, you might organize a special interest group from the class or classes in which he is working. Time might be arranged for this group to meet several times during the term. You might also suggest that he visit such activities in his home school if the college and home school vacations do not coincide. Again, you might arrange for him to visit in a nearby school in which there are extraclass activities. If he has a car, he might visit several different times during the term.

THE STUDENT ASSUMES RESPONSIBILITY
FOR EXTRACLASS ACTIVITIES

The student is ready and wishes to accept responsibility. Some students at this stage of development may be able to select, make arrangements with the faculty sponsor, and successfully assume responsibility for the activity or activities. Some will need to be helped. You also will discover some who will not be able to meet the demands of activities outside the classroom.

SELECTING THE EXTRACLASS ACTIVITY

The first problem that faces the student is his selection of the activity or activities in which he will assume responsibility. His inclination may be to select the activity in which he has most interest or has had most experience. Good practice for a student to follow is to have responsible experience as indicated in the three groupings listed below:

1. Activities in which teachers are generally expected to assume responsibility, such as noon-hour or hot-lunch duty, sponsoring parties or dances, taking tickets or sponsoring concessions at games, working in study hall or library study hall, helping with all-school carnivals or other money-making schemes.

2. A club in major field, for example, science club for science major, photography club for art or science major, sewing club for home economics major, ceramics club for art major, choral or instrumental groups for music major, athletic teams for physical education major.

3. Activities for which any teacher may be asked to assume responsibility, such as assemblies, homeroom, student council, annual, school newspaper, special events, committees.

If there is lack of time, the student should work in as many of the first group as possible. In some schools these are referred to as "common experiences" and students must demonstrate facility in all of them. A student's success in assuming responsibility in all of the "common experiences" is also used in his final evaluation. This idea is not supported by beginning teachers in the field, however.[1] They feel that classroom experiences should receive most attention, although *some* attention should be given to the "common experiences." Teachers nevertheless point to the above experiences as those generally required of all teachers in the public schools. Since experiences with extraclass activities preceding service in the field would be helpful, we recommend responsibility in the first group, although the second and third groups may have to be disregarded.

The desirability of student responsibility in one club in the

[1] Unpublished study of experiences which teachers feel should be emphasized in student teaching (Cedar Falls, Iowa: Department of Teaching, Iowa State Teachers College, 1952).

second group is emphasized by teachers in the field.[2] Sterner, in his study of teacher-sponsored activities in New Jersey, found the physical education teachers sponsoring athletic teams, English teachers sponsoring speech and drama, music teachers sponsoring music groups, and so on.

The first problem that the student faces in connection with the second and third group above is his selection of the activity with which he wishes to work. Obviously, he should be in a club with which he can succeed; that is, one in which he possesses required skills and has some interest. To place a student in a position of responsibility in a ceramics club if he possesses no skills in ceramics would not be wise. Good working relationships with the student and other staff members should enable you to plan a desirable arrangement with all parties concerned.

RANGE OF STUDENT RESPONSIBILITY

Should the student have responsibility in two clubs? Not as a general practice. You may have a student who has so much of what it takes, plus available time, that he can operate successfully with two or more clubs. Some people seem to thrive on responsibility. Those of you who have had students for several years know that one club per student is generally enough, even though he has full-time student teaching. For those with only half-day student teaching for a quarter or semester, one club plus the common extraclass activities plus the activities listed in group three might be too much. The student teaching only one hour per day can't possibly participate in any extraclass activities unless he shirks other responsibilities in his college schedule. Students who have full-day assignments are lucky.

Students having sufficient time in their schedules should also assume responsibility in the third group of activities listed above. Most teachers start their careers in relatively small schools. In these schools there are seldom more teachers than there are activities to be sponsored. Any teacher, as you know

---

[2] William S. Sterner, "A College Program to Prepare Beginning Teachers As Activity Sponsors," *Journal of Teacher Education,* Vol. II (March 1951), 28-36.

from experience, may be asked to sponsor the student council, a homeroom, or the school annual. Be sure to make these conditions clear to your students.

SUPERVISING THE STUDENT IN EXTRACLASS ACTIVITIES

In extraclass activities, as in other responsibilities, students have a right to expect good supervision. Since you cannot supervise them in all of their extraclass activities, you must arrange for other supervision. This presents real problems, especially if there are only a few supervising teachers in the school.

You must first approach the person responsible for the activity and seek his cooperation. A teacher in an elementary school wanted her students to have experiences in the lunchroom, student council, School Patrol, playground supervision, and other school activities. She talked the problem over with the principal and they decided to use several staff meetings to discuss the matter. The principal did not approach the matter by asking how many wanted to work with students in extraclass activities. He assumed that they all wanted to. The group decided in which activities students might work, what their participation or responsibility might be in each, the authority that might be exercised by the student in each, how the other teachers would keep the supervising teacher informed concerning the progress of the student, and, *finally*, which teachers would want to include students in activities under their direction.

The above procedure has much merit. All teachers in the above school, whether they wished to supervise students or not, were informed concerning the work of the students in the school. A much better attitude is developed in a school if all teachers are a part of the planning. Sometimes, however, such group planning is not possible. Getting cooperation from other teachers is entirely up to you. In such case, proceed with caution. We suggest that you make plans with one or two other people with whom you work quite closely and quite well. See how the plans work out. Student success in an activity can do a better job of selling the idea than anything *you* say.

A lone supervising teacher in a high school had no responsibility for a homeroom. She talked with a homeroom sponsor about the possibility of a student working with the homeroom. They laid careful plans and both talked with the student concerning the nature of his work. The supervising teacher had no assignment during homeroom period, so she observed the student at work. Following each homeroom meeting, she, the homeroom sponsor, and the student conferred concerning the homeroom activities and the student's participation. The student's responsibility was to meet with the planning committee of the homeroom each week. The pupils liked the situation, perhaps because more teachers were working with them rather than because one was a student. However, one of the boys on the planning committee, a member of the photography club, found the student to be interested in photography. The boy promptly invited the student to visit the club. The student talked with his supervising teacher about the problem and in turn the supervising teacher talked with the sponsor of the club. He didn't want students! After considerable discussion and swapping horses, he agreed to let the student visit. Their mutual interest broke down the barriers quickly. Before the semester ended the photography club literally had two sponsors.

The above teacher operated wisely and assured student success in extraclass activities in her school. You may have worked the problem out just as successfully in another way. Having your foot in the door, so to speak, you now face the problem of supervision. Suppose you can't observe the student because of schedule conflict. Much planning will have to be done with the sponsoring teacher or teachers in determining just how the student is going to work in the activity. Also, you will need to confer with the sponsoring teacher concerning the effectiveness of the student's work. Joint meetings with the sponsoring teacher and student are desirable at intervals, but not as a regular diet. You must not appear to lack confidence in the ability of the sponsoring teacher to supervise the student successfully. In other words, you operate more in the capacity of a concerned consultant.

Suppose a student is not succeeding in an extraclass activity supervised by someone else. One teacher was surprised to find her prize student in physical education not succeeding in the Pep Club. The sponsoring teacher came to Miss............ and reported that the pupils were not respectful to the student, were calling her by her first name and were not getting ready for each succeeding game. They attempted to analyze the problem and decided that the student was too solicitous and tried to be one of the pupils. The three (teacher, club sponsor, and student) then met for a conference and tried to get the student to determine her difficulties. The student expressed intense interest in the club but had not recognized the need for setting and observing standards, the need for businesslike organization in such a club. She was afraid of dampening their pep! The real problem came to light when she admitted that all through high school and college she had wanted to be a cheer leader but had not been selected. She was performing as a high school pupil and didn't realize it. Plans were made immediately to correct the difficulties. The sponsoring teacher helped the pupils to evaluate their effectiveness as a club and they decided that getting down to business was necessary. She then turned to the student and asked if she would like to work with the pupils in getting the club straightened out.

Your big job is to determine as best you can whether or not you think the student can succeed in the situation that exists. Also, there may be some pupil activities in which you wouldn't want students participating because of low standards maintained by the group and sponsoring teacher.

THE EXTENT OF STUDENT RESPONSIBILITY

No general statement can be made concerning the extent of responsibility that a student might assume. Many factors have to be considered. The following are quite common and may suggest others:

Administrative opposition toward students assuming responsibility in class as well as extraclass activities. In such a case you would go as far as possible in giving the student authority and responsibility.

The general atmosphere of pupil control in the school. In one school the teachers have not felt safe in giving students much authority or responsibility because of the general attitude of the pupils. In another school there seems to be a tradition of high standards of *pupil-imposed* control. In the latter, students are free to assume full responsibility unless other factors prevent.

Student growth. The student may develop so slowly in accepting responsibility in class work that he is not ready to take over in extraclass activities before the quarter or semester has ended. This condition provides a strong argument for the length of assignment being adjusted to the growth and needs of the student. You are responsible for groups of boys and girls and you cannot jeopardize their opportunities. Thus, some students may not get beyond assisting, while others may assume complete responsibility after a few weeks of participation. You have no alternative. Our best advice to you: (1) *don't jeopardize student growth* and (2) *don't jeopardize pupil growth,* by giving the student too much responsibility too soon.

The type of activity. Team coaches, music directors, and play producers often cannot give students much responsibility because they are too much in the public eye. A student might too easily jeopardize the tenure of a coach. Also, the community attitudes toward student teaching in the school might be affected if the student lost the game. We can be thankful when the "win at any cost" attitude doesn't persist through the extraclass and class activities of a school. Full responsibility could not be granted student teachers if such were the case. There is little you can do to meet this problem. Give him responsibility where you can and as much as you can. Also, see that he has the responsibility he can assume in situations which permit responsibility.

The amount of responsibility the sponsor of the activity is willing to relinquish. Some sponsors are so interested in and concerned with the activity sponsored that they don't like to delegate responsibility. This is a wonderful attribute for a teacher to possess. We wish all teachers could feel the same way about the things they are doing with boys and girls. What schools we would have!

SUGGESTED REFERENCES

Burr, James B., Lowry W. Harding, and Leland B. Jacobs, *Student Teaching in the Elementary School.* New York: Appleton-Century-Crofts, Inc., 1950. Chapter XII, "Working in the Whole School."

Grim, Paul and John Michaelis, *The Student Teacher in the Secondary School.* New York: Prentice-Hall, Inc., 1953. Chapter X, "Your Extra-Class Responsibilities."

Schorling, Raleigh and Max Wingo, *Elementary School Student Teaching.* New York: McGraw-Hill Book Company, Inc., 1950. Chapter XIV, "The Teacher's Role in the Guidance of Extra-Class Activities."

11

Building Professional Relations

A TEACHER IS A WORKING MEMBER OF A COMMU-
nity. Perhaps some teachers are able to live successfully hermit-
like within the classroom, taking little part in school or community life, but for most teachers this is not true. How many
of the teachers working with you are definitely identified with
school and community activities other than the classroom? Very
likely all of them are, and they should be. The school is the
most important community enterprise and, therefore, the school
personnel should be active community participants.

You are identified with the school and community in many
ways—a teacher of classes, perhaps a counselor of pupils, a sponsor of extraclass activities, a teacher at Sunday School and a
member of a civic club. You have stature as a member of the
teaching profession not only because of your position at school
but also because of your other identifications in the community.
But identifications not acceptable to the social mores may also
reduce your stature professionally. Every teacher has the task
of developing professional relations in the school and community that will increase his professional stature and his effectiveness as a member of the school and community.

Three aspects of your work in helping the student grow successfully in building professional relations will be discussed in
this chapter:

Your example in building professional relations.
Personal versus professional relations.
The student builds professional relations.

YOUR EXAMPLE IN BUILDING
PROFESSIONAL RELATIONS

You are Exhibit A. Students look to the teacher for examples of school and community relations. They look especially to you. They know that you were selected to guide students because of your over-all professional qualifications. They note your outlook on life (personal philosophy); your relationship with teachers, custodians, secretaries, parents, and pupils; and your attitudes toward teaching as a profession. Impressions gained from you may make an everlasting impact.

It is difficult sometimes for us to realize the effect of our professional strengths or shortcomings when working with students. Statements such as the following given by students may help us face reality, however:

Most teachers are well acquainted with this community and have its interest at heart.

This is rated so low because she didn't vote and didn't participate in community works.

The friendly atmosphere helped me enjoy my teaching and made me feel better friends with the faculty.

Teachers had excellent relations with other faculty, and students would gain good ideas for relations from this.

Teacher discussed one student's faults with the others.

Observation of teachers at PTA gives good ideas in parent-teacher relations.

The supervising teacher was polite to the custodians but gave us his own ideas of them that caused us to develop poor attitudes.

One supervising teacher in particular had a very poor relationship with the custodians.

We cannot minimize the effect of wholesome, enthusiastic professional attitudes on the part of teachers in the schools where student teaching is conducted. Professional ethics and zeal are catching. The student who reported, "The teachers spoke very highly of their work. I never heard any gripes about not getting enough money or wishing they were in a different type of work. Never heard any gossip," was no doubt grateful for the good examples of desirable professional qualities.

We must keep in mind that students may have heard much about professional ethics and the development of professional relationships but their experience may be very limited. As teachers, however, they must build the professional relationships of their environment. They learn by observing you and others and also by development of competence in building desirable relationships under your guidance.

PERSONAL VERSUS PROFESSIONAL RELATIONSHIPS

The student may never have thought seriously about the personal characteristics that appeal to one upon casual acquaintance or the personal characteristics that cause one to wear well. He has chosen close acquaintances for many years but probably never analyzed the causes for his choices. But he is now almost ready to become a member of the teaching profession. At least, he is at the stage when personal characteristics may determine whether or not he is equipped to become a teacher. He must become increasingly more aware of the personal characteristics that enable or prevent the development of good professional relationships.

An extensive list might be given but the following includes those characteristics which are most frequently mentioned as being liked in teachers:

1. Sincerity in all relationships—lack of sincerity in interest in pupils, work, or fellow workers can be detected easily.

2. Understanding of others—conscientiously attempt to understand the other person and accept him for what he is.

3. Consideration for others—recognize differences and treat each case on its own merits.

4. Cooperation with others—show sincere desire to work *with others,* not to have them work *for you.*

5. Interest in others—be sincerely interested in making acquaintance of all persons with whom you will work.

6. A sense of humor—be able to laugh at yourself, be able to give and take.

7. High standards for yourself—show desirability of high standards for yourself before expecting them of others.

8. Good taste in manners and grooming—cultivate manners and grooming that won't make you conspicuous or out of place.

You might well spend several conferences with your students considering the significance of the above qualities in establishing good professional relationships with pupils, fellow teachers, patrons, community, and professional organizations. The students might rate themselves and attempt to isolate their strengths and weaknesses. A student came to the office of one of the writers at the suggestion of his teacher recently and stated bluntly that he was not going on to get his degree in teaching. But why such a sudden decision? He had discovered that he couldn't work effectively with pupils, teachers, parents, or administration. He was a reformer and nobody seemed to respond to his ideas. Did he know why? He figured that he was impatient, arbitrary, and overbearing. He was bitter to have spent so much time preparing to teach only to discover as a senior that he could not build the professional relationships necessary for teaching success.

Your task may be more difficult than necessary because too often the student comes to you with no idea of his readiness or fitness for teaching. *Adults who worked with him may have adjusted to his undesirable characteristics.* The job of determining his personal fitness for teaching thus becomes your responsibility, together with the supervisor or director of student teaching. You have the possibilities to place the student in a great variety of situations, thus giving him maximum opportunity for growth.

The students may be able to establish good *personal* relationships quite easily but may find difficulty in establishing good *professional* relationships. For example, as a teacher, one does not choose and develop strong *personal* ties with pupils, teachers, and patrons, but concentrates on the development of the best possible relationships with all. An irritating parent is not cast off as one might cast off an acquaintance. Further, a teacher is faced with the problem of seeking out and removing difficulties that have arisen in her relationships with others.

Another difference between personal and professional relationships should be noted. An individual might move into a community as a merchant and become well established as a merchant and person. However, operating by the same social code, he might have been severely criticized as a teacher and person. Each community has a set of unwritten social standards which teachers are expected to meet as teacher and person. The two are not disassociated by the community. We should probably say that a given community has a conglomerate of social codes which teachers are expected to meet. This condition is becoming less pronounced, as you know, but nevertheless it exists to a degree in most communities.

Finally, one might not need to go out of his way in developing desirable personal relationships, but in developing professional relationships the opposite is true. One must seek out and work diligently toward the development of good working relationships with parents, for instance. The teacher cannot wait for the parents to come to him. Trouble with Johnny is so much easier for parents and teachers to face if they understand each other first. Also, it is not desirable for the merchant on Main Street to say "Saw in the paper last fall where they hired a new teacher, but I wouldn't know her if I saw her."

THE STUDENT BUILDS PROFESSIONAL RELATIONS

The student's first appearance at the school, in the classroom, in the corridor and in the community is the beginning. The first impression is strong. He should have learned this before coming to you. Regardless of the initial impression, there are definite ways by which he can *build* good relationships. These are reviewed below and in relation to personnel classifications or organizations with which he will be associated as a student and later as a teacher.

WITH THE PUPILS

The student may not have been informed concerning the relationship of his activities preceding student teaching to success or failure as a student teacher. For example, he may be a marked man when he arrives for student teaching. His mark may be due to reckless driving; loud uncouth manners in public; indiscretion in attentions to girls in public; dating of high school girls; drinking in public; or any number of other situations that happened but once and apparently went unnoticed. Because of the double standard of our society, a girl's mark may be even more serious.

These situations occur before the student comes to you and therefore you have no way to prevent them. You can, however, emphasize the seriousness of a pre-student teaching reputation with the hopes that word will get back to lower classmen. The problem is most serious when student teaching is done in campus schools, in schools in the local community or in schools in immediately adjacent communities. Gossip can spread a long way. Athletes and musicians are in a particularly difficult position because they are so much before the public.

Your chief concern is in being sensitive to pupil evaluation of and reaction toward students. You can help the student detect desirable and undesirable reactions of the pupils and attempt to determine causes. One of the responses that so often misleads students is pupil solicitation. Students, while thinking that pupils really like them, may be building up a superficial respect. This often results from over-anxiety on the part of the student to get pupils to like him. Finally one day in a position of responsibility he discovers that the pupils do not regard him with respect. They do not respond to his attempt at leadership but make remarks such as, "Oh, we don't want to have spelling to-day. Why don't you read to us?" "Why do we have to have spelling today?"

Pupils in a high school speech class had a lot of fun with a student, at first unknown to him. The student in question wished to meet as many of the pupils in his speech class as possible at a local jive-joint for coffee after school. He reported his teacher as "consenting grudgingly to my requests for coffee-conferences with the kids; a remarkably valuable weapon, I found. In fact, more valuable than anything else." The *pupil* reports of the "coffee-conferences" were different. One reported, "You ought to hear him talk with us!" "Boy, some of the stories he tells the girls. No wonder he has trouble with them in class." "Why can't he be his age?" "He tries to be silly and is *that* funny!" "At first it was funny to watch him try to be liked by the kids but now it's boring."

Students must recognize that relationships leading to respect are based upon factors such as sincerity and understanding, listed above.[1] You are in a position to foresee difficulties—in fact, you may have worked with students long enough to be able to detect symptoms early enough to prevent trouble, if you can convince the student. Frank discussion with the student is absolutely necessary. Some will sense the problems quickly and adapt quickly; others will require endless patience and repeated discussion in conference. In some cases, you will certainly want the supervisor to observe and talk with the student.

Another major problem that you may have observed involves pupil security; that is, the pupils knowing what they can and cannot do, knowing definite standards to which they will be held. The student may be able to inform pupils of standards to be followed in class, club, or playground, but may not be consistent in holding the pupils to those standards. Again, he may be able to work with pupils in setting standards, but be unable to get pupil support in upholding them. As a result, the

---

[1] Also A. S. Barr, William H. Burton, and Leo J. Brueckner, *Supervision* (New York: D. Appleton-Century Company, Inc., 1947).

pupils are never quite sure what they can or cannot do. Pupils like definite standards, unless too rigid, even though they may not be too anxious to assume responsibility in upholding them.

Students may unknowingly create problems for students who follow. A boy in third grade remarked to his father one day, "I wonder why Miss Jones doesn't talk to us now when she sees us?" The father, a member of the faculty, tried to explain that she was probably very busy in school. The boy was definitely hurt and pursued the problem further by observing, "Student teachers must not like us like our teachers do." Every student should understand the implications of this situation for future students. The student had hurt herself less than she may have hurt all students who would have this boy in their classes.

While they are teaching, students have a definite responsibility to the college. In a very real sense, the college is judged by the teachers it sends out. Also, students have a definite responsibility to future students. This is especially so in campus laboratory schools or in local schools used for professional laboratory experiences. Several student-pupil relationship policies following student teaching should be stressed with students before their teaching is completed. The following are illustrative:

1. Remain friendly with and interested in the pupils who were in your classes during student teaching.

2. Dating of high school boys or girls in schools used for observation and student teaching following student teaching jeopardizes success of future student teachers.

3. Actions of former students should be in keeping with those expected of professional persons.

4. Former students do not talk critically with former pupils about present students. (As one teacher does not talk critically with pupils about another teacher.)

5. Former students refrain from becoming companions with former pupils.

6. Former students refrain from becoming members of a "crowd" or clique of former pupils.

WITH FELLOW WORKERS

A teacher is a member of a cooperative enterprise. He is not an entity within a classroom. The successful operation of a school depends partly upon the working relationships of the faculty. You can help the student more than any other person to learn how to operate effectively as a member of a faculty.

You can demonstrate effective procedures. He senses that you do not consider yourself an entity unto yourself. Rather, he sees you and the other members of the faculty working cooperatively. He goes with you to the science office to ask advice concerning the astronomy unit in your sixth grade. He is present when the physical education teacher comes to you for information concerning a new attitude that one of the sixth grade boys has displayed on the playground. He sits in a faculty committee meeting with you, notes wide differences of opinion expressed, and marvels as a compromise agreement is reached without loss of poise.

One of the observations that impresses students most favorably is good working relationships within a faculty. In response to the question, "How did your supervising teachers help you most?" typical responses were:

The teacher created an atmosphere that made teaching with him a pleasant experience. He made us feel that we were succeeding and that student teaching should be a happy experience rather than a chore.

Pointing out personal traits to work on and by their own teaching.

Teacher had excellent relations with other faculty and students. Would gain good ideas for relations from this.

You can place them in situations in which they have opportunity to develop good working relationships. A student planned a two-hour excursion with his class and started around to make the necessary arrangements with the other teachers. A photographer, he was told, had planned to take pictures in one of the classes from which the pupils would be absent. He returned to his teacher and suggested that the trip be made anyway, only three pupils would be taken from the class. He was reminded that three families would be looking for the pictures of their children in the local paper. Also, he was asked whether or not the teacher had planned pictures featuring any of the three. He hadn't thought of such complications. Starting around again, he took a different approach—of the dates suggested for the excursion, which would conflict least with the other classes? A date agreeable to all was selected.

Students, for the most part, do not sense the entanglements resulting from activities which interrupt or change the regular routine of a high school schedule. The common use of school material and equipment may be just as confusing to the students. Lack of experience may prevent them from anticipating and averting difficulties that arise in a school. You are the one who stands by to prompt the student, to remind him of potential problems, so that he learns to avoid trouble by prearranging.

The following are illustrative of situations in which you may need to prompt the student:

1. Asking for material to use. The map may be standing unused in a closet in another teacher's room, but be sure to ask the teacher for it. The chemicals may be on shelves behind unlocked doors in the science room, but be sure to ask one of the high school science teachers for the chemicals needed unless other arrangements have been worked out.

2. Return of materials or equipment used. Costumes taken from the wardrobe are returned promptly and exactly as borrowed. The sound movie projector and screen are returned immediately after use and to the exact place from which taken. If a schedule is posted for the use of audio-visual materials and equipment, the student is responsible for scheduling.

3. Interference with schedule of another person's class or classes. One teacher does not ask for pupils from another's class unless absolutely necessary. One does not hold a class over a few minutes unless prearranged.

4. Use of another teacher's room. Materials in the room are not disturbed unless absolutely necessary, but, if so, they are

returned to their original position before the class leaves the room.

5. Joint use of room by several teachers. It is necessary for an understanding to be reached and followed. The student may not get in on the arrangement, but he is responsible for following through. If changes are to be made while the student is teaching, he makes the arrangements.

6. Planning ahead. Any plans which might in any way effect other teachers are made at least a week in advance. Sudden requests of other teachers are almost invariably irritating.

7. Individualities of faculty. To tell the student about "pet peeves" or eccentricities of faculty members, if such exist, would hardly be professional and the student might consider such information gossip. The student must be aware of the problem however, and you *can* use anonymous illustrations. Examples might be: the teacher who can't take kidding, the teacher who believes that women teachers should wear full length hose in school at all times, the teacher who believes that school is no place for joking or other such frivolous activities by teachers, the teacher who frowns upon smoking by teachers. Illustrations can also be given concerning ways of working effectively with all types of people in school. The student, being aware that such conditions exist within a faculty, must be sensitive to discover and meet effectively those present within the school in which he is teaching.

Students who have been surveyed unanimously appreciate the efforts of teachers to make them working members of the faculty and are disappointed when this is not possible. You may not be able to get all of the cooperation desirable from other faculty members, but use wisely the cooperation you can get. Be careful, however, not to take advantage of fellow workers, especially those who are not supervising students.

One of your problems in providing opportunities for students to develop good working relations will involve the breadth in types of experiences. The students may be free to go to any faculty member for advice, materials, or information. There are other types of situations that the student should experience, however. The list below is not all-inclusive but does indicate types of experiences which might be made available.

1. Participation in faculty meetings. To break the ice, the chairman of the meeting might ask the student for suggestions, opinions, or information. Later the student should feel welcome to contribute freely to discussions in faculty meetings. He always needs to be careful not to engage in argument or to offer ideas that are controversial. In other words, he must exercise extreme judgment.

2. Participation as a member of a faculty committee. Perhaps you are working on a faculty committee and can include him with the consent of the other members of the group. Otherwise, you might ask an existing committee to let him join them. If no opportunity affords itself, you could ask several teachers to meet with you (and student) to work on something of mutual interest.

3. Participation in faculty social functions. Students should be included in faculty parties, picnics, and the like. This may not be possible, however, in laboratory schools in which there may be several students per supervisor. In off-campus situations in which there are generally only a few students in proportion to the total faculty, students can participate freely in faculty social functions. Students like assuming responsibility on committees in preparation for program, games, lunch, or decorations. They usually have good ideas and like to put them into practice. They're not afraid of work, either.

4. Participation in special faculty projects. Suppose the faculty has been asked by the pep club to put on a skit for pep assembly. Include students if possible. This gives the pupils a chance to see the student in a new role. The student has a chance to experience a situation that will very likely face him as a teacher in the public school. Other situations in which students might participate or assume responsibility include community drives such as Red Cross, Community Chest, clothing to be shipped overseas, and polio contributions.

WITH PARENTS

A student had trouble with a high school pupil who would not follow precautionary measures in the industrial arts room. Finally, in a conference with pupil, teacher, and principal, the decision was made to have the parents come to school to discuss the problem. The meeting of pupil, parents, student, teacher, and principal proceeded quite smoothly through a review of the pupil's actions. Exit tact! The student responded suddenly, "You've got to teach him what authority means at home. We can tell that you've never made him mind at home. You've got a spoiled only-child situation on your hands!" The father practically dismembered the student before anyone else could move.

The father had sincerely asked for advice but the case was made almost hopeless. The student may have come from classes in psychology in which discussions were very objective and to the point. He hadn't learned, however, that parents generally respond better to a pleasant, tactful approach in reference to pupil problems at school.

There are several general principles for parent relationships that can be developed with your students, but not in one dose. We suggest the following:

1. Get acquainted with parents of your pupils as soon as possible.

   a. At PTA, try to meet parents of all pupils you have in school.

   b. Stop at homes of pupils for brief chats.

   c. At community functions (church, Sunday School, band concert, art gallery, Special Day Services, etc.) make occasion to visit a moment with as many parents as possible.

2. Be interested in many things when visiting with parents— don't always talk shop. (The dentist doesn't make a habit of talking shop when visiting in the community with his patrons.)

3. Let pupils know through conversations with them *about* their homes that you are interested *in* their homes.

4. Invite parents to come to school, and if they do come, find time to visit with them.

5. Establish a friendly basis for discussion before you go to them with problems.

6. Be absolutely frank and sincere with parents in discussing pupil problems, unless you feel that the welfare of the pupil will be jeopardized.

7. Have evidence to back up any general or specific statements you make concerning pupil progress in school.

8. Be specific in discussing pupil progress with parents.

9. Enlist cooperation of parents in treating problem situations.

10. Keep parents informed concerning the pupil program in school.

Most students learn to converse with parents rather well, but deciding how to approach the parents about Mary's problem may result in sleepless nights. Therefore, students need to be placed in situations of direct participation or responsibility with parents. These situations should be frequent and varied enough so that the student will develop a feeling of confidence in this aspect of the teacher's work.

Readiness to assume complete responsibility (for example, for a parent conference concerning an emotionally unstable pupil) is difficult to determine. In fact, you probably never can be sure from observing the student while participating with you in parent conferences. There will certainly be some who should not be permitted to assume *complete* responsibility for parent relationships, such as serious pupil or parent problems, pupil report to parents, or homeroom meeting with parents. Here, again, it is a matter of trying to determine whether or not or to what degree the welfare of the pupil, parent, teacher, student, or school will be jeopardized.

The student plans with you for conferences with parents, reports to parents, parent homeroom meetings, and so on. The partnership is established—*we* hold parent conferences and make reports to parents. You ask him to contribute to the plans, therefore you respect his ideas. He will accept rejection of his ideas if you have good reasons and take time to explain why you think they are not good. If possible, tell the student why his idea might or might not be successful. Try never to decide how to proceed without explaining why. You can't expect him to decide what to do unless you explain to him why you did what you did.

A student was informed earlier that he would help prepare the reports to parents. He understood the reporting system—a description of pupil progress but no letter or number grades. Reports written earlier in the year for each pupil were read by and explained to the student and he had an opportunity to ask questions. Also, he had the evidence that had been collected to enable the teacher to make judgment in writing the reports.

He was now ready to work with the teacher in gathering notes and data concerning the over-all development of the pupils. Both were working with the pupils. They compared notes and frequently discussed at length the growth status of certain pupils. The student was learning how to observe and what to observe. Reporting date approached and they each wrote reports for each pupil. In comparing reports, they found that the student had statements as "Ralph is doing very well but could do much better if he tried." "Sue is always interested in so many things that she might even be called a dreamer in school." "Skill subjects are difficult for Jack but he seems to be coming along all right lately."

The student had not sensed the importance of reporting specific conditions so that parents would know what the child was really doing. For example, the teacher would say, "Paul improved in spelling. He missed only one or two words each week this quarter. He seems to understand multiplication quite well but has trouble recalling the following combinations quickly—$9 \times 7, 6 \times 9, 8 \times 6, 7 \times 6$, and 7×8. He forgets how to make the following capital letters—Q, J, F, and L. His attitudes toward the other children are improving but he still interrupts and contradicts other children when they are talking in class."

Billy's handwriting gave them some trouble. Records kept during handwriting period showed definite improvement but the teacher said on his report, "Billy's handwriting is improving steadily in handwriting class but he has a tendency to be careless when writing in other classes." The student wrote, "Billy is improving in handwriting." The teacher explained that "improving in handwriting" meant over-all improvement, not just in handwriting class. She further explained that the faculty also did not report "improvement in reading" unless there was improvement wherever reading was used in school.

Many hours had been used in helping the student learn to do a good job in this kind of reporting system. But this was not enough. What kind of reporting system would the student be using next year as a teacher? Perhaps the letter system (A, B, C, D, F) or numbers (75, 86, 92). Then how would he use the data collected in making out letter or number grades? How would he use either system if each pupil were graded according to his ability? These problems were reviewed carefully and grades prepared by each. Again they compared grades and reached compromises.

WITH THE ADMINISTRATION

The principal and superintendent are directly responsible to the public through the board of education for the educational program and practices in the school. The teacher is directly responsible to the principal and superintendent for the educational program and practices in his room, class, club, and study hall. The student is at first responsible to you. When he starts assisting, however, you may be delegating tasks that make him directly responsible to the principal or superintendent. For instance, if you ask him to check supplies from the office and he forgets to leave a record of supplies taken, if he makes an error in reporting attendance, if he violates a practice in use of school equipment, or if he uses pupil personnel data indiscreetly, he is responsible directly to the principal.

The student must see sense in his responsibility to the administration. We dislike using the term "loyal to the administration" because it might imply servile obedience, which we do not mean. We much prefer that the student recognize professional inter-responsibilities and develop wholesome working-together attitudes and relationships. He should have experiences in many activities in which desirable attitudes may develop and in which he can see the necessity for close cooperation between teacher and administration. The following are examples:

1. Keeping accurate, neat records and reports. Present-day school accounting includes reports to state departments concerning attendance, transportation, hot lunch, and the school program, all of which may figure in state financial aid. If mistakes are made, the school loses money or no reimbursement is forthcoming until the discrepancies are corrected. The superintendent is on the spot to submit reports and cannot fulfil this responsibility without teacher help. Therefore, while he is with you the student should form the habit of submitting accurate, neat reports on time.

2. Using personnel data discreetly. Before they have access to the files, students should recognize the professional obligations which accompany the use of confidential information. They may have had no experience with the type of information personnel folders contain and therefore see none of the dangers that may result from "talking out of school." Misuse of the information in school may be just as bad. The student who tells a parent how his child compares intellectually and scholastically with the neighbor's child may receive a call from the neighbor.

3. Supporting policies of the school. Any school has some policies that all teachers are expected to support. In crowded conditions, they may have to do with use of the corridors, rationing of playground space, use of toilets or drinking fountains. Also, there are usually policies concerning such things as tardiness, absence, reporting illness and accidents, taking excursions, use of supplies. While working with you the student learns why policies are necessary and learns to follow them explicitly.

4. Keeping the administrator informed. The principal of the building is in a much better position if he knows about an incident which occurred at school before the parent calls. For in-

stance, two boys had a serious fight in a rest room and the student did not report the incident to the principal. He received the information from one of the parents. The student, while teaching, should have experiences in keeping the principal informed. However, he must learn what sort of information to report.

The student also should see the administrator fulfilling his responsibilities to the teacher. Examples might be:

1. Supporting you and the student in meeting a problem with pupil and parent.

2. Going over your problem of supplies for your unanticipated large grade and planning to purchase the materials needed.

3. Accepting your decision concerning a program for gifted children in your group and reviewing the plan with parents.

4. Helping you reach a decision concerning the distribution of art materials.

5. Counseling with you concerning any situation in which you feel the need for guidance.

Satisfying experiences in student teaching will give the student a good start with his first administrator in the field. The student will be fortunate if you and your administrator can give him such experiences.

WITH THE CUSTODIAN

The custodian has a real contribution to make to the educational program of the pupils and also to the student teaching program. His job is to work with the pupils, teachers, and administration in the maintenance of a clean, attractive school environment. Some students may have come from schools where the custodian was a clean-up flunky who spent much of his time in a one-man attempt to keep the building and grounds looking presentable. We hope you are in a building where the custodian is a respected fellow-worker and that the students develop attitudes similar to those reported below:

The custodial staff was one of the friendliest I've ever encountered.

We discussed this in seminar and I noticed my teachers practiced what they preached.

Custodians appreciated the consideration shown in turning off lights and shutting windows.

Teachers did not make undue demands of the custodians. When we needed help, they helped us.

The custodian talked with us in seminar about teacher-custodial relations.

Taught us to respect the custodial staff as fellow-workers.

The student shows respect for the custodian by assuming responsibility for room lights, windows, and shades; by adjusting to the custodian's schedule in room sweeping; by taking care of all situations not absolutely requiring custodial help; and by consulting the custodian before using his materials or causing his schedule to be changed. You expect pupils to extend him the same courtesies.

The cheery good morning, the brief chat, the card when he is ill, and the general friendly attitude all help in establishing good rapport. The personal relations fall down immediately, however, if the student is not considerate of him in professional relations. Leaving the windows up, calling him to get the bee out of the room, permitting pupils to leave paper strewn on the floor, asking him to clean up the mud the pupils tracked in, letting pupils drop paint on the floor without cleaning it up, arranging a room that cannot be cleaned, and calling him to mop spilled water, as examples, may nullify all efforts to establish good professional relations. Such procedures also contribute toward poor pupil attitudes concerning their responsibilities for the care of the school environment.

Some teachers make a practice of having the custodian talk with the students at the beginning of the term about his work and how he, the pupils, and the teachers work together. Other teachers have a list of practices prepared cooperatively by the pupils, custodian, and teacher concerning the responsibilities of each in the care of the building. Whatever procedure you use, the student should have experiences in working with the custodian, in sharing responsibility with him, and in directing pupils in working cooperatively with him.

WITH THE SCHOOL SECRETARY

In most school systems the secretary acts for the principal concerning certain designated matters when he is not in the office. You may have practices established in your school whereby most of your questions concerning routine can be answered by the secretary. This is especially true in making reports or in submitting requested information.

Again, the secretary is not a servant of the teacher. The student learns while working with you that material to be typed is not submitted to the secretary on short notice, that unsorted mail on the desk may not be due to a lazy secretary, that a depleted supply of Scotch tape may not be due to an unorganized office, that few secretaries know everything, and that the secretary is not being mean by asking that reports be submitted when requested. The student, by working with the secretary, comes to understand her function in the school and learns how to work with her.

You can provide many opportunities for the student to work directly with the secretary. The following suggestions are examples:

1. Check needed room supplies from the office.
2. Report loss of textbook and ask amount to be assessed pupil.
3. Prepare reports or supply information.
4. Report pupil who is dropping from school and give change of address.
5. Ask that material be duplicated for use in PTA meeting.
6. Schedule use of auditorium.
7. Submit order for film.
8. Invite secretary to room social event.
9. Permit children to use office phone only when necessary.

There are as many opportunities for you to call attention to courtesies that secretaries extend to students and teachers, for example:

1. Giving immediate notice that ordered materials have been received.

2. Stopping her work to assist in locating material, preparing reports, etc.

3. Calling the student or teacher to the phone.

4. Taking messages to the student or teacher.

5. Advising the new teacher or student concerning use of the duplicating machine.

As in other professional relationships, the personal considerations are of no value without the professional considerations. The friendly approach plus courteous requests equal good working relationships.

WITH PROFESSIONAL ORGANIZATIONS

You no doubt belong to your state education association, the National Education Association, and at least one other professional organization. The literature from these organizations is probably at school and you use it frequently in your teaching. You should familiarize the student with the organization, inform him of the services it provides, and demonstrate the value of the publications or other services to the teacher in her work. The value of membership and participation in professional organizations must be clearly demonstrated to the student before going into the field. To help you meet this responsibility, we suggest the following:

1. Belong to professional organizations. Your membership in the organization is a selling point, unless you belong just as a routine matter.

2. Endorse professional organizations. The student who wrote, "Their attitude toward NEA and English Council and participation in activities showed their belief in these organizations," illustrates the point quite well.

3. Use the services provided by the organizations. The cur-

rent publications and publications of other years may be on your shelves. Use these frequently in planning your work, assign articles that you think will be especially helpful to the student in meeting his problems, include the references to articles in your units, and frequently refer to articles from the publications during your conferences. You and the student should note references made to materials that might be helpful in your teaching and write for copies. Also, write to authors of articles asking for additional information concerning ideas or practices to which reference is made. Some articles you may have clipped from the publications to place with other materials in your files.

4. Attend meetings of the organization. If possible, take your student or insist that he attend the state or district teachers association meeting or the meeting of some other professional organization to which you belong or whose meetings you attend. Organizations such as ACEI, ASCD, AST, NCSS, Academy of Science, for example, have state or local chapters or units which you may attend and to which the students would be welcome.

5. Emphasize the contribution the teacher can make to the professional organization by his support. This not only includes financial support to maintain the organization but membership fees most often pay for the monthly or quarterly publication and the yearbook. Members have also contributed the articles, many of which the student has found helpful.

The professional organization idea can best develop while the student is with you and can see the many values of membership and participation to the teacher.

WITH THE COMMUNITY

The student may be surprised when he discovers that you are really a member of the community by registration as well as by active participation; that a teacher's activities have not ended when he leaves the school. He will soon learn from conferences with you and from your attitudes and conduct that a teacher's professional status in the community is quite generally recognized. It is necessary, therefore, that the student learn how to conduct himself as a member of the teaching profession in the community.

Ways by which you can help him might be included in the following categories:

1. Understanding of the community customs and tradition. The student may not agree with or may greatly dislike the customs and/or traditions of the community. Nevertheless, he must understand why they exist and show them due respect. He is not in the community to change the social mores. Students and teachers have jeopardized their positions in communities by ill-judged remarks in the classroom concerning some aspect of community life of which they didn't approve. To warn a student against making such statements is not to deprive him of freedom of speech, as he might think, but to prevent him from *misusing* freedom of speech. He should also recognize that he is not in the community long enough to become an established, generally recognized and accepted member of it. When he becomes established as a teacher in the field, however, he can assume a position of leadership in controversial issues if, in so doing, he does not jeopardize the welfare of the school. Many teachers have made real contributions in such roles.

2. Understanding of community standards for teachers. You can review the basic standards with him and caution him concerning conduct; for example, as regards smoking, attending community dances, language usage, dating, friendships with opposite sex, and staying in town weekends. Such standards as exist, he must accept. In the field, he will follow the same pattern, that is, determine first the standards that are imposed, and then observe the standards.

3. Attitudes toward the community. The student who enters the community with interest, with a desire to meet and get acquainted with people, with a friendly response to invitations extended, is most certainly off to a good start. *The student must accept the community before the community accepts him.*

He may be very busy at school as a student, but he still has time to exchange a few pleasantries with the clerk, the postmaster, the baker, the editor, the shoe clerk, or the parent on the street. This practice will build a wide circle of wholesome acquaintances before the quarter or semester is over. The student who hurries along the street, makes a purchase and leaves the store in haste, leaves the church service quickly without stopping to visit a bit, goes to the business district only in case of emergency, is always seen alone, and attends no community meetings, cannot expect the community to be interested in him. He should also recognize that by such actions and attitudes he is not only setting himself apart from the community but also setting the school and the profession apart from the community.

4. Participation as a member of the community. This is much more difficult because the student is ordinarily not in the community long enough to assume responsibilities in continuing activities such as Boy and Girl Scouts, Sunday School, Church Youth Groups, Community youth recreation (Teen-Time, Jim and Jane) or adult organizations. The community is not concerned that the student pitch into an organization and work intensively but it is concerned that he exhibit interest, attend (although not regularly), and participate. In this way, the student becomes identified with activities that the community considers to be important.

There are also opportunities in connection with such special days as Armistice Day observances, Memorial Day observances, Winter Carnival, and Harvest Festival. He can attend these and can take advantage of the opportunity to meet as many people as possible. Special drives such as Community Chest offer the student possibilities for service. He can either assume responsibility for canvassing or assist you in canvassing. Again, he would meet people; but most of all, the people would see him participating directly in their activities.

Teacher attitudes toward the community, developed while a student, are wonderful insurance for a wholesome community experience in the first job. The student is preparing to become a member of a profession. As a member of that profession, he has many obligations. You should acquaint him with those obligations, provide him with experiences designed to contribute to his growth as a professional person, and counsel with him concerning his growth. Your attitudes and the attitudes of the other teachers toward the profession probably have greater impact upon him than any other experiences. A high degree of skill in building professional relations, wholesome professional attitudes, and professional zeal carried into the field by every student could have a tremendously beneficial effect upon the profession.

SUGGESTED REFERENCES

Barr, A. S., William H. Burton, and Leo J. Brueckner, *Supervision.* New York: D. Appleton-Century Company, Inc., 1947. Chapter VIII, "Studying the Teacher Factors in Pupil Growth."

Burr, James B., Lowry W. Harding, and Leland B. Jacobs, *Student Teaching in the Elementary School.* New York: Appleton- Century-Crofts, Inc., 1950. Chapter XII, "Working in the Whole School."

Feyereisen, Kathryn and Verna Dieckman, *Guiding Student Teacher Experiences.* Lock Haven, Pa.: Association for Student Teaching, 1952. Pages 10-17 review briefly procedures for the student to use in effecting good working relationships with co-workers and others.

Grim, Paul and John Michaelis, *The Student Teacher in the Secondary School.* New York: Prentice-Hall, Inc., 1953. Chapter IX, "Solving your Own Problems" (Especially pages 334-338).

Schorling, Raleigh and Max Wingo, *Elementary School Student Teaching.* New York: McGraw-Hill Book Company, Inc., 1950. Chapter XVI, "Professional Growth and Personal Advancement."

Wiles, Kimball, *Supervision for Better Schools.* New York: Prentice-Hall, Inc., 1950. Treats specifically many aspects of a teacher's activity in creating good working relationships within a school.

12

Promoting Personal Development

SOMEONE HAS SAID THAT "EDUCATION IS CHANGING behavior for the better." Such a definition applies very aptly to student teaching. However, by the time a person is twenty years of age or more, behavior includes many habit patterns which may be difficult to change. Life-long attitudes and ways of doing things have become integral parts of the personality. Effective behavior in the classroom must be learned by a process of growth, and this may be a slow process. Students may be eager to improve, but just telling them their faults may not help much. One student in music put it this way, "I was told that I lacked aggressiveness but nothing specific about it. Neither was I told how, or conferred with on how, to improve in this respect (except to be more aggressive)." To have a keen urge to act and then to find the way blocked is a frustrating experience. Telling a student he needs to improve—even encouraging him to improve—is not enough. Often he needs help and guidance in discovering what to do—how to improve.

The task of the teacher who undertakes to guide a student in his personal development is threefold:

1. *Set an excellent example of good mental health:* As the old saying goes, "What you are speaks so loudly I cannot hear what you say." Your student needs an example of good teaching, but he also needs an opportunity to observe a well-adjusted indi-

vidual solving his professional and personal problems in a forthright and constructive way.

2. *Provide an atmosphere for growth:* You must be sensitive to the effect of the total environment on the student, and, most of all, of the way your own behavior affects him. You must try to discover his needs and to remove the roadblocks that stand in the way of his progress.

3. *Provide sympathetic guidance:* You can suggest, answer questions, and assist in planning, but you can't tell students they *must* do, or do it for them. The direct approach often fails. A sincere compliment and a pat on the back are often far more effective in releasing energy than direct criticism. A kindly but thoughtful answer to a frank question is worth more than hours of unsought advice.

We are making suggestions in four areas that should help you meet your responsibilities in contributing to student growth in promoting personal development:

Setting the stage for personal development.

Guiding the student as he attacks his personal problems.

Making a direct attack on certain limiting personal characteristics.

Promoting all-round student growth.

SETTING THE STAGE FOR PERSONAL DEVELOPMENT

Teachers are prepared by professional schools through professional curricula. Colleges certificate or recommend to the state for certificates only those who meet the standards set by the state. Generally the standards are set high enough so that the college is expected to vouch for the applicant's scholarship, teaching competence, character, and fitness to direct impressionable boys and girls. Certification or recommendation for certification imposes upon the college an obligation to the state. For the college to send out, as qualified to teach, persons who are incompetent or unlikely to serve as a proper influence on boys and girls, is to betray that trust. Every person who assists in guiding the prospective teacher must share some of that responsibility. As a teacher you have an important part in the total task of guiding students.

No matter what kind of selection is practiced by teacher education institutions, or how many are weeded out, some students who are definitely unsuited for the profession are bound to get to student teaching. Others will need much sympathetic guidance to develop their personal qualities to minimum levels. You should be acquainted with the situation which exists and recognize that your students will often have problems that will require careful guidance.

College guidance people realize that a well-balanced, mature student may some day become disturbed as life moves on with its problems. On the other hand they believe that they should not knowingly encourage a young person into teaching if he has major emotional problems that he cannot readily overcome.

A very brilliant student teacher was assigned to a junior high school science class. He was interested in general semantics and science fiction. One day he came to class very late, somewhat disheveled in appearance and disorganized. The teacher noted that he had never done this before, but let it pass because his work was usually very good. Later his friends became concerned and took him to a psychologist. Arrangements were made for counselling, but before this could take place the boy went berserk in his rooming house area. His power to distinguish between fact and fiction had slipped away from him. He was removed from student teaching, given several months of medical care, and graduated without a certificate. He recognized that he had no business working with groups of people and has now made a vocational and personal adjustment. Without expert medical attention, it is not hard to imagine a far more serious result. For example, suppose that he had finished student teaching, received his certificate, started teaching and then had had the breakdown. We emphasize that serious cases like this are rare and we are very thankful for that fact. They are numerous enough, however, for all of us to be alert.

GUIDANCE IS A RESPONSIBILITY OF ALL WHO WORK WITH THE STUDENT

Personal guidance of students is coming to be recognized as a responsibility of the college. Many people share in the task. The college from which your student comes may have a personnel division which organizes the program and directs the faculty, especially the designated advisors, in carrying on the work. As a classroom teacher supervising students, the college does not hold you responsible for the personal guidance of serious cases. But your opportunities while working with a student are endless. You may be able to help him in attacking his problems by your kindly and helpful attitude and by patient, understanding conversations. There may be chances to pass along to the supervisor your observations, judgments, and even hunches, just for what they are worth.

Many times both you and the college advisors will find that more competent, more highly specialized and technically qualified persons are needed to work with you on certain student problems. Unfortunately, practically all colleges suffer today from a shortage of trained personnel workers who have the time, opportunity, and training to give students needed guidance. We could definitely produce more and better teachers if more consultant services were available. In the meantime we must all work together to eliminate the poorest risks and to assist the others to make the most of their opportunities for self-improvement.

SOME PERSONAL NEEDS OF THE PROSPECTIVE TEACHER

There have been many research studies of student teacher problems. One, asking students for their personal problems, resulted in the following list,[1] arranged in descending order of frequency:

Fatigue
Illness
Family conflicts

[1] Mary Frances Brinton, "Organization and Administration of Guidance Facilities in Teacher Education" (unpublished doctoral dissertation, University of Southern California, 1948).

Conflicts with training teachers
Visiting personnel
Future employment
Marriage relations
Transportation
Conflicts with friends
Conflicts with other members of the class
Clothing
Social inadequacy
Irritations caused by pupils
Finances
Religious pressures
Hunger

The experience of student teaching, itself, is a good time for the student to discover the importance of being able to deal with many types of situations. Here is the way one student described some of her discoveries:

I found I had personal problems also, such as, "Am I aggressive enough or do I actually fear these children?" Many questions popped into my mind concerning my own mental health and attitude. This made me stop and think about the teacher and what she must face in a day's work. She, first of all, must be a teacher, but then she must be a mother in many ways, or a politician selling herself to the parents and the faculty. She must be a judge of people and above all she must be a diplomat. As I watched several teachers I gained a new insight into their role. Never before had I realized what it meant to be a teacher from a mental point of view. Yes, your first requisite is to teach, but next to that is all that a teacher must be and have in her before she successfully performs her duties. She has obligations to her pupils, the families, the faculty, and the community in which she teaches. It is something I failed to grasp before, and now I realize better the whole significance of the role of the teacher.

This student had suddenly realized the many demands that teaching puts on the personality of the teacher and the skills in personal relations that are required. If you could do no more than sensitize your student to this need you would have done much. Because of the great stimulus to learning that exists during the period of student teaching, you often are able to assist him in surprising growth in personal development.

We are all interested in having students go out well-rounded in their development and possessed of broad competencies. By the time most of them reach student teaching, they already have identified themselves with some one or two areas of subject matter. In fact most high school and special area student teachers feel closer identity with subject matter than with the people with whom they associate in everyday life.

Some students have made a very genuine *identification* with boys and girls by the time they have begun student teaching, while others, unfortunately, still have that to do. Those students who feel more at home with subject-matter than with pupils may have difficulty in identifying themselves with pupils during student teaching.

One way to characterize these twin attitudes of identification with subject matter and with groups of pupils is to recall the analysis that has been made of the stages through which our thinking about teaching has gone. Once upon a time it was thought that, *All a teacher needed was to know Latin.* Later it was thought that *All a teacher needed was to know Johnny.* More recently it was recognized that, *To teach Johnny Latin, it was necessary to know both Latin and Johnny.* Now it is recognized that, *A teacher must know himself, in order to discover the effect of his personality and behavior on Johnny as he learns Latin.* Pupil response is determined to a large extent by the teacher or by the student. Therefore, the student cannot understand the pupil unless he understands himself. He must see himself in others and be aware of his own part in the pupils' response, in order to see the pupils more nearly as they are.

This leads to one further basic concept, *self-acceptance.* The student must have accepted himself and must understand his own motivation and behavior in order to be free to identify himself with others or to remain apart. His final security lies within himself. Self-knowledge is basic in knowing people and pupils as well. It is only as the young teacher can practice self-acceptance that his pupils can be helped in self-understanding and self-acceptance. Your student, as a student teacher, may make only a beginning at developing the attitudes, skills, and abilities that you hope for him to acquire. If you can help him assess his present status, set some reasonable goals, and make some progress toward them you will have contributed much toward his potential development.

YOUR ROLE IN PERSONAL GUIDANCE

Genuine friendship and informality are the keys to helping the other fellow. Your relations with your student need to include more than just school matters and school problems. When feasible and appropriate, invite your student into your home, or find a way to include him in a social group outside of the school. Talk about his college activities, politics, the affairs of the day, and items of general conversation, so that the student will feel he knows you as a person who is interested in him and enjoys his company. This is often a revelation to him, as indicated by this report a young woman student wrote on her observation of a group of teachers working together on pupil records.

Of course, the thing that really hit me was the informality of teachers when off to themselves. I had seen signs of it in a few isolated cases, but not before en masse. Concerning a few people I have in mind, I still can't believe it. Now I know what becomes of the college bores after graduation; they go right on. I am not given to blushing at a silly remark, especially when my friends have been pulling the same ones all year, but the sudden realization that the same thing goes on on the other side of the fence really struck me. I must say that seeing teachers relax changed my attitude toward the field, and to the good, I think. A sort of initiation, I suppose, which constitutes just one plank in the bridge between being a student and a teacher.

Sound advice always is to treat a student teacher as you would anyone else. To stare at him, to talk about him, to whisper to a colleague as he enters the room cannot help but create a sense of uncertainty and frustration. Treat the student just as if he had been there all his life, and regard him as a person, like yourself at an earlier age. Accept him at face value and attempt to create friendship. Above all else, do not try to fool a student. Most people know when they are not being told the truth, or the whole truth. Once you have established good rapport, he will usually respond well to your willingness to discuss any matter with him if your manner indicates your determination to work out the right answers together. His mistakes will do little harm if you view them as opportunities for learning instead of errors for which someone should be blamed.

One of the ever-present questions you have to face is whether to use a direct or indirect approach with a student problem. The attitude of the student usually gives the key. With experience, you will come to sense whether or not your relationship together is such that it is safe to talk about matters of personal development. It is a game in which the stakes are high. Deciding how to play your part is half the battle; finesse and skill in working with the student is the other major ingredient.

This business of having a major part in directing the life of another person is a really frightening responsibility. You could worry and stew around about it until you convinced yourself you never wanted to work with a student. Your best bet is to take a genuine interest in your student as a person and then to apply all the sound principles of human relations you know, backed up by sympathetic understanding and common sense. Regardless of what the student does we must keep our perspective, which the student in his immaturity sometimes lacks, and yet we must not dictate or become guilty of too much preaching.

From the field of vocational and industrial training comes a simple plan for action which you can adapt to your task here. The following contrasting patterns for handling a man who has made a mistake are taken from a course for supervisors developed by the Utah State Board for Vocational Education.[2]

[2] *Problems of Handling People*, Book Two, Supervisory Personnel Development Program (Salt Lake City: Utah State Board for Vocational Education, 1944), p. 13.

Bawling a man out	*Reprimanding a man*
1. Is done in anger.	1. Cool off. (But don't forget it.)
2. Is done in the presence of others.	2. Take him where you can be alone.
3. Is done without checking the facts.	3. Ask why. (Be sure it is deserved.)
4. Unjust things are said.	4. Talk straight. Don't mince words.
5. Discourages a man from trying.	5. Build him up: A. Include encouragement to do better.
6. Leaves a man resentful or beaten.	B. Leave him anxious to improve.

What changes would make the directions more applicable to the student teaching situation?

In industry, the criterion for the success of relations with employees is increased production. In student teaching the criterion is the student's success in working with boys and girls. You are in a key position to help the student evaluate his own growth through resulting pupil growth.

GUIDING THE STUDENT AS HE ATTACKS HIS PERSONAL PROBLEMS

We shall now take up a few areas of recurrent personal problems of students and try to analyze them. In each case a few suggestions will be given, but you will have much adapting to do. Both you and your student have an assignment in problem solving, different only in the direction of effort. Suppose your student has a problem which is worrying him. Here is a simplified plan of attack. Have him ask himself these four questions:

1. What am I worrying about?
2. What is the real cause of my worry?
3. Can I do something about it myself? How?
4. What kind of a plan can I make to start doing something about it?

SCHOLASTIC DIFFICULTIES

If your student carries college courses besides student teaching, he must plan his time to include both types of responsibility. You should be an interested observer but not pry into his scholarly activities. College courses are subject to peak loads of work and worry—papers, exams, and the like. These should be considered in your conferences, allowances should be made, and advance planning encouraged. Sometimes you may have to suggest that your student not become the victim of his own ambitions, and encourage him to pare his load down to size.

There are a small number of students who are best described as "school dull but life bright." They enjoy working with children and adults, know how to get practical things done, but are not much interested in abstract learning. Occasionally a student will do very well in student teaching but be in real danger of failing to meet the standards for graduation. It is a case of putting first things first and meeting the practical demands of a situation. You can help such a student see that a degree may not be the most important thing in life, but that it does have a real place. For example, your state may not certificate students without a college degree. The degree represents a badge of achievement, an emblem of status, and as such is worth the effort to finish the job. Some students have developed a complex about taking formal college examinations. You can help by taking time to discuss with your student the objectives of the course, ways to prepare for the examinations, and desirable attitudes. Competition gets pretty keen by the senior year in college, and a surprising number of students really do feel the pressure of scholastic requirements.

Economic problems

Sometimes actual hunger, lack of clothing, time and pressure of outside work, and uncertainty about where the next month's expense money is coming from become all-absorbing and devastating problems to college students. This may be, and usually is, an area of great sensitivity, and one that the student is very reluctant to discuss. Helping him directly is normally unwise and inappropriate. Occasionally you will be able to think of an indirect way to bring some aid.

When you do get a chance to discuss a problem that is rooted in economics, you must handle it very objectively. Be understanding but don't destroy his self-respect by allowing him to know that you feel sorry for him. Encourage him to take an objective attitude, too. He needs to think of his expenses as an investment in himself, an investment that must be completed before it can pay dividends. Now is the time to push the rest of the "deal" through to completion. Encouraging him to take definite action, such as to apply for a loan or a scholarship, or to drop out a quarter or semester and get the money to finish, is often as far as you can go. All of life's problems loom large to him at this time, and he may forget easily that this is just one stage in the whole sweep of a lifetime.

John Winter was a student teacher in science. His teacher found that he was trying to carry a full load of college work, including student teaching two periods a day, and work a full night shift in a factory. He was married and had a family to support. To him this seemed the only way to do it. Actually his planning became so poor that he was doing a miserable job in the classroom. His teacher talked with him calmly and encouraged him to study all the various possibilities of reducing his load, which was about to break his health as well as his college record. The idea of outside help was thrown into the hopper. He was encouraged to seek a college loan. He investigated, got the loan, cut down his hours of working, and began to plan his day more carefully. In about two weeks his classroom work was definitely improving and he was on the road to the successful completion of all degree requirements. In similar situations you can rely on your own maturity and perspective. By a steady, objective attack you can guide your students to lick many tough situations.

HEALTH AND OTHER PHYSICAL PROBLEMS

The suggestions of the last two sections are applicable here.

In addition, you have the very real responsibility of leading students to recognize that teaching is hard work and requires a great reserve of physical, intellectual, and, especially, emotional energy. Why many who do not have such physical characteristics think that teaching is the field for them is hard to fathom. In conference one time a very unpromising young man said, "Why, I have a bad heart, and the doctor says that teaching is the only thing I can do." Both the boy and the doctor needed a few additional facts of life. Certainly such persons should be guided out of the teaching profession.

Students may be little more than late adolescents when assigned to teaching, having led rather sheltered lives thus far. Some have not made the adjustments necessary, considering the physical limitations within which they must live. It is always interesting to consider those of your friends who have health problems and physical handicaps and to see which have accepted them and gone on to real achievement without worrying about them. A laboratory school teacher who had lost one leg on his twenty-first birthday went about his work with crutches. He was an unusually able teacher, and it is doubtful if many of his students would ever have mentioned his handicap in describing him, because he so effectively eliminated all concern and attention to it.

James Johnson was a student teacher in mathematics who had been in an accident and lost all but the thumb and stub of the index finger on his right hand. He was sensitive about it and could not be encouraged to forget it. He refused to use that hand at all in teaching geometry, keeping it in his pocket all the time he was in the room. His whole manner was one of fear, restraint, and an unnatural approach to the pupils. Real growth as a teacher was practically impossible. For two years he tried to teach that way, but the guilt of hiding something from his pupils was a millstone about his neck. Finally, he screwed his courage and began to use the stub. For the first time his personality began to blossom a little and he was able to get some satisfaction from his teaching.

It is no disgrace for any of us to face the facts squarely. Self-acceptance of our strengths, our weaknesses, our handicaps, and our ills (provided, of course, we do not brood about them) probably has as much to do with wholesome personality development as any single factor. We must practice this acceptance ourselves to set a good example for our students.

FAMILY CONFLICTS

Seldom can you do anything to remove the problem itself, but it often becomes important to discover the cause in order to understand the behavior of the student and his problems of adjustment with pupils. Family problems are of many types.

A special teacher, who has now made a very adequate adjustment in both her work and personal life, did just passable work as a student teacher. We all knew that she had ability, that she was trying, and that she was obviously "working under wraps." She was distant, blunt, and her shell was impervious to any ordinary means of penetration. Two years later she explained that her parents were just arranging a divorce at that time, and she now realized what a surprising effect that had had on her behavior. Now she could talk about it. As a student teacher she unwisely kept it all to herself. This gives us one cue. Get your student into a relaxed situation and steer the topic of conversation around to non-school affairs. Sometimes discussing the problems others have had and worked themselves out of will open the way. There are dangers in talking too much about your own background and problems, but a little at the appropriate time does help. After you get a clue to some real personal problem which is worrying your student, just mention incidentally a problem which you had at one time and managed to work your way through. This tends to put you in the same league with the student and builds one bridge which he can use in approaching you regarding his own difficulty. But very little of this, "Now when I was a student...."

The desires of parents for their children, the conflict of two cultures or the ideas of middle age and youth, the influence of

an unwholesome background, or the disgrace that comes from
a parent's indiscretions and bad name—all these and many more
may be at the bottom of tension, insecurity, and failure to adjust.
No set rules can be given for handling these problems, but experience based on good principles of human relations will sometimes work miracles. You should consult your supervisors and
principals, for you do not have to carry the load alone. Frequently, discovering causes and problems gives others a chance
to do much more than you can in helping the student solve his
own difficulties.

Mary Jones was majoring in social studies and Spanish. She
came from a family in modest circumstances and had had an
unhappy experience working in a factory before going to
college. She had a keen mind but had been dominated by her
mother, even to the extent of preparing to teach, which was her
mother's idea and not her own. A few periods working with
individuals and small groups convinced her teacher and supervisor that Mary was not cut out for teaching. She was tense,
inarticulate, subject to long awkward pauses, and received no
stimulation whatever from her pupils. It was painful to watch.
She was finally convinced that she should never consider teaching, although even the thought of this decision was paralyzing
to her, for she feared her mother's displeasure. Her mother had
sacrificed for years to send her to college and now she wouldn't
be able to teach when she got through.

Finally the supervisor wrote the mother a long letter, which
Mary herself checked for accuracy, explaining the situation.
Months passed, but just before graduation Mary came back and
asked if she hadn't better try to teach for at least one year to
satisfy her mother. Shaking her doubts and fears was harder the
second time than the first. Finally she was persuaded to go
home, take a brief rest and seek employment of a clerical nature.
Six months later she returned to the college, and was hardly
recognized. The tranformation, resulting from successful employment of a strictly clerical nature in the home office of a life
insurance company, was miraculous. She was poised and well

groomed, her voice was full, clear, and well modulated, and she was happy and enthusiastic about life. For the first time she was free from the dominance of home. The devastating effect of her former conflict was all too apparent by contrast.

Mary's case and those with other family problems could be duplicated by the thousands, and they illustrate the great importance of family background and family relationships. You will do well to be alert for the effect of problems of this type among your students.

PROBLEMS OF ROMANCE, MARRIAGE, AND CHILDREN

Seldom does a student talk about such problems until they become very acute or until the student feels that he knows you as a person. The demoralizing effect of too much time spent in courtship, or of the broken or breaking romance, is well known. This may be the explanation for a lot of things that happen, but you are usually powerless to do anything about them. Direct intervention usually makes matters worse, whether it be by parents, teachers, or friends. With the more frequent college marriages of today many student teachers are faced with making marriage adjustments at the same time as student teaching. This combination sometimes gives even the best a rough time. Occasionally marriages don't work; separations and divorces take place. The problem of an extra mouth to feed is frightening enough to most young folks, but to the student it is often terrifying. And the divorcée who comes back to finish a degree so that she can support herself and her children usually has her hands full.

These problems often leave the supervisor and the teacher in a real quandary. We mustn't baby these young people, because they will soon have to face both life and job conditions squarely as they go out to teach. Nevertheless they can't do the impossible. We must not let them feel sorry for themselves, but at the same time we can be considerate and help them plan for the best use of their time and effort. Sometimes we must try to protect them from their own ambitious plans.

One of the special problems which has been greatly increased in frequency since the war is that of pregnant women wanting to do student teaching. Usually the decision to allow one to start is not yours. You may, however, together with your principal, be faced with deciding whether she should go on and finish, or be asked to leave and return later. The problem is sharply accentuated with junior and senior high school students, and the matter of public relations becomes a very important factor. In some subjects, such as physical education, continuance may prove unwise from a physical standpoint alone. These problems are ones which give the student a chance to show his true maturity. Sometimes moral issues come to light. We can remain sympathetic and understanding but can not compromise on principle nor risk real injury to the pupils in our charge. There comes a time when tough choices must be made. We must not dictate what these choices should be, but we can talk the problems over in conference when the student brings them up. If a student asks for our advice, we must give our best suggestions for his consideration, and let him learn to get all the facts, weigh them, decide, and stand on the results of his decisions and actions. Very occasionally there are times when we should be considerate in granting a special request: helping work out special schedules, occasional trading of responsibility, and the like. In all fairness to the student himself this must not be too frequent, for then we would be guilty of indulging him in his own weaknesses.

Feelings of inferiority and social inadequacy

The truly pathological case is one for the expert, although you should learn to recognize the symptoms, assess the causes as far as they are revealed, and turn the problem over to the college. During the first few days a student is with you it is most difficult, indeed, to tell whether a case is truly pathological or not. Don't make snap judgments here. Go about the business of building up the student's skills and wait to see how fast he can develop.

The methods are the same as at any level from nursery school to senility. People can do pretty much what they think they can. Sound attitudes become a powerful force pushing them ahead. Your skill comes in being able to select tasks which your student can complete successfully and to follow each with another which offers a little greater challenge and success. The shy student needs concrete things to do at once to take his mind off himself. You can give him a sense of importance, a feeling that he is a necessary member of the team. When you can establish the necessary rapport and the student is beginning to do some things with ease, you can often get him to talk about his feelings. Your part is to listen with interest. From this point on the judicious use of encouragement and wise choice of activities should bring real progress. Also, at this point the student may identify some of the ingredients of his total problem. When this occurs you must be ready to pick out those which can be attacked directly, suggest ways to improve and help him accomplish his objective.

Again adapting from a pattern used in vocational training we suggest this plan:

Building Confidence

1. Greet the student cordially each day. Vary the greeting.
2. Discover the student's special interests.
3. Be sincerely interested in his problems. Be optimistic.
4. Encourage him to come to you and talk over his problems.
5. Help him do something about them if at all possible.

ACUTE PSYCHOLOGICAL DISTURBANCES

Your responsibility here is the same as with the previous problem-area of insecurity. Your job is to try to get the student working at his top capacity with the group. When the time has come for him to be teaching under his own steam and there is obviously something wrong that you can't discover, don't hesitate. Call the supervisor at once. With students who seem most ill at ease in teaching it may be wise to postpone taking notes in class. However, if at all possible, take time after class or after school to make extensive notes on his behavior. Even if you are entirely lacking in advanced training in psychology, your records may well give experts enough information to be of great help to them in working with the problem.

If you begin to suspect that your student has a mild or even a severe psychosis, you should be even more alert than usual to observe his behavior whenever you have the opportunity. Instead of trying to avoid him, see if you can't arrange for him to have more contacts with you and other staff members both in and out of school. By skillful planning you can steer conversation around to many different outside topics. Your efforts must not be too obvious, but you need to learn more about his background—from him, from his friends, and from the records. Your best role is to maintain complete objectivity with the college supervisor and director of student teaching, and help them get ready for any action which needs to be taken.

The tragedy of it is that even when we get a student encouraged to seek help we may not find professional service available except at excessive cost in time and money. Because you can often get closer to the student than anyone else, you may have the best chance to encourage him to seek professional advice.

Whatever happens, stay with the student teacher as long as he is working with pupils, but continue to try to help him develop as far as he can. Make your honest recommendation to the supervisor and let the college work out the final decisions.

INABILITY TO PRACTICE GOOD STANDARDS OF PERSONAL AND SOCIAL BEHAVIOR

This weakness appears in the generally immature students. Normally they have been warned previously not to become too familiar with pupils, especially of the opposite sex; to avoid dating pupils; to follow good standards of dress, decorum, and social relations; and especially to avoid playing favorites. In addition to the efforts of the college faculty, it is a good idea for you to emphasize these matters in an early conference and to point out any local attitude that is especially important. Despite all this, some students will persist because they simply don't have adequate habits and standards of personal behavior.

You ought not to let serious mistakes go very long before commenting on them. How to do it is often a real question. You have to size up the personality of the student to judge how direct you can be. The suggested scheme given earlier in the chapter for "Reprimanding a Man" gives you some clues. A positive approach is important. Be especially sure of your facts. If you are not sure of the real truth, ask about it in a friendly way. In any event, suggest the desirable procedure as calmly and objectively as possible.

If the indiscretions continue, you had better confer with the supervisor at once. If it seems wise for you to carry the matter further, set up a situation in which you can discuss the problem in private and point out reasons. Sometimes it will seem wise to ask the principal or a college advisor to talk with a particular student. Many students have heard and talked much about the restrictions which communities formerly often placed on the private lives of teachers. The tendency of youth is to react violently against what seems to them an encroachment on their personal rights. They fail to make a clear distinction between good professional behavior and personal freedom. Therefore, your most important job is to get across to your student the professional reasons why his effectiveness with the whole group drops when he is lax in obvious personal relationships. Students themselves sometimes work out interesting approaches to some of these problems. A young woman in a high school speech class reports her reaction this way:

I sincerely tried to show no favoritism in class, and I made an effort to give everyone an equal chance in taking parts in plays, etc. I made up a secret system of finding one likable quality about each student in order to prevent giving special attention to a few.

MAKING A DIRECT ATTACK ON CERTAIN LIMITING PERSONAL CHARACTERISTICS

There are a great many personal characteristics which are a handicap in teaching and which can be attacked rather directly.

After a particular point has been mentioned in a conference a student will often ask, "What can I do about it?" You need to be able to give real help at this point. Sometimes you can lead the student to figure out a program of action for himself. At other times it is better to give one or two concrete suggestions on which he can begin to work. A very large percentage of these more minor personal mannerisms and habits can be eliminated or improved if you can get good working conditions and stimulate sufficient effort in the right direction. We shall consider briefly several groups of these problems and you can work out suitable approaches to many others.

PROBLEMS OF VOICE, PRONUNCIATION, USE OF GOOD DICTION AND GRAMMAR, AVOIDING EXCESSIVE USE OF COLLOQUIALISMS AND SARCASM

We all have to work at these skills, and students often need specific help. Your part is to make your students aware of their specific weaknesses and help them to set up a plan for attack.

The average teacher, even without special speech training, can do much to help some students with voice problems. If you feel the condition is definitely pathological, you should refer the student to the nearest clinic. For the majority of cases, the problem is one of learning how to use the voice in a particular group situation. The use of a recorder will help, but its effectiveness is not great until the student can be entirely natural while it is running. The primary objective is to help the student develop a mental image of the way he wants his own voice to sound while he is using it. Sometimes you may want to increase or decrease the volume or pitch or both.

One of the most helpful procedures is to take the student into a vacant room and let him practice until he can recognize the difference between the way his voice sounds to him when wrong and right. Some students have had little dramatic experience and do not recognize the necessity for shifting on occasions from a conversational pattern to a more exaggerated or dramatic manner. Often a student feels less self-conscious when he asks a friend to help him rather than have you do it. When the difficulty is one of low volume and lack of forcefulness, it is a good idea to have him exaggerate greatly in his practice periods, for he will naturally relax more than he should when he gets back in front of a group.

The other suggested items were more specific. Get a clear recognition of the problem by discussing it objectively. Help the student plan a concrete attack. In some cases, it means going to a style manual or other proper source; getting the rules, facts, reasons, and principles; and, for the first time, learning them for a real purpose. Substitution of the proper usage for the poor one is the next step, and it sometimes takes a bit of doing. Encourage your student to work on only one or two things at a time and master them. It is very confusing to try to change a large number of patterns at once. Usage can often be corrected more quickly by practicing writing out the same ideas rapidly several times, but oral practice is excellent when it can be arranged and still simulate class conditions.

The psychology of adjustment to a *hearing loss* is one of the most difficult problems to be faced in teacher education. This seems all the more strange when one thinks of the many people who have made good adjustments to visual handicaps. Often it is necessary actually to compel a student to wear a hearing aid before he is allowed to work with pupils. You must show him that the criterion of success is the adjustment of pupils. Watch carefully for symptoms of limitation: poor use of his voice, failure to notice student disorder, and failure to hear student questions. Observation of very able teachers sometimes will help students sense a desirable level of performance for themselves. Actual auditory competence, not just lip reading, must come first, and then the student must become so engrossed in his enthusiasm for teaching that he forgets his handicap altogether. Students who must read lips can often succeed in special areas in which they work with only an individual pupil or two, but it is hard to imagine that they can do well with groups carrying on really diverse instructional procedures.

Personal appearance and good grooming

Young people are rather style conscious, with all their opportunities to know what is the accepted standard. The common problem is one of moderation and good taste. Often you need to suggest the appropriate pattern for particular situations. Occasionally students just don't have acceptable clothes and then you have to emphasize good grooming and suggest that they get help in selecting desirable outfits when they get out on the job. We want to avoid having our students described as a high school boy did his teacher: "Yes, Dad, she does have a powerful mind, but the rest of her shifts for itself."

It is strange that in modern America, with all of our soap and cleanliness advertising, there are students who are just plain unclean. What to do is a problem. Often it is carelessness and lack of planning in putting first things first. Sometimes it represents a limited home background with the attendant extreme sensitivity. Your approach will be determined by the personality of the student. Sometimes it may be risky to speak directly, although it usually works out all right if done tactfully and objectively. Sometimes it can be done indirectly by suggesting to the supervisor that the matter could be taken up in a general conference. Often a college advisor can do it more effectively than you can. Make it a matter of professional importance and see that the student becomes aware of the problem before he finishes student teaching.

Nervous habits in front of the class

Such habits are not important individually, but cumulatively they may detract greatly from the effectiveness of our work. This is one of the areas in which experienced teachers often get into a rut and even fail to notice the hold certain habits get on them. Pupils don't fail to notice! It is best not to say much about these habits to students during their early teaching, for other things are much more important. The cure is about the same as with many of the other matters—becoming aware of the problem and substituting more desirable behavior. There is this important difference. These habits are due to nervous tension and can be increased by becoming too conscious of the problem.

Discussion of these matters with students must be relaxed and friendly. Take up only one or two at a time. Carry through to the point of helping the student to devise things to do that will make the practice unnecessary. A student may get started tossing chalk, rattling coins in his pockets, massaging erasers, swinging pointers, and many other things without being conscious of what he is doing. Emphasize with him that the act is not wrong in itself, but that a habit may become fixed and may distract the pupils from the important job at hand. Occasionally it is necessary for some students to set up very specific behavior patterns for their hands, temporarily, during certain kinds of teaching. Thus they can break the habit and gradually develop more desirable behavior.

A special aspect of this whole problem is the verbal *mannerisms* that seem to appear in some form or other with most students. All of the above observations are appropriate here for such habits as the excessive use of "All right," "Uh," "Uh huh," and other particular words and phrases. If nervous tension is the cause, then they would be treated as above. Sometimes usage of certain words has a real purpose but is inappropriate if used in excess. For example, many teachers as well as students use "all right" for approval, also for finality (with a falling inflection) at the end of a sentence, and even for the initial words of each new start (with a rising inflection). Your task is to observe until you can see the use which is being made of the mannerism and attack it directly by substitution.

A good device for this process may be illustrated by the use of "all right" for approval of pupil response. Have the student list a dozen different, thoroughly acceptable words for this purpose, and put them on a 3 × 5 card in large letters. Decide ahead of time which way the card can best be used in a particular teaching situation, whether in a book, on the desk, in the hand, or on a clip board. When the student is sufficiently conscious of the problem he can pause before using the habitual response, take time to select a new one, use it and go on. Using a mechanical, formal approach like this just a few times may get the student started on a new and more varied response pattern.

FEARS

Throughout the book much has been said about the natural, emotional strain of student teaching. Normal fears can be expected and will usually disappear in due course. There are, however, three types of fears that are almost universally present and that should be attacked directly. Skillful handling on your part can reduce them to their proper proportions.

Fear of not knowing the answer to a student's question. Honest students know they don't know everything, but, like normal human beings, they don't like to admit it. Give them a safe, sure basis for replying to pupils in these situations. They should admit their lack of knowledge frankly, encourage pupils to want to find the answers for themselves, and help them get started. *They should be certain that they also get the answers* without fail before the next day, regardless of whether or not the pupils are successful. Not to know is no disgrace, but to continue not to know is dangerous as well as disgraceful.

Fear of making mistakes. The little ninth-grade girl who said, "I don't worry about making mistakes because I have talked things over with my mother and I know that I will have some embarrassing moments anyway," was practicing sound mental health. The pupils do respect knowledge and competence in student teachers but they regard "square shooting" as an even higher virtue. Encourage your students to be honest and forthright, to admit mistakes frankly, but to be so well prepared that they seldom have to do it. Students should understand that it is more important to recognize what is correct, to be able to find right answers, and to know how to use them, than it is to try to memorize every item of an area of subject matter. If the student is otherwise reasonably competent you should be able to relieve this fear by helping him develop a more comprehensive attitude toward his whole job. A related fear of running out of something to do is usually overcome quickly. Emphasis on adequate planning should take care of that.

Fear of criticism. Much is said about this in Chapter 13 on Evaluation. No one else can do so much to help the student develop a wholesome attitude toward his own growth as you can. Your own attitude is basic. Sympathetic, informal talks about how to develop one's capacities to their highest point is a sound approach. Harsh, occasionally unjust, or habitual criticism of a negative sort, even though well intentioned, may increase this fear until it becomes an insurmountable barrier to growth. Sympathy is the answer. Put yourself in the student's place and see how you would like to be treated, and how your teacher could have helped you relieve your fears.

"Nothing succeeds like success" is sound in any attack upon fears. Self-confidence comes from achievement and the realization that, "I have what it takes to do the job." You can really work magic through providing experiences in which your student can experience success and thus throw off the shackles of fear. And, even more, you can help prevent fears in future students. Encourage the student to emphasize the positive, especially when he is talking with younger students looking forward to student teaching. If, instead of regaling his friends with the horrors of student teaching, he would point out the opportunities and the thrills that come with success, he could help build desirable attitudes for those who will come along later.

PROMOTING ALL-ROUND STUDENT GROWTH

Personal problems do not exist in isolation. Every prospective teacher combines in one personality the personal, social, and professional aspects, and they must always be approached in relation to the whole. Throughout much of this book, however, we have discussed problems in isolation, to be more specific in helping you in your work.

Great satisfaction comes from watching things grow. This is the appeal that is so universal; the architect, the gardener, the engineer, the florist, the farmer—all experience this emotion. The appeal is even greater in working with people and it explains the hold which coaching, teaching, preaching, and healing have on people who do those things. To get growth in teaching ability in its narrow sense is exciting, but to be responsible for directing the successful development of a well-rounded person with growing, broad professional competence is even more challenging. This is the opportunity that comes to you.

To illustrate the interrelationship of these various aspects of personality let us take a case situation like this:

An elementary school of 500 children, with 12 rooms, is assigned a student for one-half day throughout the semester, to work with a self-contained sixth-grade class. The student, a young man named John Campbell, comes from a rural community, where his cultural background was very meager. His family is in average circumstances and is eager to have this first child go to college and succeed as a teacher. His scholastic rating is only average.

John has been on the job four weeks but has been unable to develop any very effective performance in the classroom. Let us look in on a three way conversation between John's teacher, his supervisor, and another teacher:

JAMES MacCAMPBELL (John's supervisor from the college): It occurred to me that if the three of us put our heads together we could work out some plans for helping John get going. I asked Polly Phillips to sit in with us because she has been unusually successful with students like this in the past. Miss Borden, why don't you review for us your reactions to John's work thus far.

ESTHER BORDEN (John is her first student): Well I haven't much basis for comparison because of my inexperience, but I feel that John has ability and an intense desire to succeed. He is normally shy, emotional, speaks in a very weak voice, and is really afraid of making mistakes. He works hard, tries to think over his work, takes advice very well, and really tries to act on suggestions. When he is in front of a group of pupils he is just like an athlete working out with wraps on; he never seems to be able to cut loose and get going. He dislikes neither his work nor the pupils, but he can't seem to get next to them either. I want to help him but I haven't figured out just what to do.

POLLY PHILLIPS (An old hand with student teachers in the grades): I think from what I have observed that you have done a good job of getting started with him—creating a climate in which he can grow. Of course, it appears that he may be slow blossoming, but getting a good relationship set up is most important. Take time for frequent conferences before and after school when you can talk about many things, not just school. If it works out all right maybe he could stay and have lunch here occasionally. He has to know that you are interested in him as a person and fully as much concerned over his professional success as he is. I don't have to tell you that unless the interest is really genuine, it won't help much.

MACCAMPBELL: Being a young, single teacher, Esther, it isn't quite as easy for you to work out that kind of a relationship with a young man as it would be if he were a young woman. I believe that you have made a good start and can continue along that line with profit.

PHILLIPS: Perhaps some of the rest of us can help along that line, Esther. Suppose that two or three of us go together and have our students out for dinner. That would make it easier for you and give us all a chance to know our students better.

BORDEN: That sounds like a good idea. I'd appreciate that.

MACCAMPBELL: I have been wondering how to get John to work more freely with children. Suppose you have him play with them in the gym and on the playground and take some responsibility for directing them. I imagine he can yell if he has to, and that might be a way to get him started to using his voice more naturally. What do you think Esther?

BORDEN: That ought to work, and I hadn't insisted too much on that yet. The children asked for a story yesterday. Would it help if we asked him to read to them a few minutes every day?

PHILLIPS: That works very well. The children are one's severest critics and he will be forced to read loud enough for them to hear when he gets to an exciting part. Is he musical?

MACCAMPBELL: I understand that he does sing some in his home choir. Maybe it would work to have the children ask him to sing some new popular song they would like to learn.

PHILLIPS: That usually works well because the same restraint that applies to speaking normally doesn't affect a singer. I wonder —the big thing is to really get John vitally interested in these children. If we could really stir his emotions up over them that would help to set him afire. Let's see, Mrs. Jones, the visiting teacher is going to be working out of our school several days next week. Do you have any cases up for her attention, Esther?

BORDEN: Oh yes, I do have three and two of them live down in the hollow by the factory. What did you have in mind?

PHILLIPS: Why don't you suggest that Mrs. Jones take him along on a couple of visits. That doesn't always do the trick, but John needs to become emotionally involved with these children. Contact with some of these home environments may act like a dash of cold water in his face.

BORDEN: That sounds like an idea worth trying. Up to now I've been afraid of discouraging him too much. So, I have been ignoring and making light of his mistakes. I thought maybe he would snap out of it without my having to really put the heat on him. Is that a sound approach?

MACCAMPBELL: Yes that's a sensible way to begin. You said in the beginning that John was analytical, and tried to use suggestions. What we should do now is to help you spot specific suggestions that can be carried out easily. If we can get him growing fast enough so he sees progress then it will be easy enough to correct some of these mistakes. The important thing is that the conferences be kept informal and that mutual respect be maintained throughout. You may have to watch to be sure that his keen analytical sense doesn't get hold of too many specific failures and get him started to brooding about them.

PHILLIPS: That's absolutely right! The best way to insure that is to have him do a lot of work with small groups. He'll soon begin to feel close to those kids, and see them grow. When he gets a little flush of success the children will begin to warm up to him without our doing anything. He is good enough so that he can be left alone with groups of four to six in reading work, in numbers, construction activities for a unit, and even a trip with a committee. This is one of the best ways to get him over that shyness with boys and girls and get him ready for real leadership with the whole group.

BORDEN: I hadn't done any of that until yesterday. He went out with a group to get the materials for our next construction project. He was actually talking with Kenneth in the hall after the group was dismissed for recess.

PHILLIPS: That's the way it starts. I believe you have laid a sound beginning. Come in and visit with me whenever you want to think over your procedure, Esther. There are no certain best activities for student teachers. But for my money, for John and many another like him, real friendship counts for the most. Friendship and mutual respect. I count among my most cherished friendships some of the young people who have done their student teaching with me.

SUGGESTED REFERENCES

Burr, James B., Lowry W. Harding, and Leland B. Jacobs, *Student Teaching in the Elementary School.* New York: Appleton-Century-Crofts, Inc., 1950. Chapter I, "Getting Started as a Student Teacher." Points out personal factors significant in student teaching. Chapter XIII, "Making the Most of Conferences."

Grim, Paul and John Michaelis, *The Student Teacher in the Secondary School.* New York: Prentice-Hall, Inc., 1953. Chapter IX, "Solving Your Own Problems."

Schorling, Raleigh and Max Wingo, *Elementary School Student Teaching.* New York: McGraw-Hill Book Company, Inc., 1950. Chapter XVI, "Professional Growth and Personal Advancement."

13

Evaluating Student Growth

YOU HAVE A GREATER CHALLENGE THAN THAT FAC-
ing any other person who works with the student. Why? Because you are his constant counselor in assisting him *on the job*
in bringing his past experiences, his understandings, his attitudes, and his habits to focus upon learning to become a successful teacher.

In guiding student growth, there must be evaluation. This
is necessary to determine direction or to obtain focus. For example, in all of his work the student must be asking you and
himself, "How can I improve?" When specific need for improvement or growth is isolated, such as need to use more imagination in planning learning experiences, direction or focus is determined. The student is now able to concentrate upon an area
in which improvement is essential. Thus growth takes place, but
at a rate and to a degree dependent upon student ability.

A planned program of evaluation should begin when the student enters the teacher education curriculum. With skillful and
sympathetic guidance, most students can have a good attitude
toward evaluation and some skill in self-evaluation by the time
they enter student teaching. You can pick them up here and
guide them along until evaluation becomes a strong supporting
force, constantly directing the student's efforts toward improve-

ment. However, you must take each student where you find him in attitudes toward and skill in evaluation of growth.

In any student teaching program, there are four areas that must be clarified before you can proceed with confidence in evaluation with student teachers. The remainder of the chapter will be given to the clarification of each:

The purposes of evaluation in the student teaching program.
The evaluation program.
Use of procedures and materials in evaluation.
Special problems in evaluation.

THE PURPOSES OF EVALUATION IN THE STUDENT TEACHING PROGRAM

When the student comes to you, his ideas about why you evaluate his activities may be very unlike those you have in mind. He may think of evaluation as a method by which you arrive at his grade for student teaching. His work in each college course preceding student teaching may have been evaluated for the purpose of determining a grade. Most college students, as a result, have been conditioned to become very grade-conscious. Further, the idea may be prevalent among the students of the college that a grade of average or below is not likely to result in a good job the first year in the field. Students are very conscious of grades, and they have reason to be.

You will have a selling job to do to get the student's focus off the grade and on the real purposes of evaluation. This cannot be done by discussion de-emphasizing the grade. Neither can it be accomplished by emphasizing the purposes of evaluation. Your best approach is effective use of evaluation to achieve purposes set up by the college, by you, by you and the college, or by you, the college, and the student.

Such purposes may vary widely from school to school and from teacher to teacher. However, we feel that those reviewed below should be included in all lists.

PROMOTE DEVELOPMENT OF WHOLESOME STUDENT ATTITUDES TOWARD
   EVALUATION

The attention of the student should be focused upon the activity, not the student. For example, when discussing with a student the lesson that he has just finished directing, you should start with the outcomes of the lesson. That is, first you would analyze the results of the teaching. Then you could ask why. "Why was Dick's attitude enthusiastic today?" "Why did most of the pupils miss item 12 on the test?" You can work back to the student as one of the causal factors. Dick might have been enthusiastic because the student complimented his neat desk just before class. The pupils may have missed item 12 because the student used a phrase not known to the pupils.

Whenever possible, the procedure suggested above should be used. In the beginning the student's concern is with himself, even though you try to get his focus shifted to learning experiences. Also, the student is concerned with the grade that he will receive in student teaching and may have difficulty in getting the idea that the teacher is more concerned with his growth than with an accumulation of data to be used in determining the grade. The student must develop purposes in evaluation that will contribute to growth. In other words, he must have definite purposes for being evaluated by you and others and for growth in self-evaluation. If these purposes do not exist, but he develops a defensive attitude, there is little that you can contribute toward his growth.

OBTAIN STUDENT UNDERSTANDING OF YOUR PURPOSES IN EVALUATION

Students discover soon that emphasis is placed upon growth. Each day, you evaluate the learning or growth resulting from the experiences provided the pupils. In evaluating pupil growth, you ask, "How might I have done a better job with Jim, Nancy, Bill?" or "What caused lack of pupil interest?" Thus, you are continuously evaluating your effectiveness as a teacher and trying to determine how you can improve.

This procedure may be a real contrast to the student's previous experience in evaluation. In other words, he may be conditioned to think of evaluation as "What grade did I make?" Evaluation in student teaching is always concerned with student growth and, therefore, his concern must become not only, "How well did I do?" but also, "How can I improve?" The last question makes the real difference in student teaching.

DEVELOP STUDENT UNDERSTANDING OF BASES FOR EVALUATION

The college with which you work may have a list of competencies, experiences, and characteristics that you are expected to use in evaluating student growth. Other colleges may have brief forms that are used in reporting student growth to the advisor, supervisor, and/or placement officer. Also, you may have a list of requirements that you expect student teachers to meet in terms of growth, attitudes, habits, and experiences; or you may set no list of competencies, but, rather, evaluate the student's growth as he progresses through the term in assuming responsibility in the major areas of teacher activity. (See Chapter 1.)

Regardless of the bases used in evaluating and eventually reporting student growth, you are obligated to inform the student specifically concerning the basis or bases used. For example, if you use a competency list such as suggested in Appendix F, the student should receive a copy of the competencies and an explanation concerning how the list is to be used. This can be done in one or several conferences with the student as he starts assisting you. It also will help you eventually in contributing toward student self-evaluation. He will have in his hands a definite list of competencies in which he is expected to demonstrate growth. These he can use as a guide in seeking experiences that should contribute to the development of competencies. Further, he can see "how he is doing" by referring to the list of competencies. As you go along, you both can agree upon the competencies in which growth is commendable. These are checked so that he knows what he has done well and what needs improvement.

MAKE EVALUATION REALLY CONTRIBUTE TO STUDENT GROWTH

How successful are you in getting the student to look at evaluation objectively? Does he continue to fear evaluation, to show a defensive attitude? With each student you must determine how you can most effectively use evaluation procedures to promote growth. The student who feels that he already knows all the answers is one problem and the student who feels that he makes a mess of everything is quite another.

Those of you who have worked with students know that a different approach is needed for each. Most of them really want to know wherein growth is needed, and they want to know specifically. They are sincere in wanting to know, but they may not like the way you tell them or don't tell them. The following statements are illustrative:

The suggestions given me were always extremely good and were made in a very tactful manner.

There could have been more suggestions for improvement but I believe to find some of it for myself was good.

The teachers wrote criticisms of our work for us to read, and held private conferences for discussion of our weaknesses.

At times I would have preferred more concrete remedies, but in the long run generalities and means of self-seeing the problem and working it out were more beneficial.

There was a little too much self-evaluation. The teacher didn't really give enough concrete suggestions which might have helped a great deal. General suggestions only.

The teacher could have helped by being more critical. I was never given constructive criticism.

One time only was I ever given any suggestions.

It seemed that things that were poor were pointed out to me, and then left up to me to improve.

Comments were infrequent and often given in front of children and parents.

The teacher told me what I could do to improve but didn't tell me if I was or wasn't improving.

The teachers never really gave specific help. Sometimes they told us what to do, but not how to do it.

It would have helped if we had definite times when we were required to come in for personal talks.

Even more difficult yet may be your problem in getting the student to evaluate himself, and in promoting student growth in this respect. Two factors are involved here. First, the student may not be able to determine the quality of his performance in the activities in which he participates or assumes responsibility. For example, he may not recognize that he was more successful in working with the Science Club today than a week ago. This ability comes slowly for us all. More difficult in development is his ability to determine *why* his performance was more effective in one lesson than in another.

Second, the student may recognize differences in quality of his performance and be able to determine why one performance was superior to the other but not be able to face the facts. Some cases may be impossible to deal with. If so, the major purpose in evaluation—student growth in self-evaluation—cannot be realized.

THE EVALUATION PROGRAM[1]

We are suggesting five principles that should serve as a guide to anyone in planning and conducting an evaluation program in student teaching. These principles determine not only *what* procedures are to be used but also *how* the procedures are to be used in achieving the purposes proposed above. Specifically, it is not that you evaluate student growth during a conference period but how you proceed in the conference that determines the effectiveness of the evaluation.

[1] See also, *The Evaluation of Student Teaching,* Twenty-eighth Yearbook (Lock Haven, Pa.: Association for Student Teaching, 1949); and Pearl Merriman and Gladys Fair, *Helping Student Teachers through Evaluation* (Lock Haven, Pa.: Association for Student Teaching, 1953), 36 pages.

Principle 1: The evaluation program in student teaching is, for the most part, informal and cooperative in nature. Most of the attention to evaluation will be given by the two persons working continuously together—you and the student.

Reference has already been made to the need for a "we" relationship between student and teacher. Any effective program in evaluation makes this relationship imperative. No matter what procedures are used by you or others, they cannot be used effectively unless the student senses sincerity of purpose on your part.

Principle 2: The evaluation program is continuous. Students, in general, are concerned with their growth. To repeat, this is evidenced by their questions, "How did I do?" and "How can I improve?" If Principle 1 above is achieved, your student will most likely ask the first question at the beginning of the student teaching period; but, later in the period, he will ask the second after each participation or responsibility experience. He wants continuous evaluation, not just at mid-term and then at the end of the term or semester.

Principle 3: Student evaluation is specific. Students generally want to know specifically what they did well, what was not well done, what they might better have done, and how they can improve. Expressions such as, "You did fine today," "It will probably go better tomorrow," "Get more pupil participation," and "Don't worry about it," contribute little or nothing to student growth unless accompanied by specific suggestions.

Principle 4: The evaluation program, for the most part, is focused upon student growth in self-evaluation. For the student to graduate and enter the profession without learning to evaluate his performance as a teacher would be pathetic. Thus, most procedures you use day-by-day are of such a nature that they can be used both now and later by the student. His future growth as a teacher may depend upon his learning to use evaluation procedures while with you.

Principle 5: The evaluation program makes provision for student and teacher record of student growth. Both student and teacher keep records of the student's growth in all activities of the teacher. You and the student need the written record of his specific needs for growth and the competencies in which he needs improvement. This record can be extremely valuable to both of you at the time of final evaluation.

USE OF PROCEDURES AND MATERIALS IN EVALUATION

In keeping with the above principles and the purposes of evaluation reviewed earlier, we are suggesting a minimum program that should produce good results. You could probably adapt the procedures proposed in this program even though you had had little experience with students and suddenly found yourself with the major responsibility for evaluation.

1. Preparation for evaluation.
2. Student records and reports.
3. Use of conferences in informal evaluation.
4. Rating scales used to judge a single lesson or one area of teacher activity.
5. Anecdotal records.
6. Student-student evaluation procedures.
7. Pupil evaluation of student teachers.
8. Mid-term evaluation and conference.
9. Final evaluation and grading.
10. Final Conference.
11. Recommendations for the placement office.

No matter what college you work with or what your specific responsibility for evaluation is, you need to be familiar with all of the above procedures, and you will use most of them. The procedures suggested take time, but any thorough job of evaluation takes time. Any of the procedures suggested, however, can be used effectively even though you have had little or no experience with them. You should become thoroughly familiar with each type so that you can use it effectively.

Preparation for evaluation

You will want to secure adequate information about your student so that you know him as a person and as a prospective teacher. Factors such as limited experience with boys and girls, limited home and personal advantages, unhappy employment adjustments, very sheltered background, economic insecurity, emotional problems, and many others generally have an effect on the student's behavior in student teaching. Knowing the facts gives you, first of all, reason to be very considerate and understanding. Secondly, it may give you, or others with whom you consult, a basis for assisting the student to improve.

Student records and reports

Patterns in this procedure vary greatly, especially if the student is on- or off-campus. For example, at Florida State University the requirements set up for students who are assigned off-campus (called an "internship" in Florida) for seven weeks full-time in a cooperating school included the following:

1. Seven weekly reports, accounting for thirty to forty hours each week, whether spent in observation, preparation, or in such things as faculty meetings or other significant happenings.

2. Daily diary.

3. Three progress reports to be filed with supervisor at end of second, fourth, and sixth weeks.

4. Three analyses of special problems—due the third, sixth, and last weeks.

Colleges may require or strongly recommend some kind of a chronological diary or "log." Instructions vary, but this record can well be divided into several different sections: day-by-day records, plans, general information about the school and community, studies of class and pupils, prepared teaching materials, test materials, illustrative materials, evaluations, and any final evaluation by teacher or supervisor, or copy of one by the student himself. For many students the log becomes a gold mine of material for that first year of teaching.

The report should be comprehensive enough to keep the

student alert to his own responsibility for evaluating his work as he goes along and still not be too formal and burdensome. Special studies of pupil learning problems, the development of a resource or other unit, or other special assignments can give the student a fine opportunity for growth in recording pertinent data. In all records and reports made by the student, you need to work very closely with him at first to make sure that records are concise and pertinent. The common problem is that records and reports may become a mass of written detail and therefore a tedious waste of student time. Further, the student must see value in the records and reports.

THE USE OF CONFERENCES IN INFORMAL EVALUATION

Conferences can be the core of the whole evaluation process through which all the other activities are brought into focus and made effective. If at all possible, you should dignify these conferences in the eyes of your students by having a definite time and place for them. Failure to do this led a business education student to comment:

There were not enough individual conferences with the teacher. She told me at the end of the quarter that I should have asked when I wanted one. I wish that I had known this sooner.

In one of the first conferences, you can ask the student to observe the next period that you teach and be prepared to evaluate some particular aspect of your teaching. Make it clear that you are not infallible and that constructive criticism can help anyone. When something fails to work out as you desired, suggest in conference that you were disappointed in the results. Ask the student if he saw anything you might not have observed, or if he has any ideas that might help remedy the situation. Discuss the problem freely and frankly. This procedure should be used extensively during the student's first few weeks with you. Having established a sound cooperative basis for evaluating your work, you are ready to do the same for the student's first efforts.

It is only human nature for us to wait with bated breath until we are told how badly we performed the first time. But the student may be even more tense than you would expect. Therefore, it is essential that you place attention on the learning situation, the parent conference, the committee project, or whatever is in question. As stated earlier, the student must be helped to analyze the activity in which he has participated. You might ask, "Did the situation proceed as you anticipated?" Following this review of what actually developed in the lesson or other activity, you and the student are ready to consider *why*. This brings the discussion back to causal factors, such as teacher, references used, and setting. You can then help the student decide how the many causal factors involved might be changed, including what he might do differently. At this point, the student must have developed confidence in his ability to proceed on the next day and confidence in evaluation conferences as a real help to him.

As the student develops confidence in himself and in your sincerity in evaluation, you can shift more and more of the responsibility for evaluation of the activity and his performance in the activity on him. You can now say to him, "You don't need to wait for me to help you evaluate each situation. Try to analyze it yourself from beginning to end. When you have analyzed the situation and decided how to proceed next time or where you need some help, come and ask me." For instance, following a lesson taught by you, you might say, "I wonder if that was the best way to get the class back on the track in their discussion?" "What suggestions do you have about it?" This procedure may put you on the spot but it assures the student of your sincerity.

Another very important ingredient of successful conferences is the way in which suggestions are made. If at all possible, they should be positive, not negative. They should be sincere attempts to help; very specific at first, but often just enough to lead the student toward his own solution. Many of your comments can include a question which still allows the student to carry the ball and call the signals. For example, you could say,

"If you were to give the pupils a part in selecting the activities for the rest of the unit, how would you go about it?" Such a comment suggests an approach but leaves the student free to work on the specific procedures to be used. Informal discussion from there on makes a cooperative attack on the problem very natural.

Conferences following student activity need to be carefully timed. He needs time to form judgments, but delayed conferences may reveal that he has forgotten essential detail. If possible, conferences should be held with the student so that he has time to re-plan following the evaluation.

RATING SCALES USED TO JUDGE A SINGLE LESSON OR ONE AREA OF TEACHER ACTIVITY

Such scales exist in profusion throughout the country, but most of them are constructed locally by individuals or committees. Probably no single part of the whole evaluation process has been given consistently greater attention than these forms. Three suggestions may be of help to you in selecting and using rating scales:

1. The emphasis should be on reporting and evaluating the results obtained with the pupils and the behavior of the student in the classroom rather than on purely arbitrary judgments, such as excellent, good, fair, poor, and the like, on personal traits and professional competencies.

2. Most forms can be constructed or adapted for use as tools for student self-evaluation.

3. The informal, descriptive report is more helpful to you than most of the rating forms.

A one-page form can be used very effectively in recording impressions of a simple lesson or observation. A sample of this type of form for use in mathematics is reproduced on p. 299. You will note that a number of individual items are suggested under four major headings. Only three columns are used for checking because the major purpose is to promote growth, not to secure fine differentiation. The bulk of the form is left open for reports of specific events, descriptive anecdotes, and suggestions for improvement.

In using this form the teacher keeps a supply on a clipboard. Whenever he decides to record his impressions of a lesson he puts a carbon sheet between two forms. On any one day he might want to check 10 to 15 items, seldom more. By writing descriptions, reactions and suggestions on a few of these he has information for later conferences. Eventually the student gets the original and the teacher files the carbon by date in the student's folder. Students come to want such an evaluation and will ask for them at the close of class. The whole collection makes an excellent basis for mid-term and final evaluation.

Rating scales designed for special subjects have the advantage that special student responsibilities can be included. For example, in many subjects there is equipment to be prepared, checked, and put away. Special activities such as supervising shower rooms, library collections, projection equipment, rest periods, or recess activities can be included as needed. Another approach is to design rating forms for specific purposes; for example, the directing of an activity program, teaching through group work, coaching, conducting an excursion, and many others.

Finally, one word of caution. Rating scales can aid the teacher in organizing judgments systematically, but they are neither the end product nor even the main show in a program of evaluation. Good forms and good ratings serve as some of the raw material out of which a planned program of evaluation for growth is developed.

MID-TERM EVALUATION AND CONFERENCE

Two desirable goals make these procedures a must. A semi-official evaluation is necessary to help a student attach proper importance to the whole series of judgments both he and his teacher have been making. Verbal stock-taking and daily suggestions seldom have the necessary punch that can be gained easily by a well-planned mid-term evaluation. Occasionally a

ANALYSIS OF A MATHEMATICS LESSON

Name: Date: Subject: No. in class: Topic:

ROUTINE AFFAIRS	GOOD	FAIR	POOR	SUGGESTIONS AND COMMENTS
Ventilation				
Lighting				
Appearance of the desk				
Collection and distribution				
TEACHING PROCEDURES				
Presentation, new material				
Assignments				
Planning of lesson				
Pupil participation				
Teacher-pupil balance				
Use of illustrations				
Skill of questioning				
Measuring achievement				
Economy in use of time				
Use of drill and review				
Development of ideas				
Handling of pupil questions				
Methods of helping pupils				
Meeting individual differences				
Methods of creating interest				
Clarity of explanations				
Emphasis on important facts				
Local applications				
Attainment of aims				
Evaluation of day's teaching				
CLASSROOM MANAGEMENT				
Promotion of self-discipline				
Student cooperation				
Industry of each pupil				
Use of equipment				
Use of outside material				
Level of pupil control				
PERSONAL				
Voice				
Habits: hands, face, etc.				
Appearance				
Mastery of the day's work				
Language usage				
Breadth of knowledge				
Patience				
Habits of accuracy				
Writing on the board				
Initiative				
Knowledge of current affairs				
Pupil analysis				

Rated by

Developed by Philip Peak, University School, Bloomington, Indiana.

student will even make that concrete suggestion himself, as this one did: "Perhaps an interview with my teachers at mid-term in which they had told me how I was doing and their reasons would have been helpful."

In the second place, when confronted by unmistakable facts, the student is more inclined to reveal his own feelings and personal knowledge, which have an important bearing on his growth. In this way a solid basis can be built for the remainder of the student teaching assignment.

Ideally, descriptive statements on three to five major aspects of the student's work in which he has shown most growth and about the same number in which he shows least growth are most helpful to the student. The form used should include the basis for evaluation reviewed with the student at the beginning of the term. The student can be given the form and asked to prepare a report on himself in a few days. You agree to do the same. Then, at the appointed time, you and the student hold a conference, allowing at least a half-hour to an hour. You can go over the two ratings informally, agree on some, reconcile differences on others, select objectives for future efforts, and lay general plans. Whether your revised mid-term evaluation of the student is made a matter of record in the office is of little consequence compared to the process itself.

Timing the mid-term evaluation is a problem. Since students differ in their rate of growth, some latitude is desirable. You should pick a time after the student has really begun to show his capacity. Most teachers work within the limits of a fairly well-defined college policy, but even though the college does not require such a procedure, the teacher himself can prepare a less formal evaluation, followed by a conference.

In colleges in which grades are highly emphasized, it may be necessary to give some indication of the student's progress in grade form. One easy way to do this without committing yourself too definitely is by the use of a "grade range to date." One director of student teaching proposed that the first letter grade represent an average of the work done to date, and that the second letter grade represent an estimate of the best work done up to that time. In practice this resulted in such reports as: C to B—, or B— to B+, or B to A—. Students appreciated this type of report and the grade range was usually broad enough to allow comfortable latitude for the final grade. (Mid-term grades for special problems are reviewed in the next section of this chapter.)

STUDENT-STUDENT EVALUATION PROCEDURES

If you have more than one student at a time, or if there are several who can work closely together, they can often help each other. Many students will take judgments and suggestions from their close pals more quickly than they will from you; and, what is more important, may do more about the suggestions.

As an approach, have two or more students observe together while you teach. The observations of your teaching will be helpful in their evaluation of self and each other later. When student confidence is established they can use the same procedure in evaluating each other. Many of the attention graphs, pupil participation charts, checklists of routine items, and other specific aspects of teaching performances are well adapted to use by students as a part of their growth in evaluation. Eventually, with some adaptation, the student can use some of them on himself or have another student use them as he teaches. Your student will have gained real growth when he can invite the supervisor, methods teacher, or other teacher or student to watch him carry out a difficult process. When we are able to ask for constructive criticism we have achieved some measure of maturity.

PUPIL EVALUATION OF STUDENTS

It would be extremely unwise to say that every student should have a group of pupils evaluate him, particularly if there are many students assigned in the same school. This can be a dangerous procedure. Before using it, you should decide whether or not undesirable pupil attitudes may result. It should never be used if you think there is a possibility that it may jeopardize student growth. Occasionally students will accept from pupils suggestions which you have been unable to get across. Also, if there are sharp differences of opinion between the supervisor and yourself, pupil ratings may help to substantiate a particular judgment. These forms are easy to administer; all that is necessary is to give the pupils an honest statement of the purpose behind the procedure and seriously request their cooperation. Long experience has demonstrated that wisecracking answers are so few as to be negligible, and they are ordinarily very obvious.

Most rating forms take only a few minutes to fill out. They should be simple enough for younger pupils to use easily, and they should include space for pupils to make concrete suggestions. The example which is reproduced on p. 303 has been adapted from one developed and used for many years at De-Pauw University. You will note that it permits one general evaluation, the noting of strengths and weaknesses, and has a place for suggestions. You can readily adapt these forms to your own particular needs.

Anecdotal Records

These records can help you gain perspective on the progress of a student over a period of weeks. They can help you as you try to stimulate growth on specific points because you can refresh the student's memory and help him identify particular situations. A succession of such reports makes a sound basis for a mid-term or final rating. Although it is hard to collect enough pertinent data and harder still to use it skillfully, anecdotal information is often about the only evidence you have of student growth.

Many teachers dislike the use of a rating form for day-by-day recording of student performance and use other ways of collecting data. One of the simplest and most effective ways is to use a ring notebook for each student. Cut a piece of carbon paper to fit properly. Then, each day when you want to record anecdotal evidence, suggestions, or comments, simply date a page and start in. These memoranda are very useful in conferences,

Name of Student Teacher   Date

PUPIL RATING OF STUDENT TEACHERS

In general, how good a teacher is this student teacher? In the blank opposite the word RATING below, place a 1, 2, 3, 4, 5, 6, or 7 to indicate what you think would be a proper rating for this student teacher on this scale: (1) as poor as any teacher could be; (2) a little better than the poorest; (3) not quite as good as the average; (4) like the teacher you consider average; (5) a little better than the average; (6) not quite as good as the best; (7) as good as any teacher ever is.

RATING _____

In order to help this student teacher discover his strong and weak points, read the following list all the way through. Then check in the left hand column those characteristics in which you think he is *especially strong,* and in the right hand column those in which you consider him *rather weak. Please don't check any item on which this student teacher appears to be about as most teachers are.*

Especially Strong		Rather Weak
____1.	Is a "square shooter" and plays no favorites	1.___
____2.	Knows his subject and can really answer questions	2.___
____3.	Has work well planned with interesting things to do	3.___
____4.	Has a pleasant, easily understood voice	4.___
____5.	Helps us when we need it, but not too much	5.___
____6.	Makes class interesting with a variety of activities and materials	6.___
____7.	Gives us plenty of chance to take part and do things on our own	7.___
____8.	Is always cheerful and friendly; never overbearing or "snooty"	8.___
____9.	Is forceful and firm, but not too strict	9.___
___10.	Explains things clearly, and is patient if we fail to get it	10.___
___11.	Has many worthwhile interests in life, and shares them with us	11.___
___12.	Is neat and clean in appearance	12.___
___13.	Is willing to face the facts and admit his own mistakes	13.___
___14.	We really learn a lot when we have this student teacher	14.___
___15.	Is quick to catch on to new and different situations	15.___
___16.	Always dresses in good taste	16.___
___17.	Can be depended upon to do what he says he will do	17.___
___18.	Knows the practical side of his subject and helps us to see it	18.___
___19.	Has self-control; doesn't lose his temper or become excited easily	19.___
___20.	Has no annoying habits or mannerisms that bother us	20.___
___21.	Uses good English	21.___
___22.	Is able to see our side of a problem	22.___
___23.	Has a sense of humor and isn't afraid to laugh when things are funny	23.___

What do you like best about this student teacher?

As a means of helping this student teacher, please suggest one or two things that you think he could do to become a better teacher:

Please do not sign your name to this rating sheet.

and the original can be given to the student by just tearing it out of the book. Be sure no such comments are handed to the student unless reviewed carefully with him later. The carbon copies of your notes are in chronological order and give a quick review of the development of the student during the term.

FINAL EVALUATION AND GRADING

In many institutions, two types of final records are made: a report for the placement office which will go into the credentials, and a final evaluation for the official records. In some colleges this latter rating has been discarded and only a grade is recorded. The function of the report for placement is clear and it will be discussed later. The final rating can serve a good purpose if it is discussed at length with the student before it is reported to the proper college official. The student, if you have been successful in the ongoing evaluation program, will have a good idea of what his grade will be. But he has a right to know from you what grade is contemplated and why. Teachers who ask students to submit a final written evaluation and grade for their work very often find little disagreement between student and teacher. This, of course, requires an excellent working relationship between student and teacher.

Grading student teaching is difficult at best, and the whole process has been a matter of great controversy for many years. Students get the idea that a low grade, even a "C," is the same as a failure and that it will keep one from ever getting a job. Unfortunately, some employing officials act as if that were literally true. It is often argued that students are highly selected by the time they complete student teaching and, therefore, high grades are justified. The teachers and supervisors who know their students very well personally and who appreciate their very generous assistance often find it hard to use a realistic grade range for marks in student teaching.

Teachers should investigate grading practices of the college with which they work before they assume final responsibility for grading their students. Patterns vary so that little guidance can be offered. Using the common letter system we shall venture some suggestions that may give you some aid as you study your problem.

"F" may be reserved for those rare individuals who have been unwilling to accept advice to transfer out of the teaching curriculum, and who are obviously and unquestionably not safe risks to direct the learning of children. The judgment of several people should always be secured in making this decision.

"D" should be reserved for those students who clearly are not ready for certification and must be required to take another term or semester to bring their competency up to an acceptable level.

"C" should be the grade for those who display about the same number of weaknesses as strengths. Their major disabilities would be few and major competencies would also be few. You can't say that they are strong and neither can you say that they are weak enough to be a serious risk.

"B" should be given those who have made real growth, who have more major competencies than liabilities, but who have few outstanding abilities.

"A" should be reserved for those students who really have shown superior growth and achievement. These students should have many outstanding qualities and only one or two liabilities of any consequence. These are the students whom we judge as ready to do successful work immediately in almost any situation.

FINAL CONFERENCE

A final conference proves to be a very satisfying experience for most students. When the work is all over, the grades are in, and all books, materials, logs, and reports are properly returned, the principals in this drama can sit back, relax, take stock, and look to the future. This conference should be concerned chiefly with follow-up, as discussed in Chapter 14.

The student needs to consider what he can do to improve his competencies before he graduates, or before he starts to teach, and finally may need suggestions for making his adjustments on that important first job. Sometimes this final conference comes after the student has already signed up to teach in a certain school. Planning ahead then takes on serious purpose, for the stakes are high.

WRITING RECOMMENDATIONS FOR THE PLACEMENT OFFICE

This is a very important task. You want to be fair to both the student and to the employing officials. You want to tell the truth and still not damage your student's chances for the best position for which he is qualified. The job is especially difficult because you are dealing with the student's potential and must predict his success on that basis. To give only factual statements of progress to date would scare off most employers, for they tend to forget that student teaching must, after all, be primarily a foundation for growth and not a finishing school.

In some colleges only a rating form is used, in others a descriptive statement is required, and many use a combination of the two. If you are working with students for the first time, you would find it helpful to go to the placement office and ask to read a group of reports from previous years. Colleges vary in their practices and this is another point at which it is most helpful to become acquainted with the established pattern.

Laboratory school teachers are often required to prepare reports for the placement office, but public school teachers seldom are expected to. Even if you do not have full responsibility for preparing these evaluations you are likely to be asked to supply data for the supervisor. Sometimes you will prepare a joint report. But even if your regular duties as a teacher do not include writing a recommendation there is always the likelihood that one will be requested from you by some employing official.

What does an employing official look for in reading sets of credentials? Curiously enough, he is especially impressed by what isn't there. This suggests that these reports should be comprehensive enough to be worth while. Administrators also look for anecdotal and documentary evidence to back up the qualitative descriptions. No one who is asked to write a reference for a set of credentials is in as good a position to give evidence based on actual behavior as the teacher and supervisor who have jointly directed the student teaching.

Unfortunately, administrators frequently screen out two or three credentials from a larger number for purposes of interviews. This is time-consuming and, as they hurriedly read through these folders, they are likely to be influenced greatly by rather minor matters, particularly if these stand out. This is why a blunt negative statement of fact may do a lot of damage, far in excess of its importance. Just imagine reading for an hour and coming across this sentence, "Miss Jones was never able to handle the discipline in this class, but——." The tired administrator reads to the comma and tosses that one aside, never bothering to read further.

Here are a few suggestions to serve as a guide in writing these reports:

1. Describe briefly the setting of the assignment—grade, subject, school, term. Add any very unusual facts about the teaching situation which greatly affected the work of the student teacher. Be careful not to describe the bad features of the situation so bluntly that the officials of the school would be embarrassed if they saw the credentials.

2. Give evidence of the behavior that bears out the qualities you ascribe to the student.

3. Be fair to the student. Give his strengths and weaknesses, being careful not to overdo either.

4. Be careful to avoid the overly blunt statement in presenting the weaknesses of the student and give any compensating factors in the same sentence, or at least in close proximity.

5. Give your honest judgment of the student now and a reasonable prediction of his probable future development. If he will need more than a moderate amount of assistance to succeed, be tactful, but say so.

6. Identify the type of situation in which you think the student has most possibilities for success.

7. Recall the student's most outstanding achievement. Try to include reference to it in a sentence or two.

8. Be sure the written description corresponds with the rating and grade if the grade and rating become parts of the credentials.

Most of the above points will be illustrated in the samples included here. (Usually the setting has been omitted for obvious reasons.) Analyze them in the light of the above suggestions. Do you see how they are or are not well written? Here are three reports on student teaching that are practically worthless. Why?

A fine young teacher! (Grade was A.)

Mr. Mansur is a reliable, hard-working man. He will make a good teacher but will need encouragement from his administrators and supervisors. He lacks self-confidence and is easily disturbed. He is a fine person and will be willing to work in the community. I respect him highly. (Grade of B in Vocal Music.)

Juanita Kern is a superior young teacher and will become a very effective teacher. I found her cooperative, hard working, and reliable in every respect. She will be an addition to any school staff and will work well in a community. (Grade of B in Science.)

Here are more complete descriptions for two persons whose grades were above average. Can you note any inconsistency in either one? Are they well written? Do you feel that you know something about these students after you have read the reports?

General: Miss McVickers is a delightful young woman of about medium stature whose most noticeable asset is a dogged determination to do her very best every moment of every day. She doesn't complain or make excuses. She just tries hard and the results are very satisfactory.

Discipline: Her control of the classroom situation is above average. No discipline problem worthy of mention has come up.

Informational background: Miss M. doesn't seem to have a great fund of information which, of course, is normal among beginning teachers, but she prepares so carefully each day that her deficiency is almost lost from view.

Responsibility: This student teacher, through her willingness to prepare carefully each lesson has demonstrated a very fine sense of responsibility.

Likelihood of Professional Growth: On the basis of her friendly manner and willingness to work hard, her ability to control her class, her persistent effort to learn more, and her fine sense of responsibility, one predicts a successful future in teaching for this student teacher. (Junior High Social Studies, Grade of B.)

Mary Camp is the type of young lady who, when she enjoys something, lets everyone know that she is enjoying it. She has a poise and dignity about her that will carry her far. She worked with an alert group of fourth graders on a project of the community. Although the unit was a little slow at the beginning, she soon put into practice the suggestions that were given her, and success was achieved. Mary was always attractively dressed, and was able to take suggestions in a mature manner. She accepted responsibility nicely and was co-chairman for the student teacher tea. She has a good musical background. She was especially well grounded in mathematics, her secondary major, and seemed to be more than able to put across many good ideas in this area. Control within her group never appeared as a problem and good working relations were apparent. She was well liked by her pupils and I feel she will become an above average teacher once on her own. (Fourth Grade, Grade of B.)

The following examples describe serious deficiencies. Note how effectively the writers have stated the facts tactfully, given the extenuating circumstances, and thus made the whole statement a fair assessment but one which might not damage unduly the applicants' chances. Such statements may give employing officials clues concerning ways to assist the young teacher.

Her major weakness is the fact that at present she tends to be over-tense and ill at ease in the classroom. Apparently this has little effect upon her pupils. As Miss Kain gains additional experience, I believe that she will acquire more self-confidence and become more relaxed, and hence more effective, in the classroom. (Eighth Grade Social Studies, Grade of B plus.)

Early in the quarter Ruth had a little difficulty with control. This, I think, was due to the fact that noise did not bother her. When we helped her to become aware of the noise her control improved. (Fifth Grade, Grade of B plus.)

Miss Long's academic record in English courses is fairly good, but not outstanding. She did, however, take pains to make herself thoroughly familiar with all aspects of the subject matter she was presenting to her class. (English 11B, Grade of C.)

Miss Wanger is not aggressive. As a matter of fact, she is perhaps a little too humble and will need some encouragement from her principal. She "blossoms" under praise and works extremely hard to merit recognition. (Kindergarten, Grade of B.)

We shall complete this section with three recommendations which are very well written, representing three different levels of success. Check them against the suggestions given earlier.

Miss Canfield made outstanding progress during student teaching. She sought and found effective means for overcoming a problem with group discipline and eventually had such good control that she could be left alone without hesitation. She was very effective in using experience charts, films, resource people, and trips, and her ability to draw children into planning grew rapidly. In fact, they became so enthusiastic that her chief problem became one of helping them to limit intelligently the amount of work which they set for themselves. Miss Canfield soon realized the necessity for setting a good example and improved her writing, sentence structure, and punctuation through continuous practice and requests for criticism. She made good use of incidental experiences for functional learning and showed much insight in planning areas of the day around individual needs. Her unit on "Community Helpers" was very successful. She was cooperative, resourceful, and willing to spend the time necessary to make her teaching successful. She is aware of her need to gain more confidence and experience in the area of music. I am confident that she will work until she gains competency in any area in which she feels a bit insecure. I feel sure that she will be a strong teacher and will work with a school staff on a highly professional basis. (Second Grade, Grade of A.)

Miss Cameron's performance in her student teaching was very good. At first she showed some hesitancy in entering into the situation as fully as could be expected, but as soon as this was overcome, she was able to assume full responsibility for her classes. Her use of voice was especially good, and the classes responded to her readily. Her main difficulty seemed to be in working with individuals. She tended to lose the interest of a few among the group when a large group activity was in progress. However, she made great improvement in this respect as she began to plan her work more flexibly. She made good use of resource materials. Her analysis of situations was good, and she was able to work very well within the limitations imposed. Her evaluation of her own performance demonstrated a great deal of learning and growth, and she has developed a great deal of sensitivity to teaching problems. (Seventh Grade Art, Grade of B plus.)

Miss Sample made a slow beginning in her student teaching because of her seeming unwillingness to assume responsibility. Even though we gave her many specific suggestions, she escaped as many situations as possible by giving excuses of illness, etc., and did not profit as she should have from the help she received. A further deterrent was lack of careful planning, which often made it necessary for me to come to her rescue. When we found it necessary to give her a choice of dropping student teaching or of proving her ability within a week's time she settled down to work and made satisfactory progress during the last two weeks of the quarter. In fact, she became enthusiastic over activities related to the unit of study and was rewarded by a corresponding growth in the children's interest in their work. Miss Sample will need to continue to work on the problem of separating her personal and professional life. Conferences revealed that inability to resolve certain personal problems was the underlying factor behind her slow adjustment to teaching. If she sincerely works at this problem, I believe that she might make a satisfactory teacher with sympathetic and constructive supervision. (First Grade, Grade of D.)

SPECIAL PROBLEMS IN EVALUATION

The preceding review has covered just the usual aspects in evaluation. Unfortunately, this is a process in which all the deeper problems of the whole curriculum, the student teaching program, and the individual students sooner or later come to light. Every director of student teaching or coordinator of laboratory experiences recognizes that one of his primary functions is to serve as a trouble shooter. The channels should be well known and should be kept clear. For you, if you teach in a public school, there are two routes. For most matters which are strictly in the field of teacher education you go through your immediate supervisor to the director of student teaching. When the problem is one which concerns the school in which you teach or is one which jeopardizes the best interest of the pupils, the principal should be brought into the picture at once. The two of you should work with the college through the supervisor. If you teach in a laboratory school, you will confer first with the administrative official of that school.

THE INCOMPETENT STUDENT TEACHER

With well-planned induction procedures and careful daily supervision, lack of student fitness for teaching can be discovered and remedial measures applied before many weeks have passed. If these do not work it is usually possible to get the student to recognize his unsuitability for teaching, or to embark upon a longer remedial program.

There are several specific steps and cautions which should be applied before reaching the stage of making radical decisions in a given case. First of all, don't get alarmed and jump to conclusions. If you sense trouble in the offing call the supervisor and begin a cooperative study at once. Inform the principal that you think the student is weak but that you are working closely with him and will see to it that the pupils' best interests are protected. Close supervision of the planning and the teaching done by the student, your continuous presence in the room and assistance in the actual work of the pupils can often keep the learning at a fair level. This can usually be done without seriously impairing pupil progress, but obviously the student is not going to be prepared to accept a position in the public schools.

Students whose failure seems almost certain tend to fall into three main groups. There are those who don't care, those who aren't ready to do the job, and those who just don't have what it takes to do the job. Stated another way; there is lack of attitude, lack of preparation, or lack of ability. It would be very helpful if you could just find out which cause is the real one in a particular case.

The students who don't want to teach, don't plan to teach in the immediate future, never did want to teach but want a degree now they have gotten this far along in college, often try to bluff for a while. The second group often performs in much the same way. Their trouble may be lack of time, too many outside responsibilities, failure to plan their time, or just plain procrastination. Whatever the cause, the result is the same. They either don't have the drive or don't make the preparation that is needed.

Start working with both groups in the same way you work with all of your students. First, try to help them through gradual induction, friendly discussions in conferences, and assisting activities. If this isn't working too well, stress the importance of doing a good job and what they need to do to improve. Often the truth won't come out until later in the term, but you must keep trying to raise the level of performance. If you are satisfied the student is able to do good work, you have tried to help through generous conferences, and you are sure he hasn't done even a reasonable job of preparing, temporary removal from teaching may be an effective approach.

Before actually removing the student from assisting or teaching responsibility, be prepared to do it with kindness and consideration, but firmly. You might say something like this, "We have talked about your progress repeatedly and we both realize that you are not yet getting the results we would like. I may be wrong but I doubt that you are likely to get the progress we want by continuing in the way you are going now. I suggest that we stop, take stock, and start over. Suppose you not assist for a few days. We will plan for you to observe my teaching. Outside of class you can be planning for some assisting activities for next week. Bring your preliminary plans in and let's go over them together. Take them back and polish them up until you have the best preparation you can possibly make. Then, when we are both satisfied you're ready, you may try again." If the student really has what it takes the next teaching usually is noticeably better. The student may realize that thorough preparation pays dividends. This procedure may have to be repeated and the student may never get to responsible teaching.

The result of starting over, plus any information or attitudes revealed at the mid-term conference, will usually enable you to determine whether your student is a "don't want to teach anyway" case or one who just isn't making adequate preparation. With this knowledge you can act accordingly. Those who lack interest in teaching also may be guilty of professional irresponsibility. We can usually forgive one indiscretion or two if there really were extenuating circumstances. We doubt if you have any right to waste your time and energy and the pupils' indulgence with a student who fails to show up for class without making previous arrangements or notifying the school. A student should be expected to be just as responsible and dependable as an employed teacher. If he hasn't those habits now he isn't likely to acquire them later. A warning or two should be enough. If the delinquency persists without adequate reason the supervisor should be asked to consider his removal.

With wise guidance students who don't plan to teach often can be led to succeed rather well. Here is the way one student evaluated her own adjustment in that situation:

As I am sure you are aware, my dreams and plans for the future do not end ultimately with becoming a successful school teacher. Nevertheless, as I started to plan to meet the challenge of student teaching, I was determined to do absolutely the best job of which I was capable. I thought possibly this might be the only time I would spend teaching, and I wanted to see just how much I could accomplish above and beyond the "ordinary" classroom situation to which I had so often been exposed.

We must try to help others do as well.

Those few cases that really try the souls and the patience of teachers and supervisors alike are the students who are incompetent to become teachers. Making the decision on incompetence is exceedingly difficult at best, especially with our present state of knowledge and supply of measuring instruments. The difference between complete inability and reasonable potential for success is hard to define and harder still to work with. Teachers generally are inclined to give the student every break and to avoid decisions which might be unfair to the slightest degree. Our basic principle is clear—the pupils come first, now as well as later. We must give students a reasonable chance to grow, a chance to show what they can do, *but student teaching should never be used as an experience for the student at the expense of the pupils.* Occasionally advisors, parents, doctors, even psychiatrists will ask that a student be given a student teaching experience because some measure of success will be good for him. *Unless there is reason to believe that the student is a fair-to-good prospect for the profession we have no right to be a party to such exploitation of pupils and schools.*

If you have done your best to guide a student into success, and by mid-term or after he shows no prospect of ever being able to do a fair to satisfactory job of teaching, it is time to take stock at once. Call the supervisor and talk with the principal. Encourage both to study the student's behavior in the role of a teacher under varying conditions. Keep adequate anecdotal records and be as objective about the whole affair as possible. Furnish all the data you can to the others and make your own recommendation. College personnel should take the lead in calling a conference of those concerned. Normally the responsibility falls on designated college personnel both to make the final decision and to carry it out. There are several alternatives. A personality clash between you and the student or some other situation might have been a big contributing cause. Most likely the student doesn't have the background necessary, needs more training and experience, needs a different placement for a second try, or needs to be guided out of teaching. Your duty is to act in a thoroughly professional manner, and the college must carry the full legal responsibility.

GUIDING INDIVIDUALS WITH SPECIAL PROBLEMS

Some student teachers just get moving in high gear about the time the assignment is over. Unfortunately, there are some whose rate of growth is so slow that they do not reach this level. What should be done about them is always a knotty question. Most of the students in this situation need a different level, grade, or subject, or in some way the stimulation of a new environment. Usually you will not have to make this decision, but the supervisor or the student's advisor may ask for your advice. When the student has another term or semester the problem becomes one of the college arranging another student teaching assignment for him.

Seldom will you have the decisions to make in those cases, yet you do have the very great responsibility of making an early estimate of the student's probable success. This is in that difficult area of prediction again, where it is so hard to know what to do. The earlier you get a hunch that the student will need more time than the assignment provides the better. When you get such a hunch, confer with the supervisor at once. Refrain from discussing it with the student until the two of you are sure that it would be a good idea. Begin holding out the bait of gaining greater confidence and building competence with more experience. Don't press the issue but give the student time to think about it. Then when the final decision is made by the supervisor it won't come as a shock, and the student may be more receptive.

The major contribution you can make in evaluation is to help the student develop a high degree of proficiency in self-evaluation. He sees how *you* evaluate your activities and how you revised procedures as a result of your evaluation. He develops wholesome attitudes toward evaluation, develops skills in using evaluation procedures, and revises plans and methods accordingly.

All evaluation with the student is continuous through the term, is specific in treatment of strengths and weaknesses, and is, insofar as possible, focused upon the activities of the student rather than upon him as a person. Serious problems should be reviewed with the supervisor or laboratory school administrator, as the case may be, when you feel the problem to be one in which the college will need to make a decision.

SUGGESTED REFERENCES

Burr, James B., Lowry W. Harding, and Leland B. Jacobs, *Student Teaching in the Elementary School.* New York: Appleton-Century-Crofts, Inc., 1950. Chapter VIII, "Evaluating Your Work"; Chapter XIV, "Completing Your Work."

Feyereisen, Kathryn and Verna Dieckman, *Guiding Student Teacher Experiences.* Lock Haven, Pa.: Association for Student Teaching, 1952. Pages 25-27 review briefly pertinent aspects of evaluating the student's growth.

Grim, Paul and John Michaelis, *The Student Teacher in the Secondary School.* New York: Prentice-Hall, Inc., 1953. Chapter XI, "Evaluating Your Work."

Schorling, Raleigh and Max Wingo, *Elementary School Student Teaching.* New York: McGraw-Hill Book Company, Inc., 1950. Chapter XV, "The Broader Concept of Appraisal."

Merriman, Pearl and Gladys Fair, *Helping Student Teachers Through Evaluation.* Lock Haven, Pa.: Association for Student Teaching, 1953. Specific helps in evaluating student growth and in helping the student develop responsibility for his own evaluation.

14

Preparing for the First Teaching Position

THE STUDENT IS LOOKING TOWARD HIS FIRST POSI-
tion before his student teaching is completed. He is trying to
decide what sort of position he would like, where he would like
to teach, what combination of subjects or what elementary
grade he would accept, and so on. He has brought to you many
personal and professional problems. He has learned something
about assessing his strengths and weaknesses in relation to job
possibilities. And above all, he has learned that success in teaching is measured by quality of performance in meeting the responsibilities of a teacher.

You are in an excellent position to give him guidance in his
final relationship with you as a student and teacher. His growth
in learning to be a teacher has been guided by you. Both must
agree that he is or is not ready to accept a position in the field.
If both agree that he is not, then decisions will have to be made
concerning next steps. Decisions must be made, and many of
them will be difficult. These are trying times. We can not help
you with each situation, but we have selected points that should
give clues or suggestions for some of your problems. These are
organized under the following subtopics and each is reviewed
in some detail for you.

The student is informed concerning teaching conditions.

The student plans for service in the field.

Guidance in securing a position.

Making plans for a specific position.

Continued relationships with your students.

THE STUDENT IS INFORMED CONCERNING TEACHING CONDITIONS

Your student may ask you at any time, "What should I do if I had only a textbook to use in my first job?" "What should I do if a discipline problem like this came up in my first job?" "Would I be likely to find units in the files next year?" or "Could I get books and things for my teaching after I get on the job?" Having some idea concerning the possibilities of conditions is necessary for the student. He also needs suggestions in answer to the oft repeated question, "What should I do if ——?" Knowledge of conditions teachers meet in the public schools and how they adapt to those conditions is absolutely necessary for you in counseling your student about his first job. Ideas you may suggest will be a boon in helping him until he really gets "on his feet."

PRINCIPLES TO FOLLOW IN HELPING THE STUDENT BECOME INFORMED

There are several principles that should be followed in talking with the student about conditions in the public schools.

References to conditions in the field are made in a matter-of-fact manner. Be careful not to be derogatory about practices unlike those in your school. Suppose the student asks about pupil reports to parents. Review the practices followed but refer to each practice in an objective manner. You can compare any or all of the practices followed with the system in your school but refrain from speaking of them as "old-fashioned," 'obsolete," "too progressive," "a fad," or "antiquated." The student must enter his first position (or any position, for that matter) with respect for the school as it is. The conditions in a particular school may have been obtained through years of work by the faculty.

Realistic suggestions are given the student concerning his part in effecting changes in public schools. In the new job, the teacher gets acquainted with the conditions that exist and makes the necessary adjustments. Each school functions in its own way. Even so, there are many illustrations of how a teacher may operate with individuality; for example, he may like for the pupils to select their seats rather than to be seated alphabetically, require correct spelling in social studies papers, require science students to keep a list of key words and know their meanings, or not require all pupils to use the same size paper for work to be handed in.

The student also needs to become well acquainted with and follow the many established practices in the school. Examples might be: a common form used through the school in friendly letters, business letters, and other compositions; weekly tests in each academic subject in high school; homework in academic subjects for all senior high school pupils; no voices in the corridors during classes; teacher plans for the week submitted to the principal on the preceding Friday; no voices in study hall; a monthly report of progress in each class submitted to the principal; or all teachers reporting at a given time morning and noon and remaining at school until a specified time.

Perhaps the student will not approve of some practices discovered in the school where he will teach. No attempt should be made to bring about any change until he is established as a member of the group. Even then, he is a beginner. There are probably specific reasons for the practices he discovers and time will be necessary for him to determine those reasons. The beginning teacher must be very sensitive toward faculty attitudes regarding his individualistic ways of doing things and concerning his suggestions for change. There is some indication that beginning teachers do not take advantage of opportunities they have to use improved methods of instruction.[1]

[1] William A. Oliver, "A Study of Lag between Teachers' Educational Beliefs and Their Classroom Practices" (Doctoral dissertation, State College of Washington, 1950).

The student is given practical suggestions concerning how he may use initiative and imagination in his teacher activities. After he has become oriented to the school, he is ready to operate as one of the group, but not yet as a highly vocal member. Suppose there is little bulletin board space in the room and he needs more to make use of the bulletin board as a contribution to learning. First he would talk to the principal about the problem and have definite suggestions to make. The principal would probably want to know how he is using present bulletin board space and how he intends to use additional space. The student also should be ready to designate items intended to be purchased for his department or room but which he would relinquish in favor of the bulletin board. The principal might go with him or send him to the superintendent who would make the final decision. In these times many school budgets can accommodate few special requests, unless by substitution as suggested above.

Procedures to follow when other staff members are involved vary greatly from the above procedure. Suppose the teacher wishes to obtain more supplementary reading material for her first grade. But there are two other first grades in the building. He cannot go ahead and ask for the books. This time he must start with the fellow teachers. Select an informal situation in school when the three are together and casually raise questions such as, "What do your strong readers use when they have finished the basic series and the one supplementary series?", or "Do you have enough pre-primer materials for your very slow groups?" In this discussion, the new teacher may get no farther than just discussing the problem. Be patient.

Later he can pursue with questions or comments such as, "I have two children who have brought books from home to read to the children. In fact, all they have to read now is books from home or from the library. I've a notion to talk to the second-grade teachers. Maybe we could work out some scheme so that I could take these two on into second-grade readers. Have you ever tried that?" The response at first may be noncommittal.

Don't worry about it, but try later. Eventually the first-grade teachers will talk with the second-grade teachers. Later, perhaps in time to order books for the coming year, the teachers will review the problem with the principal and/or superintendent. The second year they may be squared away.

The suggestions given above have emphasized the fact that change takes place slowly in the public schools. This is a desirable feature, a necessary protection against spontaneous changes that have not been well thought through. The deliberate nature of the process of change, however, is rough on impetuous youth. It is for this reason that students should be counseled concerning the nature and processes of change while with you. *It is very possible that the professional zeal of young teachers would not be lost if they understood how change occurs in the public school and why change takes place slowly.* They must also recognize the tremendous potential for desirable change that they possess if they only know how to proceed effectively.

Ways of keeping students informed

We now turn to the methods you may use to inform the student and to teach the student to keep himself informed. In general, they are the same methods you use to keep informed.

Relate student teaching experiences to conditions in the public schools. Students are well aware of the need to be thinking about conditions in the field and will appreciate your help. Your conference periods provide opportunity for you to think through situations that occur during student teaching in terms of situations that may occur in the field. When asked to evaluate their teachers regarding the principle "The teachers related your work in student teaching to the conditions you would probably meet in the field," students gave the following characteristic responses:

When questions arose as to behavior or curriculum, it was always brought up as to what we might find in other teaching situations.

I felt that, as a department, the science teachers were particularly interested in the coming years in the field. They made valuable suggestions to me about my work.

Gave good coaching suggestions.

This was handled through seminars especially; also constant comparison by my teacher of situations and materials here with those probably in the future.

She talked abstractly about ethical things and constantly ignored giving practical advice.

There were some relations but they were too sparse when they could have helped the most.

Suggestions should be specific and should be given in all situations that you think will help the student in his first teaching. Be careful to avoid saying, "Now when I was teaching at ——," or "I had this situation arise and this is the way I handled it." One advantage of keeping posted concerning many public school situations is that you can keep the personal pronoun "I" in its proper proportion.

Use your file of information from former students. You may already have such a file, but if not, you might try one. Notice the attitudes of your students toward the information revealed. For ready use, the material could be filed by topics, such as: "Public School Schedule," "Problem Solved," "What Next?" "Extraclass Activities," "Parent-Teacher Relationships," "Using the Community," "Just Kids," "Prompted."

Such a file gives you examples to illustrate the idea that there are many ways of accomplishing the same thing. Teacher ingenuity becomes significant. Students also soon recognize the great variety that exists in public school practices. You should remind the student that this is a direct result of the American tradition of local control in public education.

Caution students about copying procedures verbatim. Students often want to copy suggestions or procedures. Let them copy all they want, but be sure to emphasize the fact that the solution in one case might be "bad medicine" in another case even though the two seem identical. The personality factors involved in any two cases are sure to be different. One teacher might produce desired results with a pupil by a given method but the same method employed with the same pupil by an·

other teacher might fail. The difference in facial expression, tone of voice, previous experiences with the two teachers, mannerisms at the moment, emotional balance, or any number of different conditions occurring immediately before or after the incident might make the difference. Suggestions are to be used only as suggestions. They cannot be lifted from one situation as a solution and be expected to produce magic results in another.

The student must understand that one may select elements from many suggestions in deciding what to do in a particular set of circumstances. Sometimes a given suggestion might work as is; sometimes a combination of suggestions might be best. To have a mass of ideas cached and ready for use when prompted is one thing, to be able to use them successfully is another. The student who has had rich experiences in meeting situations during student teaching can approach his first teaching job with more confidence than the one who had a tendency to use suggestions verbatim, rather than selecting and making application in each situation.

Take the student to public schools with you when visiting. Such an experience would help him understand that great differences in practices do exist from school to school. The experience could also be of help to him when applying for a position. Perhaps you've been amazed at the meager information brought back from interviews by students.

The visit could be made a trial run for the student in trying to decide whether or not he would like to teach in the school or whether or not he would be the person for the position. What characteristics, philosophy, practices, methods, materials of instruction, pupil attitudes, teacher initiative, and administrative procedures, as examples, would he want in a school in which he were to teach? How would he get the information he wanted and needed in order to make a studied judgment? Would a person with his characteristics and competencies be suited for the position? Upon returning to home grounds, you could go over the information obtained and attempt to reach a decision.

Notices of vacancies from the placement office cannot give

the information that the student needs in order to select the position best suited to him and to which he can give best service. Neither can the placement officials give information sufficiently complete. Therefore, the visitation experience with you, the process of getting desired information, and the very real problem of trying to analyze the school visited in terms of his qualifications is valuable experience for the student. Perhaps many more beginning teachers would realize greater success and retain the real professional zeal they carried from college to the field if more attention were given to helping the student select the first position.

Take the student with you to professional meetings. The student who attends such meetings has the privilege of meeting the people and of discussing their experiences with them first hand. The personal enthusiasm conveyed by the teachers with whom he talks cannot be so well conveyed by you.

A student was present in a group in which a teacher of six weeks volubly exclaimed the thrills he was experiencing in a community with a low economic level. He told of the eighth-grade girl who, with her father, was left responsible for ten children; of the family for which he had collected clothing in a nearby community, of the seriously undernourished children in a certain family and how he had obtained a doctor to examine them, of the drinking water problem and how the state was helping, and of the meetings they were having for the mothers to discuss ways of getting more for their money for their children. The student sat and listened, evidently bored at first, and finally commented, "All you've talked about is the work you do in the community."

The first-year teacher only paused long enough to hear the question, then responded, "I'll bet the most important work I'm doing is in the community. I lived in the country and my folks aren't rich but we never lived like that. Why if I can get those kids dressed and fed and slept right, I'll have the biggest problem at school licked. You can't expect kids to learn if they're hungry, sleepy, cold, and sick. If you . . ."

The student interrupted, "But how do they act at school? I mean, what are their attitudes like?"

"In a way it's pathetic. Their lives aren't interesting so everything unusual you do with or for them, they love. You should have seen them when we got the room fixed up with pictures, books, tables, and interesting things on the tables. Then we got flowers and a large aquarium with fish. The kids helped fix everything up and were as proud as peacocks. Have I taught much reading and arithmetic yet? No, but the day's coming when I can."

You know the effect that sort of thing has upon student teachers if you have been through such an experience. Certainly impressions can be created that would be beyond you. The negative influence, however, can be just as great. A first-year teacher was deploring the lunch situation in her school in the presence of two students reared in the city. She described the students coming to school with their dinner "buckets" and placing them on the corridor floor under their coats, the condition of the sandwiches by lunch time, and the smell of the classroom when the buckets were open and on through the afternoon. She was as forceful as the teacher quoted above and equally as effective in creating an impression.

One finds much less of the latter situation, however, when visiting with beginning teachers. We recommend, therefore, that you take your student with you whenever it will be possible for him to visit directly with beginning teachers.

The following types of meetings are suggested:

State Education Association

District meetings of the State Education Association

Saturday conferences on college or university campuses or in centrally located cities

Local chapter meetings of ASCD, ACEI, AST, PDK, etc.

County or parish institutes.

Encourage the student to correspond with beginning teachers. Perhaps your student is already corresponding with beginning teachers; his friends who graduated last year or the year before. In this case, your job might be to offer explanations concerning statements made by the teacher. One teacher wrote that "The faculty is a 'lollapalooza' to listen to. We never get anything done." No further mention was made of the faculty, even though the student asked for explanations. Explanations in some situations, however, wouldn't be so difficult. For example, a teacher wrote back to a student saying that it was almost impossible for her to teach in the school because she couldn't get anything she needed, then listed what she might have expected in three or four years! She had taught in a campus school which was very well equipped and somehow had missed being counseled on the problem of supplying and equipping public school classrooms.

What explanations to offer may present real problems. A student was quite perturbed about a statement made by a friend, "The teachers here are really upset. The new superintendent won't get a substitute for us so that we can visit another school. We have to pay our own substitutes! He says it's O.K. for us to visit schools but we're afraid it isn't. If it were, why would we have to hire our own substitutes?" There may be very logical explanations for a situation of this kind, or the explanation might seem to lack the kind of professionalism that one would like.

Problems such as the above, in one letter after another from friends in the field, may cause the student to develop an unwholesome attitude toward teaching. This may reveal the real reasons for undesirable student attitudes that you have attributed to other causes or that you could in no way explain.

Students who are not corresponding with friends now teaching should be encouraged to do so, if for no other reason than to get information concerning public school situations. They should be getting enthusiastic reports from friends in the field and should also be getting negative criticisms. You then have opportunity to clarify problems presented and to prepare the student to face imperfections as challenges.

It is strange how we react toward imperfections in a derogatory manner, blaming any or all parties associated with the school. If we could only bring ourselves to look upon undesirable conditions objectively and to apply our knowledge of how to solve probems, our profession would certainly be a happier one in which to work. One of your very important jobs is to look upon school problems objectively and to work on them enthusiastically, as challenges. Simultaneously, you may have to work overtime to convince the student that defeatism has no place in the teaching profession. There has been entirely too much "singing the blues" in the teaching profession instead of accepting problems as challenges and trying to do something about them.

THE STUDENT PLANS FOR SERVICE IN THE FIELD

The student has been making plans for teaching as he found out about conditions which he might face. While assisting you and while teaching, he has decided to try many different things when on his own. Preparations must be emphasized while the student is with you, although they should have been started when he first entered the professional part of his program. The major preparations are reviewed briefly below:

BIBLIOGRAPHY OF INSTRUCTIONAL MATERIALS

The student knows or should know something of the curriculum in the public schools. If the state course of study is followed in the different fields in all schools or in schools other than the large city systems, he will find the preparation of a bibliography easier. Many of the books, booklets, pamphlets, and bulletins that he used while teaching with you he would want to include in his bibliography. In case the state course of study is used only in the rural and small town schools, he will need to get from you, or from friends in the field, some idea of the curriculum in the grades or by fields in high school. His bibliography should be annotated. Under each item might be included information such as reading level, authenticity, date, comprehension level, purpose of publication, readability, and general résumé. The bibliography should be organized by fields and should include content materials for pupils and teacher: maps, graphs, charts, tables, films, filmstrips, flat pictures, concrete materials, periodicals, equipment, supplies, sources of materials, and any other listing of materials which he wants to record for future use.

The most valuable aspect of the bibliography to the student is his experience in the selection and evaluation of materials of instruction. Your biggest problem may be to get the student to evaluate and annotate instead of writing down the name of all the publications he sees.

PROFESSIONAL LIBRARY

Whether or not the student has started a professional library, there are several things you can do. He will be using professional books, periodicals, bulletins, booklets, and manuals with you, and he should recognize their value to the teacher in his everyday work. Those materials he finds useful in his teaching can be included and annotated in a professional library bibliography. We have little confidence in student bibliographies unless annotated. The student will also need to include cost, date, and publisher. Also he should be required to use consistently acceptable bibliography form.

You frequently receive, through the office of the superintendent or principal, notices of new professional materials and, sometimes, sample copies. These should be referred to the student and the relative quality for particular purposes should be reviewed by you and the student. When textbook representatives visit your school and you have opportunity to talk with them, be sure to include the student. Attendance at professional meetings and visitations in other schools give you further opportunity to work with the student in building a bibliography for a professional library.

INSTRUCTIONAL PROCEDURES

The student will want to save units that he has prepared and used and also he may want to copy units prepared by you or other students. The latter practice is not recommended unless he realizes the dangers of trying to copy and use verbatim units that have been prepared by others. You can judge the desirability of such a practice for a given student by the initiative and imagination exhibited while with you.

Other materials such as clippings and descriptive articles should be filed according to use. The student should start such a file, if one has not already been started, and should develop an organization which he can use. For example, a folder might be used for each of the following: standard achievement test samples, teacher-made test samples, homeroom, individual differences, homework, pupil counseling, school clubs, class schedules, pupil reports to parents, parent-teacher conferences, school assemblies, discipline, radio, care of equipment, left-handedness, pupil seating, physical examinations, and school insurance.

Miscellaneous materials

Most teachers eventually start a file to include clippings to be used with or by the pupils in the teaching-learning process. The file might include pictures, maps, graphs, tables, diagrammatic drawings, recipes, patterns (home economics), and compositions. He should devise an organization for his file based upon subjects, units, fields, or some other logical arrangement.

Students teaching in most high school fields and in the elementary grades also have occasion to collect samples. The high school English teacher may collect copies of poetry and prose selections and pupil composition samples; the music teacher, samples of compositions for orchestra, band, chorus, glee club, and ensembles; the art teacher, samples of glaze, paper, leather, yarn, paint, clay, pictures, designs, and pupils' work; the mathematics teacher, samples of geometric shapes and fractional parts made from wood; the fourth grade teacher, samples of rocks, woods, minerals, historical objects, and materials characteristic of countries and climates and raw materials to manufactured products.

Storage is the major problem in the collection of samples. Perhaps you've seen teachers' rooms cluttered with such materials. You can help your student avoid this problem by demonstrating the value of keeping only the sample type of material that is used and that really contributes to learning. Before leaving you, the student should be counseled repeatedly concerning the necessity for keeping files and shelves cleaned of materials that cannot be put to good use.

GUIDANCE IN SECURING A POSITION

The experiences and counsel you give students in helping them bridge the gap between student teaching and their first jobs are real professional services. The climax of your counseling comes as the students start receiving notices of vacancies. Most help can be given to them if they are being considered for positions at the time they are teaching with you. Those who taught with you in the junior year or early in the senior year may return for counsel if you are close enough. Also, they may write you or may call you. Their contact with you at the time of placement may depend upon the confidence developed for your judgment during teaching, upon the experiences you provided in helping them understand public school teaching, or upon the attitudes you took toward conditions found in public schools.

Counseling with the student concerning his first job presents many difficult problems for you. In each case, you are attempting to size up the situation in order to predict student success in a particular situation. Also, you are attempting to decide which position offers the student best possibilities for success in his first job. There are so many intangibles, so many conditions in each position that you don't know about, so many student characteristics to consider in relation to each position, and so many personal and professional pressures and relationships that are not known to you. Each time a student considers a position, an entirely new problem is presented in attempting to analyze the situation in terms of probable student success.

Realizing the problems you face, we are offering suggestions which may be applied to any situation.

No student should accept a position without visiting the school and community. While he is there he can make necessary observations and ask questions to give him the information he needs to make a decision. Your biggest contribution at this point is the assistance given the student in deciding what information he needs. He then has to formulate questions which he hopes will provide the information. We suggest that the student might well know something about the aspects of the school-community situation listed below. The questions are not intended to be used as stated but are intended only as suggestions.

1. *The general philosophy of the school.* Are subjects taught as such in the elementary school or are reading, arithmetic, spelling, science, and social studies taught in relation to large units? Is discipline rigidly imposed by the teacher or are pupils given the opportunity to develop self-control, to develop independence, and to direct their own activities? Do pupils learn how to solve problems or do they study subjects? Is the secondary school college-preparatory or does it attempt to meet the needs of all high school pupils?

2. *The school curriculum.* Does the school have a written curriculum or does each teacher follow textbooks? Is the curriculum determined by the faculty or by the administration? In the elementary school, are teachers required to follow specific outlines? Does the curriculum allow pupils to explore vocations? Is the curriculum strictly academic, with music, art, drama, speech, and journalism relegated to extraclass status? What is the course of study in the particular field or fields of student interest?

3. *Instructional materials.* Are references a definite part of the instructional program or is the textbook the basis for instruction? Is provision made for individual differences in reading in high school classes? Can instructional materials be ordered dur-

ing the year? About how much could a fourth grade teacher (or science, math., social studies, English, or home economics, as the case might be) expect to be spent for instructional materials in his room each year? What instructional materials are available now? How much are audio-visual aids, including excursions, used in the school? Could more money be spent on this part of the program?

4. *Extraclass activities.* Are extraclass activities included as a part of the school day? How much emphasis is placed upon athletics for girls and boys? Does the school participate in contests in music, speech, drama, and the like? What clubs are now sponsored in the school? When do clubs meet? How are clubs financed?

5. *Supervision.* How much does the principal (or superintendent or supervisors) supervise? Is the teacher welcome to counsel with the principal concerning problems? Does the administration stand back of the teachers? How closely does the principal work with the teachers in programs of school improvement? What work in school improvement has recently been done by the principal and staff? Are staff meetings regular? What are staff meetings used for?

6. *Pupil reports to parents.* What kind of reports are used? How often are they issued? How are they issued? How are they liked by the parents and staff?

7. *Teacher load.* How many classes and what classes are considered a teacher load? How many extraclass activities such as clubs, school lunch, playground supervision, study hall, student council, or drama might be included? In elementary school, are art, music, industrial arts, and physical education taught by special teachers? What committee assignments might be made? What reports are expected?

8. *Opportunities for professional self-growth.* Are teachers permitted to visit other schools, attend conferences falling on school days? When the teacher is absent for school visitation or conferences, is the substitute paid by the school or by the teacher? How much of a professional library is maintained in

the school? How is it financed? Are a part of the teacher's expenses paid when he attends conferences? If so, how much?

9. *Teacher turnover.* About how much turnover is there each year? What causes the large turnover?

10. *Class size.* What is the maximum class size? How large are the classes now? Why are such large classes permitted?

11. *Building adequacy.* What plans are made to take care of increasing enrollments in the building? How soon will additional building space be available? Why won't the community vote bonds for additional classroom space?

12. *Restrictions on teacher activity.* Is the teacher permitted to attend community dances? Is he permitted to smoke in public? Is he permitted to smoke at school? If so, where? Are teachers required to remain in the community a certain number of weekends each month? If restrictions are placed on teachers, by whom are they placed?

13. *Pupil population.* What is the background of the pupils who come to the school? What changes do you see in proportion of rural to urban or low economic level to high economic level?

14. *The specific assignment.* Specifically what would my assignment be the first year? What might it be the next and the next? Does the teacher have a choice concerning change of assignment?

15. *Community attitude toward the school and teachers.* Is there a PTA? How active is it? What percentage of the parents are members? Do parents visit school? Do parents cooperate with the school and teachers? Is the community divided into factions because of differences of opinion concerning the schools? Are teachers accepted as members of the community? If not, why not? Are teachers included in community activities? Do teachers belong to community organizations and work in community activities?

16. *Cultural opportunities.* Is there a good lecture concert program supported by the community? Is there such a program in a nearby town? Is there a good community library? Are there

good shows at the theater? Are art shows sponsored by the community?

17. *General characteristics of the community.* Is it growing? Is it progressive or does it enjoy being old fashioned? What are the churches? Is new industry coming into the community? What is the predominant nationality? What traditions should one know about?

18. *Teacher salary.* (This item is last because other aspects of the position may be so unsatisfactory that the interview will not reach salary.) What would the salary be for this particular position? Is there a salary schedule? Is it a single salary schedule? What is the annual increment according to the salary schedule? What additional increment is provided for additional preparation? Is additional preparation required periodically?

With information in mind, the student is then ready to look at the job seriously in terms of his qualifications.

THE STUDENT SHOULD LOOK AT HIS QUALIFICATIONS FOR THE POSITION

There is a difference between what the student had dreamed his first job might be and the features of real jobs. As you acquainted him with actual teaching conditions in the field, you hoped that the Utopian features of teaching would be replaced by reality. Facing real jobs is much easier for the student who has learned what real jobs are like.

Self-analysis and self-appraisal may yet be difficult for the student. If so, he will have difficulty in looking at a job in terms of his qualifications. Suppose he cannot see wherein he has difficulty in working with people. He grew up in a small town, however, and wants to return to a small town to teach. You are afraid of the problems that he will face in a small community where everybody knows everybody else and where no one can isolate himself from the group. Another student may have difficulty in enlisting the cooperation of pupils and, even with your help, he has grown little in sensitivity to the problem. He likes a position in a school in which there is a very informal pupil control. You feel that this would be a disastrous combination.

You have no alternative but to be very frank with the student in warning him about personal or professional qualities which make him unsuited for a particular position. He will make the decision, of course, but you will have done all in your power to get him to select the position in which you feel he has greatest possibilities for success.

Keep in mind that the student is probably counseling with people at the college, with relatives, and with friends in the field. Your objective, analytical approach becomes even more crucial as you realize the superficial reasons others may be using to influence him. There are always factors brought in by the student and others, such as getting a position near home, near the fiancée, or in the same school with his girl friend, in a certain sized community, near the college, in the mountains, in a dry climate, and so on. You may have difficulty in getting the student to look at the specific nature of the position unless it is located *where* he wants it. All of your good counseling may have gone for naught, but at least you tried.

MAKING PLANS FOR A SPECIFIC POSITION

The student who accepts a position during the term that he is teaching with you may get plans well set up for his first year. Again, those who are not teaching with you when positions are accepted may contact you for help. It is important that you give all students every assistance possible, but especially those who accepted positions against your better judgment.

Specifically you can help the student in the following ways:

Planning for the first week of school. Students who have not had the "September Field Experience" or who did not teach with you the fall quarter or semester may have little idea how to start the year. Specific plans might be made for the first week or two weeks for each class.

Planning for extraclass responsibilities. The student may know what extraclass assignments he will have, or at least he should know before accepting the position. Again, specific plans should be made for the activities of the group or groups. In case the student doesn't know what groups he will be sponsoring, he might make plans for groups known to be active in the school.

Planning best use of facilities, community resources, and school instructional materials. The student knows that he will have trouble with the physical education program because of inadequate facilities, equipment, and supplies. How can he make the most of what he has? Social studies references are inadequate. How can students learn to use references when so few are available? How might more be obtained? Films are scheduled for the school each week, but most often they do not fit into the units being studied at the time. How can the films be used effectively, for example, when the forestry film comes in January and the forestry unit is in the Fall?

Planning a program for an adult-education class. The student was informed that she would be responsible for an adult-education class in home economics one night per week. She has had no experience with adult-education programs. Tentative plans could be prepared for the year, including alternative activities. Reference also should be made to available literature on the subject.

Planning for community relationships. If the community is small, the student may have serious problems in adjusting to the lack of recreational, social, and cultural features found in larger communities. Other problems may be presented by the student's religious preference, community customs, lack of community activity other than Church and Sunday School, lack of teacher social and recreational activities, lack of housing in the small community, teaching in the home community, teaching in a school with brothers or sisters as students, and presence of school factions in the community. Your experience and judgment can contribute to a good community start by the student.

CONTINUED RELATIONSHIPS WITH YOUR STUDENTS

Some say, "The student is on his own now. It's time he is weaned from his teacher." We do not agree. Students are inclined to wean themselves too soon from the professional college and their counselors. They just don't grow up professionally that fast. So, stretch your apron strings to your student no matter how far away his first teaching job may be. He learned your steadying influence, your confidence, and your counsel while a student. As a teacher, he may yet need your help for a while. If he needs only your assurance of standing by in case, make sure that he has your continued interest and desire to help. You may never have a more important task at the moment than to respond to the plea for help that just came in the morning mail.

There are many ways by which you can continue your service to the student. Please note that at the same time you are also growing in your ability to better serve future students. We suggest that you try the six methods listed below if you haven't already tried them.

Make sure that the student recognizes the sincerity of your interest in him following his teaching with you. This idea can be developed to a large degree by his confidence in the sincerity of your interest in him while he is teaching with you, while he is selecting a position, and while he is preparing to start in the new position.

Review specifically with the student the competencies that require continued evaluation and improvement. Both of you should keep a detailed record of your discussion; that is, a list of the competencies discussed with specific suggestions concerning ways by which they might be improved. For example, a given student might be quite weak in his ability to develop good working relationships with other faculty members. This would be listed in terms of a competency with suggestions as follows:

Competency: ability to work effectively with other faculty members. Suggested ways to improve:

Be friendly by greeting other faculty members in hall, playground, or wherever you see them; smiling; visiting with other faculty members whenever the opportunity arises; joining other faculty members for refreshments after school; joining other faculty members in jokes played on one of the group; and being a good sport.

Share experiences you are having in your classes or in other professional activities that might be of interest to other teachers.

Share ideas when a discussion calls for ideas; for example, when a problem is being thoroughly reviewed in faculty meeting.

Give the other staff member a chance to explain his idea before commenting.

Be tactful; it is often not *what* you say but *how* you say it that causes hard feelings.

Accept reversals without griping to everyone, as when another point of view prevails by faculty vote.

Invite other faculty members to your room to observe or get their reactions to specific situations (a general invitation won't work).

Consult other faculty members who may be able to help you with a problem.

Be sincere.

The student should go on his way to the first job with a notebook containing suggestions concerning specific ways by which his growth as a teacher may continue. Individual differences being great, the time spent with the student in this task, the notes made by the student, and the value of the suggestions to the student after he gets on the job will vary tremendously. The value of this type of assistance to the student and to the profession, however, makes all your efforts worth while.

Ask the student to correspond with you so that you may know how he is getting along in his work, what problems he faces with which you may be able to help him, and how the suggestions made to him concerning continued growth in competencies are working out.

Specific information and insight into conditions existing in public schools can be most helpful to you in continually relating conditions in the student teaching situation to conditions in public schools.

A former teacher wrote each of his students of the preceding year and asked for the following information:

1. A copy of the schedule showing his class responsibility.
2. A list of extraclass activities superimposed on the schedule.
3. An orientation of the building showing the classroom space available for his classes.
4. A list of the instructional materials available.
5. A statement of the philosophy of the program.
6. The basic method of instruction, textbook, or unit with references.
7. The factors that contribute to high or low morale in the school.

The material collected by the teacher referred to above is kept on file for specific examples in discussions during conferences. Also, the materials are available for student perusal or study at any time.

Make tentative plans to meet the student for a visit at some conference or during the meeting of the state teachers' association. A good visit in a situation of this kind will give you better insight into the goings on with the student than correspondence. You can also catch the degree of enthusiasm that may not be revealed by letter.

Perhaps the college or university from which you receive students conducts conferences each year. Your participation with former student teachers and with other public school teachers would be a great help. Not only would you be able to help former students but you would also learn more of existing public school practices, which would be helpful to you in working with future students.

Make tentative plans to visit the student in his school next year. Such plans can be made in advance, with the time to be settled later by correspondence. Some students may want to be visited in the fall and others not until spring. They will want to be sure that things are going well before you come. The visit enables you to talk with the beginning teacher on the job and to see his problems first hand. Arrange for the visit through the administration of the school, indicating time to visit, particular field or grade, and purpose of visit.

While visiting, you may also be able to obtain specific information that otherwise would not be available to help in counseling other students. The information you need to be most helpful to the student in relating experiences in student teaching to conditions in the field often may be obtained only through questioning. This type of questioning may be pursued with a former student but might not be welcomed by someone not known to you. Examples of information that you may be able to get only through questioning are:

1. The attitude of the administration toward teacher initiative.

2. The program followed in developing and maintaining good working relationships with parents.

3. The encouragement given to staff to attend professional meetings.

4. The degree to which the staff works toward improvement of the pupil program.

5. The practices in promotion and grading.

6. The attitudes of the community toward the total educational program versus, for example, interest in contests.

7. The extent to which the school is used as a community center.

8. The policies concerning homework.

9. The philosophy of the school concerning pupil control or discipline.

Encourage the student to subscribe to professional publications that report public school practices. Articles published relating to instructional practices are often criticized because they are not adaptable to public schools in general. We do not accept this as a valid criticism. You certainly have found helpful suggestions in publications and experienced no difficulty in adapting their use in your teaching. One state teachers' association journal includes a section in each issue devoted to "This

Is How We Do It."[2] Another includes an article in each issue entitled, "It Worked For Us."[3]

REWARDS

Most of your blessings you'll never count because you'll never see them, never be aware of them. You may catch glimpses, in correspondence or in visiting with former students, of the wealth of experiences; the assuring, practical counsel; the variety of responsibilities; the sincere concern for growth; the specific evaluation and suggestions; the final recommendations for continued growth—in all, a tremendous contribution to a future teacher. Most recognize and appreciate your efforts, and those who do don't need words to tell you so.

You have seen student growth from the faltering first steps to confident success in the activities of the teacher. You have seen pupil confidence and interest in the student shift to "trying him out" and back to confidence and respect. You are surprised each time, after assessing the student's possibilities, to observe the nature of his growth, unpredictable and unlike any other. You have been forced to desperation by more than one student only to hit upon procedures that seem to help him get hold of things. Or was this only delayed actions; that is, previous procedures just taking effect? You'll never know; none of us know for sure, because we're working with a human mind nurtured by a vast, complex background of experiences.

You saw John Jones work with pupils as an aggregate, neither recognizing nor providing for individual differences. You saw him eye the pupils skeptically, afraid and distrustful because he could not predict their reactions and responses and was terrified by questions. Later you noticed him relaxed, not trying to smile, purposefully stimulating thought and action. Finally, you

---

[2] *Midland Schools,* Iowa State Education Association (415 Shops Building, Des Moines, Iowa).

[3] *Louisiana Schools,* Louisiana Education Association (418 Florida Street, Baton Rouge, Louisiana).

observed his plans develop into wholesome teaching-learning situations for each boy and girl in the group.

Latest report from the field: "John Jones is one of our best young teachers." Reward enough?

SUGGESTED REFERENCES

Burr, James B., Lowry W. Harding, and Leland B. Jacobs, *Student Teaching in the Elementary School.* New York: Appleton-Century-Crofts, Inc., 1950. Chapter XIV, "Completing Your Work"; Chapter XV, "Looking beyond Student Teaching."

Schorling, Raleigh and Max Wingo, *Elementary School Student Teaching.* New York: McGraw-Hill Book Company, Inc., 1950. Chapter XVI, "Professional Growth and Personal Advancement," gives specific suggestions to help the student in finding a position, making application, preparing for interview, deciding upon a position, and getting started in the first position.

Appendix A

PERSONAL AND PROFESSIONAL DATA[1]

ELEMENTARY SCHOOL STUDENT TEACHING DURING ___ QUARTER, 19___

Name _____ Advisor _____

Home Address _____ Tel. No. _____

College Address _____Tel. No. _____

Classification _____ Estimated date of graduation _____
        (Year)   (Quarter)

Curriculum _____ Major _____ Minor _____

Date of Birth _____ Where raised: (circle) rural, town, city
      (Month) (Year)

Size of your family: _____ Your place in your family (1st child,
   2nd, etc.) _____

1. Courses in education (please put course titles) you will have before student teaching (if a transfer student, indicate institution where courses were taken):

2. List learning experiences you have observed (indicate whether elementary or secondary)

3. List school activities in which you have participated (indicate whether elementary or secondary)

4. Give your schedule for this quarter; and hours of outside work, if any:

[1] Prepared by Dr. Tom Horn, formerly principal, College Elementary School, and Campus Elementary School Staff, Iowa State Teachers College, 1950.

5. Experience in teaching: (indicate total)

   a. Teaching in field   *Years*   *Grade*   *Place*

   b. Student teaching _____

             (Date)   (Quarter Hours)   (Grade)

   _____

       (Building)   (Place)   (Supervisor)

6. a. Experiences in working with children: (Sunday School, 4-H, Baby Sitting, etc.)

   Description of experiences   *Length of time*   *Hours per day*

   b. Other work experiences:

7. Travel Experiences: *Description*   *Time*

8. Leadership activities with classmates or adult groups; including off campus (4-H clubs, etc.)

   a. _____

       (Positions held, and where)   (Time)

   b. _____

9. Present membership in social organizations or interest groups: (KPBA, Elementa Chi, etc.)

   a. _____ b. _____ c. _____

10. Present membership in educational organizations: (IEA, etc.)

   a. _____ b. _____ c. _____

11. Talents, skills, or interests which may be assets in teaching:

Do you play piano? Well enough to accompany an elementary class?	Can you lead children in singing? List instruments you can play:	List hobbies & other talents:
	_____	_____
	_____	_____

12. Type of position you hope to obtain upon graduation and your future plans:

Appendix B

STUDENT TEACHER WEEKLY PROGRAM
(Social Studies)

STUDENT: Donald Porter DATE: Sept. 15 WEEK: 1 COUNSELOR: Mr. Wells

	M	T	W	Th	F	Sat	Sun
8:00	Attend general faculty meeting	Attend meeting of homeroom sponsors	Assist principal and supervising	Participate in B. I. E. Day (Business, Education, Industry)	Meet with Secondary Staff		
9:00	Social period	Attend meeting of extraclass sponsors	teacher register		Committee studying reporting	Complete preparation	Attend Sunday school and church
10:00	Continue general faculty meeting	Luncheon with homeroom sponsors	new pupils			for opening	
11:00		and chairman of homeroom parents				of classes	
12:00							
1:00	Attend secondary staff meeting	"	Work with supervising teacher in		Attend general faculty meeting	Shop and	
2:00	Meet with social studies teachers	Work with super-	organizing materials and planning for the		Work with supervising teacher in	meet people in the busi-	
3:00	Secondary staff social period — Building orientation	vising teacher in preparation for opening of classes	opening of classes		preparation for opening of classes Monday	ness district	Attend school board
4:00	with supervising teacher		Visit softball practice				open house for teachers
EVENING	Faculty picnic	Attend PTA council meeting	Student teachers have dinner together and attend theater				

347

STUDENT TEACHER WEEKLY PROGRAM
(Social Studies)

STUDENT: Donald Porter   DATE: Sept. 22   WEEK: 2   COUNSELOR: Mr. Wells

	M	T	W	Th	F	Sat	Sun
8:00	Assist in checking schedules and organizing homeroom	Assist in organizing American history class	Assist pupils in selection of references	Participate in current events review	Assist pupils in use of references		Attend Sunday school and church
9:00	Assist in checking textbooks to American history class	Participate with pupils in organizing unit	Assist pupils in selection of references	Participate in current events review	Work with committee in selection of maps for class use	Preview films	
10:00	Attend assembly	Attend Radio Club	Attend student council	Attend parent conference in principal's office	Select American history references of low reading level	at college	
11:00	Observe organization of orchestra	Observe organization of band	Visit orchestra	Visit band	Study data given in pupil personnel folders	audio-visual center	
12:00	Help supervising teacher at hot lunch program						
1:00	Confer with supervising teacher	Confer with supervising teacher	Confer with principal and superintendent	Confer with supervising teacher			
2:00	Visit principal, school nurse and library with pupils	Prepare American history bibliography in library	Visit American literature class	Participate in current events review			
3:00	Assist in organizing world history class	Participate with pupils in organizing unit	Assist pupils in selection of references	Student teacher seminar	Plan bulletin board with committee Attend pep assembly		
4:00	Attend general staff meeting	Student teacher seminar	Visit scenes of historic interest with 2 American history pupils		Ride school bus with pupils		
EVENING	Visit public library with pupil Civic Club Dinner				Take tickets at softball game	Attend teen-age party at recreation center	

348

STUDENT TEACHER WEEKLY PROGRAM
(Second Grade)

STUDENT: Betty Mantle DATE: Sept. 1 WEEK: 1 COUNSELOR: Miss Hill

	M	T	W	Th	F	Sat	Sun
8:00	Attend general faculty meeting		Assist principal in registering new pupils		Tour other school buildings and/or	Complete preparation	Attend Sunday school and church
9:00	Social period	Attend meeting of elementary teachers with superintendent			rooms with supervising teacher	for opening	day school and church
10:00	Continue general faculty meeting	Social period				of classes	and church
11:00		Check supplies delivered to room, add to inventory	Assist teacher in room organization		vising teacher		
12:00							
1:00	Attend elementary staff meeting	Plan daily schedule	Attend meeting with teachers and principal to discuss testing	Participate in B. I. E. Day	Attend general faculty meeting		
2:00	Social period	Compare daily schedule with other teachers at staff	Work with supervising teacher in planning pupil program		Work with supervising teacher in	Shop and meet people	
3:00	Continue elementary staff meeting	meeting and			preparation for opening of school	in the business district	Attend school board open house for teachers
4:00	Building orientation	remove conflicts	for the first week		on Monday	ness district	house for teachers
EVENING	Faculty picnic	Attend PTA council meeting	Student teachers have dinner together and attend theater				

349

STUDENT TEACHER WEEKLY PROGRAM
(Second Grade)

STUDENT: Betty Mantle DATE: Sept. 8 WEEK: 2 COUNSELOR: Miss Hill

	M	T	W	Th	F	Sat	Sun
8:00	Assist with last minute preparations	Help supervise playground		Conference with teacher			
9:00	Meet pupils with supervising teacher, assist in distribution	Observe reading instruction		Work with advanced reading group		Visit possible sites for social studies excursions	
10:00	of books and other materials	Observe music and sing with pupils Observe physical education and play with pupils when appropriate					Attend Sunday school and church
11:00	Adjust seats to fit pupils	Participate in introduction of social studies unit		Help committee plan bulletin board	Help committee complete bulletin board		
12:00	Eat with pupils and teachers in hot lunch program						
1:00	Participate in introduction of science unit		Show and discuss film with pupils	Go to high school science room with committee to get	Assist committee in preparing aquarium		
2:00	Hear vacation stories Recess—play with pupils		Observe number work	aquarium; assist with number work			
3:00	Start reading story to pupils	Continue reading story to pupils					
4:00	Conference with supervising teacher	Student teacher seminar	Ride school bus with pupils	Student teacher seminar	Conference with teacher		
EVENING	Civic Club dinner			Picnic with principal and other teachers			

350

Appendix C

"ASSISTING" AND "FLUNKY" ACTIVITIES

The following illustrations of student activities may help you further in differentiating between an assistant and a flunky:

Assistant	*Flunky*
1. Takes care of lighting until you are sure that he is sensitive to lighting conditions, then only when he is teaching.	1. Is responsible for lighting at all times whether or not he is teaching.
2. Student learns functions of office in school by going to office for different purposes, such as: to obtain paper, chalk or pencils; to obtain permission for group to use gym; to give explanation of pupil injury in corridor; to report need to repair teeter-totter; to request use of school bus for excursion; or to ask for information concerning a school policy.	2. Student runs all errands to the office.
3. Pupils, student and teacher tidy room for next day.	3. Student tidies room.
4. Student and teacher close windows and turn out lights before leaving room at noon and evening.	4. Student assumes complete responsibility for room lighting and ventilation.
5. Student, teacher, and pupils wipe paint from floor in kindergarten.	5. Student regularly wipes paint from floor in kindergarten.
6. Teacher and student check pupils' papers while teacher is responsible for class; student	6. Student always checks pupils' papers.

and teacher check pupils' papers while student is responsible for class.

7. Student, teacher, and pupils return materials to proper places after class.

8. Teacher and student prepare chairs and music racks for orchestra.

9. Student records and reports attendance to office until he learns procedure and then assumes this responsibility only when teaching.

10. Student learns how to duplicate materials and then duplicates materials only when needed for his teaching.

11. Student types materials needed in his teaching or for his use.

12. Student and teacher share responsibility for keeping pencils sharpened in first-grade room.

13. Student, pupils, and teacher share responsibility for putting away materials and cleaning up science laboratory.

14. Student and teacher supervise shower and dressing room.

15. Student, pupils, and teacher cooperate in cleaning art room following class.

7. Student always puts everything away so the pupils can go ahead to next class.

8. Student responsible each day to have chairs and music racks ready for orchestra.

9. Student records and reports attendance during entire period of student teaching.

10. Student does all duplicating for teacher.

11. Student does all typing of materials for instructional use by teacher.

12. Student keeps pencils sharpened in first-grade room.

13. Student puts away materials and cleans science laboratory.

14. Student supervises shower and dressing room.

15. Student and teacher always clean art room following class (teacher also flunky in this case).

Appendix D

TYPES OF ASSISTING ACTIVITIES

All of the assisting activities listed below might be desirable for a particular student. For another student, a few of them might be desirable, and for still another, few of them would be desirable. Their use with a particular student depends upon the readiness of the student and your answer to the four questions listed in Chapter IV.

Non-teaching routine
   Care of lighting (artificial lighting and shades)
   Care of ventilation
   Care of cleanliness (dusting, paper off floor)
   Care of orderliness (tables neat, books well arranged on shelves, supplies arranged on storage shelves, tools on panels)
   Care of room displays (arranging, dusting, collection of materials, repair of materials)
   Keep room records (books checked to pupils, books returned by pupils, books lost by pupils, pupil payment of fee for hot lunch, pupil payment of book loan)
   Inspect pupil lockers and desks
   Repair equipment and supplies (sharpen tools in art, industrial arts, and shop; sharpen pencils for first grade pupils; repair books with torn pages; repair damaged athletic equipment)
   Cleaning of materials used (kindergarten toys, floor under easels in primary-grade rooms, science laboratory tables)

Teaching-learning activities
   Assemble materials needed for instruction (physical education equipment, specimens for science, references for study, materials for art class, display samples for social studies)

Prepare materials for classes (prepare seatwork for first-grade reading, prepare experience charts for second-grade social studies, duplicate graph for study in safety unit, mimeograph copies of song written by pupils, mount pictures to be used with opaque projector, make slides for use with microscope, prepare units and tens blocks for primary grade arithmetic, demonstrate for science teaching)

Select materials for classes and pupils (references for particular reading level of pupils, glaze for pupils in ceramics class, wood finishes for individual projects in shop, materials for individual projects in science, bulletins for committee use in report to class)

Locate aids in the instructional program (area to observe soil conservation practices, historical markers to be observed on excursion, references in libraries to be checked out and used in class, pictures to use in illustrating point in social studies, farms to visit in studying good land use practices, stores to visit in studying retail practices, samples of tree disease and surgery)

Organize instructional materials (write up successful procedure used in demonstrating spontaneous combustion, revise test after its use, place materials in files after the unit is complete, prepare display table with help of pupils, arrange materials for use by groups in science class, place music in cabinets, place instrument repair supplies in newly acquired case, place tools on folding panel for industrial arts, place complete set of supplies in each sewing machine in home economics class)

Assist directly with the teaching-learning process (student writes problems on board as they are raised by pupils and teacher, student and teacher evaluate editorial written by pupil for school paper, student and teacher give science demonstration, student and teacher demonstrate on trampoline for class, student works with individual band members during practice, student and teacher assist pupils during study of problem as assistance is necessary, student and teacher assist pupils in sewing projects as necessary, student and teacher work with individuals in arithmetic)

Bit teaching—small groups and individuals (demonstrate service in volleyball and work with several pupils having difficulty, teach superior reading group for several days in first grade, teach golf foursome in physical education class, teach superior group in tumbling class, give extra time to pupil besides helping him in class, give special instruction to pupil in geometry, help pupil with trombone part in orchestration, give special help to second-grade group in development of phonetic sense, demonstrate and work with pupils learning swan dive, give special speech training to pupil, instruct two pupils in use of acetylene welding, help committee prepare outline to use in making report to class, assist joke editor of school paper in deciding what type of jokes are appropriate, demonstrate for waitress committee a table setting for formal party and answer questions raised, show pictures to boys in home economics class and discuss desirable wardrobe for junior-senior banquet, give corrective exercises to physically handicapped child)

Bit teaching—the entire class (prepare demonstration of volcanic action and develop explanation with pupils, pronounce spelling words and supervise pupil correction of mistakes, use ten minutes of art class to talk with pupils about paintings made on previous day, show samples and give history of tintype in science class, lead discussion concerning interpretation of map in social studies class, read new directions for fire drill to pupils and answer questions, introduce new song to chorus, and work through it two or three times, conduct discussion concerning larva brought to school by third grade pupil, introduce and work through problem with pupils in trigonometry class, use ten minutes at beginning of period to conduct discussion of current event, introduce and help pupils learn folk dance)

Extraclass activities

(Work with pupil on radio project in science club, assist secretary in preparing notes on council meeting, give special assistance to high jumper in track practice, work with baton twirlers, work with assembly committee in preparation for an assembly, supervise pupils playing on swings on playground, assist tumblers in intramural program, play with and assist saxophone section of school dance band, help committee set up program for school party, help sell concessions at athletic contest, assist school annual committee responsible for formal, help school group plan for and carry out a paper drive, assist committee preparing student handbook for the next academic year)

Intrafaculty relationships

Social activities: (Assist teacher in collecting assessment for faculty picnic, plan games for faculty picnic, call square dances at faculty party, participate with faculty in preparing stunt for assembly, lead singing at faculty pot-luck)

Professional activities: (Work with committee in curriculum revision, assist teacher in preparing new fire drill organization, discuss social studies unit with high school social studies teacher, arrange with another teacher for cooperative use of reference materials, invite another teacher and her pupils to attend a room party, arrange with another teacher to miss class because of an excursion, contribute to the faculty professional bulletin, arrange with another teacher for change of music period, volunteer help in faculty meeting, help repair furniture for faculty lounge)

Administrative relationships

(Prepare monthly attendance report for office, discuss mistakes on monthly attendance report with principal or superintendent, obtain permission from principal or superintendent to take pupils on excursion, prepare excursion report for office, obtain interpretation of policy concerning pupil payment for lost books, prepare requisition and talk with principal about purchase of materials, accompany pupils to office to report broken window, make inquiry concerning assistance for underprivileged child, talk with principal concerning parent who objects to restricted activity of pupils during noon hour, plan with principal for use of school auditorium for evening play practice, obtain principal's reaction to invited guests at school party)

Parent relationships

(Accept invitation to walk home with pupil to meet parents, arrange for social call after school, get acquainted with parents at PTA meeting, visit with parents at homeroom parents' meeting, discuss pupil progress with mother who visits school, assist teacher in preparing pupil reports, assist teacher in discussing pupil reports with parents, assemble material and assist teacher in discussing pupil growth at parent-teacher conference, call parent concerning child who is ill at school)

Community relationships

(Accompany teacher to newspaper office to discuss possibility of one issue per week containing school news, visit lumberyard with committee of pupils to obtain sawdust for homecoming bonfire, accompany teacher and committee of pupils to plan excursion to cheese factory and to obtain samples for class use, accept invitation to sing at meeting of community club, talk with wholesale grocer concerning possibility of visit by general science class)

Appendix E

EVALUATION OF STUDENT TEACHING

Student _____ Term _____ Year_____

School _____ Grade _____ Section _____

Curriculum Classification _____ Supervisor _____

Previous experiences with children:

Teaching _____

_____

_____

Other _____

_____

_____

Student teaching assignment (class, grade, club, guidance, administration, noon-hour, etc.):

_____

_____

_____

_____

* Key to symbols:

A Indicates student is outstanding, exceptional, definitely advanced in professional development.

B Indicates student is superior, above average, shows promise of superior development.

C Indicates student is adequate, average, satisfactory.

D Indicates student is undeveloped, below average, inadequate.

F Indicates student is definitely not qualified to assume a position in the teaching profession.

I. *Maintains a good physical environment in the school*
   1. Manages mechanics of heating, lighting and ventilation to best advantage. _____
   2. Maintains orderly and effective arrangement of facilities. _____
   3. Secures cleanliness of the environment. _____
   4. Secures personal cleanliness and other health habits. _____
   5. Maintains conditions of safety. _____
   6. Uses arrangement, color, texture, etc., to create an artistic atmosphere. _____
   7. Obtains pupil growth in development of responsibility for good physical environment. _____

II. *Provides atmosphere conducive to social and emotional growth of children*
   1. Functions with vitality. _____
   2. Displays a wholesome sense of humor. _____
   3. Displays consistently a happy, cheerful disposition. _____
   4. Displays social sensitivity. _____
   5. Works in a manner which shows confidence, poise, and relaxation. _____
   6. Uses voice effectively. _____
   7. Shows good taste in grooming. _____
   8. Responds to children in terms of their personal needs. _____
   9. Guides children effectively in solving individual social problems. _____
   10. Succeeds in effective teacher-pupil planning. _____
   11. Secures individual and group development in pupil control. _____
   12. Secures discernible social and emotional growth in children. _____
   13. Meets effectively the spontaneous demands of pupils. _____

III. *Maintains a wholesome learning atmosphere*
   1. Uses knowledge and skills essential to successful teaching. _____

2. Provides for maximum individual growth. _____
3. Uses imagination and independence of thought. _____
4. Appraises individual pupil and group needs. _____
5. Stimulates broad interests in pupils. _____
6. Evaluates pupil growth effectively. _____
7. Makes essential skills an inherent part of the learning situation. _____
8. Contributes to pupil growth in self-evaluation and remediation. _____
9. Succeeds in obtaining pupil attitudes of responsibility for learning. _____
10. Secures discernible pupil growth. _____
11. Secures assistance of school and community personnel in contributing to pupil program. _____
12. Organizes learning experiences effectively. _____
13. Selects learning materials and activities suited to individual pupil and to group needs. _____
14. Guides learning experiences effectively. _____
15. Secures pupil purpose in learning. _____
16. Holds standards commensurate with ability and progress of individual pupils. _____

IV. *Sees the child in relation to his home and maintains effective cooperative relations with parents*

1. Discovers and properly records pertinent facts concerning the pupil's out-of-school experiences, especially relating to their homes.
2. Uses constructively in pupil and parent counseling, the information he gathers relating to the pupil out-of-school. _____
3. Meets parents well and maintains relations of mutual respect and cooperation. _____
4. Helps parents and others understand the aims and program of the school and gains their cooperation in the development of the aims and program. _____
5. Helps parents understand specific needs, interests, and problems of their children. _____
6. Cooperates with parents and others in meeting

the needs of the children in relation to their out-of-school activities. _____

7. Cooperates with the PTA and other parent groups in activities which are consistent with the aims of the school. _____

V. *Contributes to the welfare of the whole school*

1. Cooperates with fellow workers. _____
2. Accepts his rightful share of responsibility for the successes or failures of the school or its program. _____
3. Uses tact and courtesy at all times. _____
4. Takes responsibility for any child in the school in circumstances dictating need for action. _____
5. Makes a creative, positive approach when problems arise. _____
6. Meets responsibilities promptly. _____
7. Uses critical judgment in contributing to group discussion. _____
8. Spontaneously senses and accepts unassigned responsibilities. _____
9. Adapts readily to change.

VI. *Functions as a part of the community*

1. Responds as a mature individual according to the standards generally acceptable in respected citizens. _____
2. Knows and understands the outstanding characteristics of the community and its life. _____
3. Assumes a share of the responsibilities as a member of the community. _____
4. Senses the relations of the curriculum to the needs of the community. _____
5. Enriches the curriculum by relating it to community activities. _____

VII. *Initiates and maintains professional growth*

1. Makes professional growth consistent with his ability. _____

2. Performs independently in study essential to interests of school and profession. _____

3. Volunteers services for advancement of school and profession. _____

4. Shows a developing sense of professional responsibility. _____

Appendix F

EVALUATON OF SUPERVISION

During the past quarter you have been learning how to assume successfully the responsibilities of the teacher in the school and community. You have worked in a school and in a community. The opportunities for your growth as a teacher were many, perhaps many more than you had time to encompass.

The supervisors with whom you worked were not only interested that you avail yourself of as many experiences as possible but also that in having an experience you grow as rapidly as possible in stature as a member of the teaching profession. To have conferred with parents was not enough, the worth of the experience being judged by how well you progressed in your ability to work with parents. Perhaps fewer experiences would have been more desirable with greater emphasis upon appraisal of progress in each.

Our special concern as supervisors, however, is how well we have helped you to develop your potentialities as a teacher. We are asking your assistance in attempting to determine how well we have met *our* responsibilities as your supervisors.

Below, you will find a series of supervisory practices which we consider to be of major importance. You can help us by rating the supervisors with whom you worked on each according to the example given below. Number one is the highest rating and number five the lowest. The symbol O denotes that you did not have sufficient observation to form judgment. Space is provided for comments following each item. Comments explaining *why* you gave a certain rating will be very helpful and very much appreciated. Note sample comment following sample rating.

EXAMPLE:

The supervisors held the student teacher responsible for evaluating his progress. (A part of the time the supervisors gave me written comments or told me what was wrong instead of asking me to evaluate my teaching.)

1	2	3	4	5	0
		X			

The check (X) above indicates that the supervisors with whom you worked did not consistently hold you responsible for evaluating your progress, take time to counsel with you in evaluating your work, hold you accountable for evaluating your work, or impress upon you the necessity for self-evaluation.

	1	2	3	4	5	0
1. The supervisors provided that you plan the unit to be taught and the materials to be used in the teaching.						
2. The supervisors gave you specific, understandable suggestions concerning the improvement of your work with boys and girls.						
3. The supervisors related your work in student teaching to the conditions you would probably meet in the field.						
4. The supervisors made you feel a definite part of the school.						
5. The supervisors respected your suggestions concerning the classroom and school in general.						

	1	2	3	4	5	0

6. The supervisors created an environment that enabled you to maintain good pupil control in the classroom and school in general.

7. The supervisors encouraged you to use available personnel resources in school and community which could contribute to the school program.

8. The supervisors demonstrated the advantages of participating in the whole school program over confining themselves to the classroom.

9. The supervisors planned carefully with you for experiences outside the classroom.

10. The supervisors encouraged you to assume responsibility inside and outside the classroom as you demonstrated readiness for such responsibility.

11. The supervisors created an environment that enabled you to develop and maintain good relations with the custodial staff in the school.

12. The supervisors encouraged you to develop your own teaching personality, not to teach as they taught.

	1	2	3	4	5	0

13. The supervisors demonstrated effective ways of meeting individual differences in reading, composition, voice ability, and interests.

14. The supervisors held high standards for themselves and student teachers in voice usage, English usage, and handwriting.

15. The supervisors held the teaching profession to be a worthy profession.

16. The supervisors demonstrated effective procedures in developing good pupil-teacher relationships.

17. The supervisors showed a sincere and informed interest in the community in which they taught, and they expected the same of you.

18. The supervisors created an environment that enabled you to develop and maintain good relations with the faculty in the school.

19. The supervisors held high ethical standards for themselves and for you.

20. The supervisors gave you a feeling of working *with* them rather than *for* them in planning and conducting the educational program for boys and girls.

	1	2	3	4	5	0

21. The supervisors were concerned with your growth in each student teaching experience.

22. The supervisors held definite and specific standards for your achievement as a teacher.

23. The supervisors created an environment that enabled you to develop and maintain good relations with the secretarial staff in the school.

24. The supervisors made opportunities available for you to use your special interests and abilities in your student teaching experiences.

25. The supervisors planned with you and made additional experiences possible for you in areas where you showed least ability or growth.

26. The supervisors were concerned with pupil growth in responsibility for room and school housekeeping and therefore such responsibilities did not become routine chores for you.

27. The supervisors held you responsible for self-evaluation and self-improvement.

28. The supervisors held themselves and you responsible for high scholarship.

1	2	3	4	5	0

29. The supervisors, if recognizing lack of effort, initiative, or willingness to assume responsibility on your part, helped you to meet the situation successfully.

30. The supervisors created an environment that enabled you to develop and maintain good relations with the community.

31. The supervisors, at the beginning of your student teaching experiences, informed you specifically concerning your opportunities and responsibilities as a student teacher.

32. The supervisors informed you specifically concerning the characteristics and competencies by which your growth as a teacher would be evaluated.

33. The supervisors helped you to recognize the importance of understanding each pupil in relation to all of his activities (home and school) and not just as a pupil in your classroom.

34. The supervisors contributed effectively to your social and professional contact with parents.

35. The supervisors contributed to your learning to attack and plan solutions to school problems with other student teachers and/or staff members.

Index

Index

A

Activities, planning for initial student, 59-62

American Association of Colleges for Teacher Education, 37

American Association of Teachers Colleges, 1

Assignment, problems in providing extraclass activities, 222-224

Assignment, student, progression in while teaching, 103-104

Assignment, student teaching:
types of, 34-35
  final assignment, 35
  full-day assignment, 35
  initial assignment, 34-35
  limited assignment, 34

Assisting, during induction period:
distinguished from flunky activities, 71-72
nature of assisting activities, 71
progression in assisting activities, 75-76
types of activities, 72-74
working *with* you, 71

Assisting activities during induction period:
criteria by which determined, 72-77
  aid in developing poise and confidence, 75-77
  co-worker with teacher, 72-73
  identification of student as essential, 73-74
  learning experience for student, 74-75

Association for Childhood Education International, 326

Association for Student Teaching, 326
The Evaluation of Student Teaching, Twenty-eighth Yearbook, 1949, 11, 291

Off-campus Student Teaching, Thirtieth Yearbook, 1951, 37, 95

Association for Supervision and Curriculum Development, 326

B

Belongingness, student:
as related to rights and responsibilities in use of material and equipment, 56
at beginning of student teaching, 56

Bit teaching:
during induction period, 76
importance of, 104-105

Brinton, Mary Frances, 260

C

California Statement of Teaching Competencies, 11

Climate, for student growth:
function of faculty in providing, 8
function of pupils in providing, 8-9
function of teacher in providing, 7-9

Clubs, college, 36

College supervisor, responsibilities to teacher, 20-21

Community, student adaptation to mores of, 135-136

Competencies essential for student success, list, 11

Competencies, teacher, 14-18

Conferences:
in developing student focus and purpose, 12-13
initial, items to be included in, 62-63
student-teacher, characteristics of, 80-84
  arranged to meet immediate needs, 83-84

371